The Archivist's
and Records
Manager's
Bookshelf

Archives & Archivists in the Information Age

Richard J. Cox

Neal-Schuman Publishers, Inc.
New York   London

Published by Neal-Schuman Publishers, Inc.
100 William St., Suite 2004
New York, NY 10038

Printed and bound in the United States of America.

The paper used in this publication meets the minimum requirements of American National Standard for Information Sciences–Permanence of Paper for Printed Library Materials, ANSI Z39.48-1992.

Library of Congress Cataloging-in-Publication Data

Cox, Richard J.
    Archives and archivists in the information age / Richard J. Cox.
    p. cm.—(The archivist's and records manager's bookshelf ; no. 1)
    Includes bibliographical references and index.
    ISBN 1-55570-530-8 (alk. paper)
    1. Archives—United States—Administration. 2. Archivists—United States. 3. Professional employees—United States. 4. Personnel management—United States. I. Title. II. Series.
    CD3021.C696 2005
    025.1'97—dc22   2004028982

Table of Contents

Series Editor's Foreword

Archives and Archivists in the Information Age by Richard Cox launches the first volume in Neal-Schuman's new series, *The Archivist's and Records Manager's Bookshelf*. As technology, the information explosion, and current events expand and renew the importance these jobs play in the digital age, this guide fully examines the traditions of the field—appraisal, retention, organization, preservation, and access—in a new light. It also explores modern trends and demands—technology, compliance, outreach, finance, facilities, and more—that face today's information professionals.

Archives and Archivists in the Information Age offers a powerful statement of why people engaged in this arena not only continue to be of value to organizations but have also become essential to today's organizational structures. Dr. Cox utilizes his experience in archival education to investigate the changing educational requirements of professionals, examine the value of experience and to inspect continuing education and the debate over archival certification.

The author's unique and enlightened point of view affords impressive insight into the role consultants play, the construction of job descriptions, and the importance of public scholarship. These areas add new dimensions to the traditional concept of archival work. This call for readers to enter the public discourse is welcome. It comes at the perfect time as our culture has increasingly realized the significance of keeping and preserving sound records in order to steer clear of scandals and media attention.

Created with the author's keen sense of the knowledge age, *Archives and Archivists in the Information Age* will help readers understand what is happening within their own organizations by observing the changing trends in administration. The chapters travel from the most mundane level of daily activity to the large value systems that place them in context. Ideas like reengineering or managing knowledge illuminate the effect of the digital age on records keepers, including the changing definitions of information, documents, and records.

Richard J. Cox has produced a history of where we have been and proposes a vision for where we might go. This first volume of the series *The Archivist's and Records Manager's Bookshelf* not only contributes to our professional growth and identity, it also brings to light the changing role of the archivists and the transforming dimensions of information and definitions of our organizations in the digital age.

Gregory S. Hunter, Ph.D.
Long Island University
The Archivist's and Records Manager's Bookshelf
Series Editor

Preface

To many people the term archivist evokes sepia-toned mental snapshots of experts in the cloistered rooms of ivy-covered buildings filled with solitude, dust, musty smells, and ancient manuscripts cribbed in ornate handwriting. In reality, though, archivists to this archetypal image contend with compelling and complex matters including copyright and intellectual property; preserving digital information; authentication and ownership of documents; controversial or concealed materials; and sanitized or censored information. *Archives and Archivists in the Information Age* examines many of the primary issues involved in this constantly changing role. For example, what are the proper identities, loyalties, educations, public profiles, and credentials? How does one consider these qualities in the context of shifting notions of work and organizations?

The fact that all archivists work with critically important evidence and information, and often manage these sources in difficult situations, is one common theme. Beyond these tricky circumstances, the worker may be difficult to manage in their own right. Their loyalty is often placed elsewhere (to their profession and its mission, or to their own interest in working with historical documentation) than with the institution employing them. Turbulence may erupt both inside and outside the organizations where they labor.

Many of this book's chapters—like how to hire an archivist or an archival consultant—describe practical matters in a straightforward manner. Others raise questions and grapple with contentious issues about a professional where responsibilities, credentials, and loyalties are changing.

Chapter One, "Why Organizations Need Archivists," considers the importance of the archivist's work in an organization. What role do they play? What responsibilities should they have? Which functions do they carry out? What position do they hold in records management programs? This chapter shows how to determine the right kind of person for a given position including how to establish educational and other employments requirements; and ways to write an advertisement and sell the position.

Chapter Two, "Why Organizations Need Archival Consultants," discusses key aspects of this important statement. It shows how to set up what the position requires, define expectations, formulate questions for candidates, select from the pool of applicants, use multiple consultants, and more. This chapter also deals with cost, cooperation, and completion of consultant products.

Chapter Three, "How Organizations Define Archival Positions," examines the profession through a study of job descriptions from the past thirty years. Ample clues about the desired qualifications abound in numerous job announcements. This chapter presents interesting findings that relate to the growth of technology and how it impacts the traditionally sought functions of the job.

Chapter Four, "Why Records Professionals Need to Explain Themselves," debates the nature of public scholarship and relates the implications and importance to archivists and records managers. It also comments about how these kinds of individuals might achieve greater success in public scholarship. How can they position themselves as authorities when important, records-related issues—restrictions on presidential records, corporate scandals, etc.—surface in the news? How can they create a sustained presence that makes clear the importance of the documents and the value of the experts who organize the materials to our society?

Chapter Five, "Archival Credentials and Professional Identity," explores the various aspects and arguments surrounding certification and the creation of an archival academy. An ongoing quarrel has raged for the past century about how members define themselves, their careers, and what they might become. This chapter looks at how people in the field and society in general need some way of distinguishing archivists from the larger information profession including librarians, curators, historians, and even information scientists.

Chapter Six, "Archives, Records Management, and Distance Learning: Weighing the Options," explores this vital issue. After long relying on workshops, institutes, and conferences to sustain and strengthen their knowledge, the emergence of more opportunities for such experiences via distance education only seems like an extension of what has been going on for some time. Upon closer examination, this chapter finds that distance education is not a neutral delivery mechanism for additional training. Nor is it a universally welcomed answer to the profession's education needs.

Chapter Seven, "The Archivist in the Knowledge Age," recognizes that organizations and their workforces remain constantly in flux and people are challenged to stay current with their employer's operations and structure. This chapter draws from some of the seminal writings in knowledge management (such as by Thomas Stewart) urging readers to be both alert and adaptable.

Chapter Eight, "Records, Documents, and Stuff in the Digital Era," considers the relationship of these materials, and the compulsion to save everything in the new Digital Era. In the last decade, everyone involved with the organization and preservation of information have grappled with its broadening scope. This chapter examines how they employed a variety of research, scientific, technical, historical, and mathematical approaches.

Chapter Nine, "Forming the Records Professional's Knowledge," surveys and evaluates the changing patterns of publication and its impact on professional knowledge— including the tensions between scholars and practitioners. Drawing on my own work as the Society of American Archivists' Publications Editor and as the author of a number of books (both manuals and monographs), I address the general state of archival knowledge as well as its future prospects.

Chapter Ten, "Putting It Altogether: Case Studies of Four Institutional Records Programs," provides guidance for both establishing and re-energizing records programs, drawn from an assessment of four institutions (two local government and two religious organizations). These examples, reflecting the typical conditions found in many institutions, place in real world context the importance of hiring an archivist (Chapter One), hiring a consultant (Chapter Two), composing job descriptions (Chapter Three), and the continuing debates about the credentials of managers (Chapter Five).

Please note that throughout these chapters I have tried to be specific when I address the particular needs of an archivist versus a records manager, but I often revert to using the term "records professional" when I am addressing broad issues cutting across all professionals. I have not made up my mind whether archivists and records managers will converge into some sort of information professional—many might call this a "knowledge manager." I do know that whatever the future of these disciplines, we cannot lose sight of the importance of managing records. Many of these chapters have been updated and revised from articles I originally wrote for *Records and Information Management Report*. This volume is also intended to complement the author's earlier works on managing institutional archives (1992) and records as part of information policy.

ENDNOTES

1. Richard J. Fox, *Managing Institutional Archives: Foundational Principles and Practices* (New York: Greenwood Press, 1992).
2. Richard J. Fox, *Managing Records as Evidence and Information* (Westport, Conn.: Quorum Books, 2001).
3. Richard J. Fox, "Archives and Archivists in the Twenty-First Century: What Will We Become," *Archival Issues* 20, no. 2 (1995): 97–113.

Acknowledgments

Many thanks to Lynn Taylor and Jane Lerner, with whom I worked for many years. Lynn founded *Records & Information Management Report*, a journal that has brought articles from both the archival and records management fields together. Jane has done much over the years to make my writing better than it deserves to be.

1

Why Organizations Need Archivists

INTRODUCTION

If organizations and society are to see success in the maintenance of organizational archives, then it is imperative that the archival profession and its allies labor to establish and nurture institutional archives. The era of massive collecting by archival and historical records repositories, the primary means by which the archival records of organizations like corporations have been saved (when they have been saved), is ending (if it has not already ended) as an effective strategy to protect important archival records because the volume and complexity of records lessens the utility of outside acquisition. Most existing repositories are already at or near capacity, and the great volume of records produced by many of these organizations would strain them even if they had more space and resources. Even if space was not an issue, the increasing use of electronic records technologies has made it harder to visualize how these records could be collected and their viable use maintained by second-party agencies.

These are the types of themes that I have explored in many of my writings over the past decade, and that continue in the essays in this volume written in the past few years. These writings have most often been composed from the perspective of the archivist; that is, they have tried to contend with what archivists can, might, or should do in society to ensure that they play a viable role in the modern information or knowledge fields. There is a more important perspective that needs to be added to these themes, however, and that is the matter of the critical roles archivists play *within* their organizations.

This essay looks at the matter of hiring an archivist, built on the premise that archivists are essential to the basic work of any organization. The chapter describes what an archivist is, how an archivist fits into a records management program, and the essential functions of archival work. It also considers the educational requirements of an archivist, how experience and training produce the necessary qualified archivist, whether the certification of archivists is the solution for identifying qualified archivists, how to write an advertisement for hiring an archivist, where to advertise for archivists, the elements of carrying out interviews for archivists, essential salary and related remuneration requirements, and whether to use a consultant in the search for an archivist. There are also suggested readings to help an organization think through the process of hiring an archivist. All of this is offered while trying to help an organization determine *whether* it should hire an archivist.

WHY ORGANIZATIONS SHOULD BE CONCERNED ABOUT ARCHIVAL RECORDS

- Archival records are not old records; rather, they support the organization with evidence and information of continuing value
- Archival records are an organizational resource critical to its effective management and work

All organizations should be concerned with managing their archival records. This does not mean that an organization should be concerned with administering its *old* records. Archival records are those records that are identified by an organization as possessing *continuing* value. Continuing value means both that the records contain evidence and information of current use to the organization, as well as that the records contribute to the organization's knowledge about its own activities, past and present. Archivists or individuals playing such a role within the organization (archival responsibilities might be carried out by others with different position titles) are essential if an organization is to take the necessary holistic view of its records and information. The first step, inherent in all that is discussed below, is whether an organization should employ its own archivist or make some other arrangement for its archival records. *All* organizations, for their own purposes, should provide for the management of their archival records, but the means for doing this might vary from organization to organization based on size, type, business, and other elements.

The "National Association of Government Archives and Records Administrators Statement of Preferred Qualifications for Directors of Large-Scale Government Records and Archival Programs" provides an excellent description of why *records* and *records professionals* continue to be valuable even in the modern electronic Information Age. According to this professional association.

> Records and archives programs are essential to the sound, effective, responsive operation of government. Government at all levels is changing and adapting to meet shifting public expectations, service needs, resources levels, and changes in our economy and society. Its records and information resources are essential to the sound management of government itself, to the delivery of services, and to the documentation of its work. Records represent a major investment of time and governmental resources. The widespread use of computers, telecommunications technology, and the dramatic shift to the creation and use of electronic records and information present records management problems of unprecedented magnitude and complexity. Managing government records and information today is a demanding challenge that requires skill, dedication, understanding of management techniques, and a capacity to adopt new techniques to meet changing issues and needs.[1]

One could easily take this statement and revise it to match the interests of other organizations, such as for-profit corporations and not-for-profit community associations.

WHAT IS AN ARCHIVIST?

- An archivist is not merely an individual paid to work with archival records, but also someone who understands records and recordkeeping systems—especially those providing records with continuing value
- An archivist works on identifying, preserving, and providing access to records possessing continuing value and relevance to an organization

At one time, an archivist would have been defined simply as someone employed to work in an archives with archival or historical records. In other words, the *place* of employment and the nature of job responsibilities would have been the determining factors in identifying an individual as an archivist. Or such individuals would have been defined by what they were *not* doing. They were not working with books and printed materials, so they were not librarians. They were not working with current or active records, so they were not records managers. They were not designing information systems, so they were not information scientists. Such problems with definitions have come from a notion long harbored by many archivists that people actually understand what archivists do, or, worse, that there was some advantage in the prevalence of ambiguous notions about archival work.

Even today, archivists continue to be partly defined by what they are *not*. The Society of American Archivists provides on its Web site a pamphlet text entitled "So You Want to Be an Archivist: An Overview of the Archival Profession." After a paragraph describing the "primary task" of archivists, there is a slightly longer paragraph noting how archivists are distinct from other professions. Comparisons of tasks and responsibilities are made to librarians, records managers, museum curators, and historians.[2] In some ways, this approach to defining an archivist is a legacy of the slow evolution of the archival profession, as well as the multitudinous means by which individuals seem prone to enter the field.

There are a number of reasons why such a definition (or anti-definition) would once have been operational. There were few formal educational programs for training individuals to work as archivists. Most entered the field either in a serendipitous fashion, or as a second career option (in lieu of not being able to secure a position in their first career choice). Individuals working as archivists often identified themselves as historians, curators, librarians, or other professionals—with the determining factor either being their source of training or even their own personal interests.

Much of this stemmed from the field's low public profile, where individuals often discovered archives as a field by chance. While the newspapers and other media covered stories about archives and records, the lot of archivists was uncertain. While this chameleonlike approach has some advantages for archivists fitting into virtually any environment—from government and corporate to cultural and non-profit—it does pose problems for human resources officers as they try to develop advertisements and position descriptions for hiring archivists. Can a human resources specialist write a job description or announcement for an archivist by describing what an archivist does *not* do? This is not, of course, an option in our highly regimented and legalistic organizations.

This accidental archivist is very real to me, since it is basically how I entered the field (and how most of my long-term colleagues also joined the profession). I did not set out to be an archivist. Rather, I knew that I wanted to work in some field where I could use my interest in history. In between graduate programs, at a point in my life when I was not certain what I wanted to do, I contacted a former professor of mine who directed me to a historical society that suddenly needed to hire someone in a hurry. I became an archivist with no formal preparation and started immediately to learn on the job. Lest anyone think that this should confirm the lack of importance of graduate education programs in archives or records management, let me disabuse them of any such idea. It took me half-a-dozen years to come to terms with what it meant to be an archivist, and nearly a decade to fully appreciate the nature and importance of archival work. This is precisely how *not* to support a profession, and, in fact, it makes archives look more like a medieval guild than a real modern profession.

Fortunately, much of this is radically changing. There is a decided shift to more comprehensive graduate archival education programs, with a concentration of courses and some programs planning for separate masters degrees. This educational transition is drawing individuals with specific career objectives; in other words, archives administration is not a secondary or tertiary choice of vocation. Most individuals going to the better educational programs will gain an understanding in a year or two that it took me in my apprenticeship a decade to achieve. Moreover, the need to manage archives and legacy records systems is increasingly being recognized by organizations and society as an important function.

Archivists have been identified as representing a "hot" field, partly because it is being better identified. There are clearer roles for archivists, even if they are sometimes muddled in novels or movies. Some graduate archives education programs are also shifting their approaches to encompassing more than preserving historical records for use by historians and other scholars to include a focus on accountability or to stress archives as part of something broader like knowledge management.

What is an archivist? An archivist should be defined by the roles he or she plays within an organization (which is the focus of this essay—you can extrapolate to determine the broader societal values). The archivist is, in the most obvious way, responsible for identifying, preserving, and providing access to records possessing continuing value. This mission was first articulated by the Society of American Archivists (SAA) in the mid–1980s as part of its Goals and Priorities planning effort. The SAA definition of archivist notes that the "primary task of the archivist is to establish and maintain control, both physical and intellectual, over records of enduring value." The selection, arrangement and description, preservation, reference and access, and management of records are then briefly mentioned as the critical functions.

The "values" notion of records can throw off some people as being too subjective. The idea of "records possessing continuing [rather than enduring] value" can be transformed into the concept of records helping an organization to be compliant and competitive in its daily work. In this way the role of the archivist becomes one in which he or she identifies records possessing information that contributes to an organization's current work (in the sense that knowledge managers describe this). The primary difference is that the records that the archivist is responsible for tend to be the older records that must be maintained because of legal, fiscal, administrative, and corporate memory requirements. However, even here the archivist's distinction from the records manager is changing because of information technology uses for recordkeeping systems, the obvious advantages of the records continuum model for conceptualizing records management, and the developing notions of ideas like knowledge management that blend together archives, records, and information management ideas and objectives.

ARCHIVISTS IN RECORDS MANAGEMENT PROGRAMS

- Records are managed to support organizational purposes, and the boundary between active and inactive records has blurred as organizations adopt Information Resource Management (IRM) and Knowledge Management (KM) concepts and approaches
- The unifying principle for both archivists and records managers is that records are important to the organization as a source of evidence, information, and knowledge

There have been many viewpoints concerning the relationship between archivists and records managers, ranging from partnerships to troubled marriage to competitors to professionals with hopeless conflicted missions. We can also examine the historical relationship between archivists and records managers, showing that records managers initially grew from the archives field. This historical circumstance is not meant to imply that somehow archivists are senior or superior to records managers. To the contrary, this development suggests that archival work and the archival mission—without some ability to relate it to current or active records—is missing a critical component. All of these investigations often lead to self-conscious concern about the future of the records professions. There is, however, a better means to consider this relationship.

The notion of the records life cycle, now replaced by the records continuum, provides the initial clue as to how to view archives and archivists within records management programs. From up close, archivists and records managers may see the differences between them stemming from education, outlook, and job title. Yet, from the vantage of managing records, such distinctions appear superficial. Records need to be managed to support organizational and societal purposes, and it is often the case that a record of value to an organization may cross the boundary line between active and inactive record without its current use really changing. In other words, this boundary line is often a phantom. Australian educator Sue McKemmish provides this description of the power of the records continuum:

> A continuum is something continuous of which no separate parts are discernible, a continuous series of elements passing into each other. A records continuum perspective can be contrasted with the life cycle model. The life cycle model argues that there are clearly definable stages in recordkeeping, and creates a sharp distinction between current and historical recordkeeping. The records continuum, on the other hand, has provided Australian records managers and archivists with a way of thinking about the integration of recordkeeping and archiving processes. The life cycle model sees records passing through stages until they eventually "die," except for the "chosen ones" that are reincarnated as archives. A continuum-based approach suggests integrated time-space dimensions. Records are "fixed" in time and space from the moment of their creation, but recordkeeping regimes carry them forward and enable their use for multiple purposes by delivering them to people living in different times and spaces.[3]

Looking at a model like this, we see that a record that is important to an organization for administrative or legal reasons almost always becomes an archival record. Sometimes, archivists will identify records that lack obvious administrative or other closely related values because of some social, scholarly, or other research need. At this point, organizations need to understand that their records sometimes possess a value beyond their immediate use, which is why many corporate archivists spend considerable time relating their work to public relations possibilities. As long as such possibilities do not become the *only* reason why archival records are justified, this is an important function.

There is a more direct way of characterizing this relationship between archives and records management. Records management programs without any provision for archives cannot really be designated as fully functioning records management operations. If a record needs to be maintained for a long time, up to a status as a permanent record, then should it be described as a current/active record or as part of the archives? Records managers might be prone to designate such a record as active, because for many, an archival record has the sense of being old or having value only if one needs to write a history of the organization. The SAA's definition of archivist mentions that archivists and records managers are "closely allied," but then it goes on to emphasize a difference. The "records manager controls vast quantities of institutional records, most of which will eventually be destroyed, while the archivist is concerned with relatively small quantities of records deemed important enough to be retained for an extended period."[4] This is a gross and misleading distinction.

Rather than making such artificial distinctions, archivists and records managers need to consider the importance of records to an organization as being their common ground. Traditionally, or so it seems, archivists and records managers seemed to approach the management of records from very different perspectives. Records managers emphasized the economical and efficient administration of records. Their main objectives were to make sure that current records could be found quickly when needed and to ensure that obsolete records were disposed of as quickly as possible to reduce costs in storage and handling. Records center administration, with lower storage costs, became a major focus for records management programs (regardless of whether the records center was an internal operation or outsourced to a commercial provider).

Archivists, on the other hand, could contribute to the cost-effectiveness of organizations by enabling critically important records with continuing value to be produced at a moment's notice (such as the retrieval of an engineering drawing when a company building suffered damage or needed renovation or upgrading), but it was more likely that the long-term maintenance of archival records would add to the records costs of an organization. Preservation, specialized access systems, and other archival functions add costs to an organization's records regime, and the benefits of such costs have to be measured in ways other than purely economic ones.

The relationship between archival administration and records management has also changed as organizations have shifted to emphasizing information resources management or knowledge management approaches. These more recent perspectives stress the administration of the evidence and information found in records and other sources rather than the management of records as objects or artifacts (although the archivist plays an invaluable role in enabling the organization to understand when the original record needs to be maintained for evidence and information). While there are many nuances to IRM and KM, both bring the important contribution that records have value to the organization as they relate to organizational-critical functions and activities and that modern information technologies will be used to expedite the use of these records. Yogesh Malhotra, a consultant in the rapidly growing domain of knowledge management, suggests, "Knowledge management caters to the critical issues of organizational adaptation, survival, and competence in face of increasingly discontinuous environmental change. Essentially, it embodies organizational processes that seek synergistic combination of data and information-processing capacity of information technologies, and the creative and innovative capacity of human beings."[5] To a certain extent, looking at records from the IRM–KM perspective blends together the work of archivists and records managers. Records are seen as one of many information-knowledge sources, along with other sources such as the Internet/World Wide Web and the individual memories of long-term employees. The archivist/records manager can become one of the key information or knowledge workers within an organization, *if* the organization has hired the right kind of individual to work as an archivist (one who is forward-looking and a promoter of the value of records to the ongoing work of the organization).

ARCHIVAL RESPONSIBILITIES AND FUNCTIONS

- Organizational archivists and records managers both first approach their work understanding the implications of external warrants dictating or influencing the creation of records
- Archival functions include appraisal, arrangement and description, reference and access, and preservation

Archivists have developed a core set of functions in order to meet their mission of maintaining the records that make up the archives of organizations and the documentary heritage of society. These functions follow a continuum of records, from their point of creation to their final disposition (either destruction or designation as archives). Records managers also follow on the same records continuum, mainly because records are records and share certain universal characteristics in their creation, use, and maintenance. Traditionally, archivists and records managers have viewed this continuum differently because of diverging final objectives—one stressing ongoing use and the other seeming to emphasize destruction. A better focus on the value of records as integral aspects of an organization's business brings archivists and records managers together and unites them in a broader objective of managing information or knowledge based on the nature of its business.

Appraisal

Archivists have generally viewed the beginning point of their work as being appraisal, the identification and selection of records with continuing value. The United States Environmental Protection Agency's glossary of records management terms provides this fairly typical definition of appraisal: "The process of determining the value and thus the final disposition of records, making them either temporary or permanent." This term is cross-referenced to "evaluation," defined as "in records disposition, the process of assessing the value of records to recommend or determine their retention periods, making the records either temporary or permanent."[6]

This seems like a straightforward process, but any archivist or records manager will tell you how difficult such analysis can be. Appraisal generally has focused on the broad values of evidence and information or concentrated on the values of administrative, fiscal, legal, and research uses. The values approach has led to considerable commentary on the subjective process of appraisal, leading some to see this function more as art rather than science. This perspective tells us more about the limitations of how archivists have approached this part of their responsibility, as many archivists have seen their task to be to assist scholars and research. There has been a remarkable shift in attitudes and ideas about archival appraisal within the past two decades. While it is impossible to capture briefly all of the nuances associated with the shifting ideas about appraisal, the most salient point is to understand how appraisal is most often now associated with both the mandates for the creation of records and with the elemental functions of any organization.

Archivists, as well as records managers, start from the premise that the records that need to be maintained are first and foremost connected to the primary external warrants for recordkeeping and the identification of the most essential functions of the organization. As I described the concept of a recordkeeping warrant elsewhere, "Developing the concept of a warrant for the recordkeeping functional requirements has also provided a clue to a new mission. The idea of the warrant drives records professionals to cite external regulations, legislation and best practice as the primary mandate for the management of recordkeeping systems, rather than a more vaguely defined argument for the historic value for records or the rationale of fiscal efficiency and economy in administering records warehouses."[7]

The recordkeeping warrant transforms the concept of appraisal in several ways. First, appraisal is moved from an entirely subjective process based on values that can vary in extreme ways between different archivists. Second, the warrant ties the mission of the archivist to the objectives of the parent organization, the records generator. Records are appraised to have value for how they support the organization, rather than only for how they support researchers who may have little investment in the organization. And third, and finally, appraisal is shifted to focus on the systems that generate records, encompassing the full range of elements that make up records systems, rather than as discrete objects containing isolated information. Archival principles like provenance and original order become more meaningful and valuable when entire records systems, are inspected and linked to the activities and responsibilities of the organization.

Archivists working within institutional contexts still need to bring extra sensitivity to functional responsibilities such as appraisal—especially responsibilities like this one. Terry Cook, examining the appraisal of voluminous case files, writes, "Appraisal has been termed 'the greatest professional challenge to the archivist' by the author of a leading manual on the subject. Yet appraisal has often been done in a random, fragmented, uncoordinated, even accidental manner, producing a biased, distorted archival record." Cook assigns the source of this problem to conducting appraisal on a "'taxonomic' stage, that is to say, a descriptive categorizing of various values of records (such as evidential and informational, primary and secondary, and so on). . . . Appraisal, therefore, generally occurs in isolation, where various of these 'taxonomic' values are applied to each series one by one." Cook argues, "While general approaches to appraisal apply to all records, it has been rightly recognized that personal information, especially when aggregated in modern, voluminous case files, is a 'separate problem' and requires special treatment." Cook recognizes that the "archivist's task of appraising modern records containing personal information is made considerably easier, however, by the existence of sound records management in the agency creating the records," especially since the "archivist can obviously use many of the tools of the records manager to aid in the identification and transfer of a better archival record."[8] However, appraising records with personal information like the kinds that Cook describes requires both an extra sensitivity to matters like privacy and the importance of records for broader social and research purposes.

Arrangement and Description

If appraisal is the foremost service archivists might perform for most organizations, then archival arrangement and description (or what is sometimes termed archival representation) is the next critical function. Description has been defined as "in records management, the process of giving a written account of the contents and characteristics of a record series or system" and "in archives administration, the process of preparing finding aids."[9] Archival representation within institutional archives is the responsibility to make these records available to the organization. Within an organizational context, archivists create descriptions by developing links to the functions that cause records to be created in the first place. Archivists tend to think of writing scope and content notes, descriptions of the agency producing the records, and some sort of list of records. The objective of the archivist is to reflect records so that they can be readily identified, found, and used in an effective fashion. Preparing archival description is not an exercise in creative writing, rather it is an exercise in clear and concise prose that allows the records to speak for themselves. The evidence of the records must be obvious, along with the links to critically important organizational functions.

What makes archival representation an important archival function is what makes records important to begin with: that they represent business transactions, providing evidence about the activities of an organization. The description of records is done so that they can be utilized by organizations in fulfilling their legal, administrative, and fiscal responsibilities. Organizational theorists and managers now use concepts like data warehousing and data mining to capture the importance of reusing older information for continuing or new activities. A typical computer glossary defines a data warehouse as a "generic term for a system for storing, retrieving and managing large amounts of any type of data.

Data warehouse software often includes sophisticated compression and hashing techniques for fast searches, as well as advanced filtering." The same glossary defines data mining as "Analysis of data in a database using tools which look for trends or anomalies without knowledge of the meaning of the data. Data mining was invented by IBM who holds some related patents."[10]

Archivists and records managers have written about the nature of records that might be produced within data warehouses,[11] but they need also to utilize similar techniques to make their records available. Archivists, within organizational settings, need to determine ways to describe their records in ways that make the records highly visible to people working in the organization. This requires that they understand how the organization makes information available to its employees, meaning that archivists need to be prepared to use intranets, employee newsletters, bulletin boards, policy and procedure manuals, and other commonly used mechanisms for disseminating information. It also means that organizations need to find individuals who understand records, know what makes certain records possess archival value, and appreciate how new and emerging information technologies affect the creation and maintenance of records.

Archivists, in approaching the representation of records, also need to understand when and how their records will be used internally and externally. This has been a difficult aspect of work for institutional archivists, because the archival profession's orientation is so overwhelmingly slanted toward service for scholars like historians and other researchers. Institutional archivists exist, however, to provide services to the institutional creators of records. Obviously, this raises substantial issues about how they separate these groups of potential users.

The most logical manner for institutional archivists to proceed is to put their emphasis on providing access to internal researchers, while developing policies and procedures for access in case researchers from the outside seek to use their organizational records. In the realm of archival representation, this means that the archivist needs adopt professional standards for describing records—such as the use of Encoded Archival Description (EAD) for publicizing their holdings on the World Wide Web—while understanding that this promotion about the availability of records may have limitations. As the official Web site for EAD states, "The EAD Document Type Definition (DTD) is a standard for encoding archival finding aids using the Standard Generalized Markup Language (SGML). The standard is maintained in the Network Development and MARC Standards Office of the Library of Congress (LC) in partnership with the Society of American Archivists."[12] Since this standard is intended for placing inventories and registers on the Web, there is nothing that precludes it being used as part of an intranet for an organization. Clearly, when an organization seeks to hire an archivist, it needs to bear in mind the need to find an individual who has a good feel for professional standards while being aware that there are limitations in allowing access to organizational records.

Reference and Access

Such concerns relate as well to another major aspect of archival work, reference and access. Early in the development of the archival profession, archivists viewed their role to be to gather up the records and to provide access to researchers as they came to the repository. This perspective has shifted dramatically in the last couple of decades. Now archivists see their responsibility in this function to identify who is using the records and who should be using the records, thus promoting the use of their records at every possible opportunity. While being proactive in this area, archivists also need to be sensitive to matters like personal privacy, donors' wishes (if they are responsible for donated records), and a wider constituency of users who may bring very specialized needs as well as extra sensitivities to social concerns like multiculturalism.

Privacy and access, like preservation and access, are logically opposite ends of the spectrum of archival functions and by even their most basic definition can generate tensions. These tensions can be more intense within institutional archives. Obviously, some of these challenges are enhanced in organizational archives, where archivists may be responsible for proprietary information while working in an institution of such economic and historical significance that there will be a steady demand for use of the records from individuals outside of the organization. This is made even more complicated by the fact that most of the recent discussions about privacy in the Information Age has focused on *personal* privacy;[13] the institutional archivist must bring an extra sensitivity to privacy that is relevant to an organization's proprietary information.

Institutional archivists should approach the administration of reference and access to their records in a manner that ensures that their records will be effectively used first by others within the organization. This may be a challenge, as many within the organization will be focused on the current information needs and may view archival records as old and obsolete (if they have any sense that there is an organizational archives at all). Institutional archivists need to take their resources to the organization, and this can be accomplished in a number of ways. Archivists must be active within the organization, aware of and actively participating in any function that either impacts on the creation and maintenance of records or that could make effective use of the information and evidence found within archival records.

Archivists should use the most common means of communication within an organization. If organizational professionals generally communicate via electronic mail, then the institutional archivist should use this means to send information about new records, suggest better approaches to using these records, and highlight records that might be of particular interest to newly formed task forces and work groups. The old days of waiting for the researcher to arrive at the archives facilities are over, at least if the institutional archivist wants to see the records actively used within the organization.

Institutional archivists also carry the heavy responsibility of ensuring the long-term maintenance of their organizational records. This responsibility has often proved to be a problem for archivists working within organizations because it is a time-consuming and expensive process. The financial costs of institutional archives can only be hidden at the expense of burying the archives itself, so the better option is to invest time and resources into demonstrating the practical uses of archives. Institutional archivists, as with records managers, have often been loath to discuss preservation or long-term maintenance issues because they can appear to be a bottomless pit of financial expense.

Such issues have become more complicated as many have shifted their attention to access, such as through the use of digitization, and as many have written, access and preservation are not the same issue—although both can be very expensive. While preservation enhances access, digitization, which enhances access even more, is not a stable preservation option. As Paul Conway argues, digitization can protect originals by developing surrogates for use, but these are not equal responsibilities.[14] Whatever the institutional archivist does to provide for the long-term maintenance of records within an organization, the degree of success will be directly proportional to how relevant the organization sees its archives as being to its current activities.

APPLYING THE ARCHIVAL FUNCTIONS IN AN ACTIVE WAY

- Archival functions are all directed towards supporting archival records as having active value to an organization
- Archival functions will be most useful to an organization when the archivist takes an active approach to understanding organizational culture, how decisions about recordkeeping systems are made, and current projects demonstrating the creation and use of records

Archivists, and records managers as well, are often prone to adopt personas of being misunderstood within their organizations (and society, too). This may be the result of not making archival records relevant to an organization's current work, primarily by expecting organizations instinctively to know how to use archives. The archivist's responsibility is to know what the organization does at all levels and across all units, not the other way around. If archivists are to appraise records, for example, they must comprehend the full range of an organization's functions and related activities, and identify those that are critical (hence providing a focus on the most important records of an organization).

Likewise, the effective description of archival records requires tying these records descriptions to the work of the organization in a manner that can be readily understood by non-archivists. As those who have written on appraisal and description have demonstrated quite effectively, such knowledge comes from study and research; archivists are both students of records and recordkeeping systems as well as of the organizational generators of the records. Such knowledge also derives from archivists who are active within their organizations in as many facets of their work as possible.

The work of archivists, and the nature of the work that undergirds all archival responsibilities, can be understood by looking at practical, strategic approaches. The first example relates to teaching principles about institutional archives. Many of my archives students, either because of their previous experiences working in an archives or through their reading about and visiting archival programs while students, often ask just how they should approach their first professional positions (especially if they accept a position with responsibility for developing an archives operation). Some of these same students worry about aspects such as processing backlogs (records needing description already held by the archives) and running traditional reference services to the archives (staying with the archives and waiting for the researchers to appear). In a sense, these individuals think they need to tether themselves to where the records are stored.

My advice is simple. Get a beeper and always be *virtually* available, but get out into the organization and become known. Learn about the organizational culture. Discover where decisions about records and recordkeeping systems are made and get involved with these groups. Identify current projects that may have substantial implications for the creation of records and become an observer of and advisor to the project. Find projects or institutional activities that may be failing and see if information from the archives might help. All of these kinds of actions testify to the potential and actual importance of records within the organization for its main mission.

All of the above kinds of activities also attest to a critical observation: the administrators and chief policy makers of organizations may have very limited perceptions about what an institutional archives is about and what an archivist does. Their perceptions may be as much based on popular conceptions (really, misconceptions) about archives and archivists in which archives are old records and archivists are antiquarians with a slightly musty odor about them. Rather than worrying about such perceptions, archivists ought to see within them an opportunity to chart the direction for their own work that allows them to build archival programs within organizations that are best suited for the organizations. One state archivist determined that essential state agencies and task forces did not know about the archives and the scope of its responsibilities. Rather than wringing his hands about this problem, the state archivist went to the meetings of these groups first as an observer (they were, after all, open to the public). After the groups knew him, the state archivist became formally invited to participate in these groups. Another state government archivist built a strong archival and records management program by emphasizing both public outreach and advocacy activities. He worked to bring a relationship with state legislators, and he encouraged his staff to work with various professional associations that had a vested interest in records management. While such activities required long-term vision and patience, they paid off by providing a solid legislative, administrative, and fiscal foundation for developing a comprehensive records program.

This final aspect of organizational archives work relates to the institutional archivist as an administrator as well as a records specialist. The above scenarios suggest that an organization, if it is serious about an archives program, needs to be careful in finding the right individual to become the archivist. Being able to position oneself on important policy making groups or develop good political relations with key individuals who can support a records program requires a person who is not only an adept archivist, but also is committed to the importance of archival records to a degree that they will be an active promoter of the value and use of such records. Although many individuals, as they prepare for and enter into the archival profession, often do not see the importance of management to their roles as an archivist, they will generally understand that they must think of themselves as administrators even if they are in charge of only themselves or a small staff of one or two others.

Organizations should seek to hire archivists who possess a professional and institutional mission, are committed to the organization by making archival records relevant to the organization's functions and activities, and who can think outside of traditional ideas concerning archival records. Success in finding such an individual requires the organization to know where to find the qualified archivist and how to define the archivist's position.

EDUCATIONAL AND OTHER EMPLOYMENT REQUIREMENTS FOR ARCHIVISTS

- Organizations need to look for individuals possessing an educational background supporting their understanding of recordkeeping systems, the purpose of archival records, and how the maintenance of archival records relates to the organization's mission
- Organizations need to define what subject and other knowledge, beyond a foundation in archival studies, is appropriate to archival work in their environment rather than relying on bottom line professional standards such as certification

Organizations find all sorts of ways to hire individuals to work as archivists. Some hire consultants with expertise about the field who can help them determine the kind of individual needed for their position. This is especially useful for organizations that have little awareness of the archival field other than understanding that the field exists and that they need to hire a competent archivist. Other institutions transfer employees into an archivist position and support the individual obtaining education appropriate to this field. The danger here may be that the individual brings some entrenched opinions about the organization and may be already associated with a particular area of responsibility in the organization. The advantage is that the individual already knows the organization's corporate culture, administrative style, mission, functions, and activities. Some organizations create and post position descriptions in the appropriate job employment services and on various listservs and electronic bulletin boards. Here the key is knowing about the elements of a job description, a topic discussed later.

All of these approaches can be successful. An organization should avoid hiring individuals who have no experience or educational background in archival work, or who seem to possess only related experience such as in library or history work. The organization must remember that it is making an investment in an individual to assume very important responsibilities, and it wants to hire someone who has the best prospects of paying off for the organization. Moreover, while many aspects of library or historical work may appear to have affinities with archival work, there may well still be very different perspectives involved. For instance, a librarian may have a strong orientation to public service and access, but the organization may need to employ an archivist with sensitivity to restricted access and use. A historian, even one in public or applied history, may be oriented to the use of the informational content of records while the organization requires an archivist who comprehends that informational content is only useful as it relates to concepts like recordkeeping warrants and business processes.

That organizations may seek very different means to find someone who can work as an archivist has much to do with the wide array of avenues by which people find themselves in the archival profession. In New Zealand, for example, the following advice is offered to someone inquiring about entering into an archival career: "Archivists need to have at least an undergraduate or postgraduate arts degree in one or more of the following areas: history, art history, anthropology, archaeology, Latin, English literature, Maori studies, public administration, politics, law or economics. It is also advisable to gain a postgraduate qualification with an archive, museum studies or library component." The smorgasbord approach of background education is understood when one is also informed, "There are no other specific entry requirements for archivists." More emphasis is placed on previous experience: "Historical work, research work, or work as an archive assistant is useful experience for archivists. Library and museum work are also relevant to this area of work. Experience in information management or working in a government department may be helpful, and any work that involves dealing with people, such as customer service or teaching."[15] This type of advice has been typical for individuals inquiring about archival careers in North America as well, although the situation is better now as graduate archival education has grown and continued to mature. The Society of American Archivists annual education directory at least provides advice on career preparation starting from the premise of an educational background: "Individuals can prepare for a career in archives through a variety of educational programs. Most entry-level positions require an undergraduate and a graduate degree, together with archival coursework and a practicum." The directory also suggests, "Particular knowledge of certain subjects may be important for work in archives that have specialized topical emphases. Training and experience in conducting research in primary and secondary sources are also helpful."[16]

Professional definitions of archivists often avoid the matter of educational background. General promotional material from the New England Archivists defines an archivist in the following manner: "Archivists are trained professionals who decide what records to preserve, organize them, keep them in good condition, and share them with the public. We make sure people have access to the information they need, for today and for the next millennium."[17] This description begs the question of what constitutes a "trained" professional? Is it a particular type of education? Is it a combination of education and experience? Or, is it a combination of education and experience that is appropriate for the type of organization seeking to hire an archivist? Even the Society of American Archivists' standards and guidelines about graduate education of the past decade or so are somewhat ambivalent about how one prepares or enters the archival profession.

The difficulty of considering the appropriate background for any organization can be seen in the minutes of the Corporate Archives Forum. At this group's second meeting in June 1999, the following struggle with the placement of archives within businesses suggested that hiring an archivist and establishing an institutional archives can be more complicated than first meets the eye: "One commonality to much of the above discussion was a struggle over what to call an archives. Should it be the 'museum,' 'historical resources,' 'heritage center,' or some other name? Does this indicate that we no longer are comfortable with the standard definition of archives? Perhaps it indicates that a business archives first and foremost must demonstrate a business purpose for its activities. The group concluded that what matters most are the *relationships* that you establish with others within the corporation, rather than the *name* of the department."[18] In the same fashion, organizations need to look for archivists who possess an in-depth understanding of records and recordkeeping systems, the purposes of archival records, and how the maintenance of such records fit into the organizational mission and mandate. When organizations go out to accomplish such aims, they can find many conflicting and confusing ideas about what this means.

Educational Background

What is the appropriate educational background for an institutional archivist? An organization should look for an individual who has been grounded in archival theory, methodology, and practice. Organizations should look at the nature of graduate coursework an individual has taken in archival science and records management courses. An appropriate educational background should include at least an introductory course in archival administration, a course in records management (or a closely related field like information resources management or knowledge management), and at least several advanced archival courses, preferably focused on basic archival functions like appraisal, arrangement and description, and access and reference. Organizations should also want an individual who has had at least some coursework in preservation management.

Organizations also need to understand that not all graduate archival education programs are the same, either in philosophy or comprehensiveness of curriculum. Organizations should try to determine educational programs that are good fits with their missions and cultures. An institution involved in the entertainment industry would do well to develop contacts with the archival program at UCLA because "UCLA offers multi-level courses, experiential components, and research opportunities addressing everything from archival theory to electronic record-keeping to state-of-the-art techniques in digital preservation, asset management, and multimedia development for historical and cultural materials." A high-tech business corporation might do well to work with the archives program at the University of Michigan because it has the following mission statement: "The School of Information (SI) offers an integrated, multi-disciplinary degree (Master of Science in Information) with an optional specialization in Archives and Records Management. Distinguishing features of our program include breadth (we offer seven courses in ARM), emphasis on modern records and modern technology (electronic records management, digitization, and on-line access systems), and the mixture of classroom instruction with practical engagement." A cultural organization (such as a museum or historic site) might develop connections with the North Carolina State archives program with its mission being "NCSU's M.A. in Public History program is grounded on thorough training in history and in public history. Students select a sub-concentration in Public History (archives, manuscripts, editing, museology, historic preservation) and minor in some field of history." Finally, organizations needing individuals to work with complex records problems and technologies might want to work with the archival educators at the University of Pittsburgh, pursuing a mission that states that "Graduates become experts in records and recordkeeping systems, the evolution of new technologies, and the interdisciplinary nature of research about records and recordkeeping systems. The program is designed to help students understand that archivists and records managers work to administer records as evidence rather than only as information or cultural artifacts."[19]

Samples of Work

Formal coursework is not the only criteria by which an organization should judge hiring a potential archivist. Organizations interviewing such individuals should ask to see samples of the individual's work produced while a student or, if experienced, while working in other archives and records programs. Prospective institutional archivists should be able to present examples of written papers on archival topics, products such as an archival finding aid or archival appraisal report, and evidence of applying formal coursework to real-life situations. Organizations will also want to see evidence of work that may help them assess an individual's potential for working in their particular work environment, emphasizing either their analytical and/or communication abilities. Organizations should let applicants know in advance what kinds of particular or specialized evidence they might want to see, so that prospective employees can come to the interview prepared to present their best and most relevant work.

An Important Consideration: The Needs of the Organization

The degree to which an organization wants to consider the educational background of its applicants for an archivist position might depend on whether the organization seeks an experienced or relatively new entrant to the field. Many organizations assume that the best kind of individual for their archivist position will be one who has considerable experience, especially since the North American archival profession has stressed experience over formal education (the field has always operated with the assumption that a masters degree is the entry degree along with experience). However, organizations wanting an archivist need to ask themselves what kind of experience is desirable and then set criteria for evaluating such criteria.

Not all experience is equal. Institutions should consider applicants who have experience in similar kinds of organizations or with the kinds of records that they might need to work with in their own institutional setting. However, beyond such considerations, organizations need to ask themselves a series of questions about the emphasis on particular archival functions that their institutional archivist should possess. An experienced archivist who has worked extensively on arrangement and description and the use of descriptive standards may be of little use to an institution that wants its archives primarily for use within the organization and that has intricate and complicated archival appraisal challenges. Likewise, an archivist with experience in working only with traditional paper records will be of little use to an organization that needs an archivist to work almost exclusively with electronic records systems.

Most individuals working in the archives field also possess a subject masters or a specialized bachelor's degree in a discipline very different from archives and records management. Organizations need to consider whether a subject degree is essential or desirable and search for individuals who possess such a degree in addition to formal graduate coursework in archival studies. Archivists with degrees in fields such as public administration, law, a science, or some other such discipline can be matched up to organizations that might have a focus in such a field. A law firm or law school, for example, could do well with an individual trained as an archivist or who has a degree in some aspect of law or who has received training and experience as a paralegal. A corporation in the field of agribusiness would like to have an individual with archival education and a degree in some discipline related to agribusiness. The critical key to such hirings, however, is making sure the prospective archivist understands primarily records and record-keeping systems, rather than only approaching the documents and their systems from a content perspective.

Many archivists contend that both history and library science—the disciplines playing host to graduate archival programs in North

America—constitute additional subject degrees. While both fields are helpful, it depends on the nature of the courses that the individuals completed as to whether these would constitute subject degrees. History degrees can come with many different emphases, from a particular era of American history to broader designations such as European or Asian history. The most useful aspect of a history degree would be the extent of focus on the study of historical methodology and the use of archival sources for research, but this also varies considerably from program to program.

Organizations that want to establish institutional archives, by hiring an archivist, need to reflect on what field of history is necessary or useful for an archivist to have. A high-tech firm, for example, would do well to hire an individual with a degree stressing the history of science and technology. The same is true for individuals holding degrees in library and information science. Information studies is a broad field, and students can focus on very diverse topics ranging from a particular kind of library to a technical dimension such as telecommunications. Again, organizations need to consider the nature of the specific courses taken, and they might do well if they are an institution working in the information industries. For a long time it was assumed that individuals with degrees from library and information science schools would do well working with electronic records requiring technical expertise or in an environment emphasizing access and the use of descriptive standards. Here again, it is necessary to focus on the educational experiences of the individual from such schools.

Organizations hiring individuals with archival education and a specialized subject degree may encounter some problems in accomplishing this objective. Some institutions with highly specialized needs might find it difficult to find individuals who meet both criteria, and they should consider whether it is easier (or better) to hire an archivist who can learn about the discipline or a subject specialist who can be supported in formal archival education. Both approaches have been successful.

Organizations should be open to interviewing individuals who fall on either side of this professional fence, and should try to find the individual most suitable for the particular circumstances of the organization. This is a problem that may be disappearing as archival education programs expand and as a more diverse group of individuals are attracted to the field. A decade ago it was very difficult to find individuals who possessed both archival knowledge and technical expertise; now many archival education programs are equipping individuals with knowledge about both.

Archival Certification

Some organizations may look to archival certification as a means of identifying prospective archivists. This is especially the case in archivists joining records management programs, since this field has stressed individual certification in lieu of developing stronger graduate education programs. The Academy of Certified Archivists, established in 1989, exists to provide a "leadership role by defining the knowledge and abilities necessary to be an archivist," via "certifying archivists, ensuring professional archival standards, and promoting the employment of Certified Archivists." The Academy further explains its role in this way: "The academy participates in the definition and advancement of professional archival education, concepts, and issues. It identifies and promotes understanding of archival goals, ethics, and standards. Professional certification provides the only available standard by which employers are able to judge the qualifications of prospective staff members."[20] Whether this self-promotional information is accurate or not is debatable. For example, very few job advertisements state any employment qualification requiring certification. Furthermore, graduate archival education has developed largely on its own, with some modest encouragement from the SAA and few incentives from the Academy. From my perspective, and this includes being on the SAA governing council that voted to approve certification, the Academy's first decade has been a disappointment.[21]

Despite such qualms, the question remains as to whether an institution should seek to hire a certified archivist. Certification ought not to be the only criteria, nor should any organization consider certification to be the primary means of establishing professional standards. Organizations should first consider the other attributes of a prospective archivist: knowledge of records and recordkeeping systems, expertise with archival systems, other disciplinary knowledge relevant to the organizational mission and work, personal characteristics such as ability to communicate and to work well with others, and so forth. The only time an organization might want to consider certification is when it opts to hire an insider and to provide this individual training in archival work. Individual certification might then be a reasonable benchmark and target for professional achievement, although this, too, might be far less important than the ability to succeed in the organization.

WRITING AN ADVERTISEMENT AND ADVERTISING THE POSITION

- Organizations should provide specific information about all the elements of the archivist position in an advertisement, after the organization has worked to visualize the kind of person it desires to have as an archivist and the nature of its archival program
- Organizations should use the various electronic venues for advertising their archivist positions to reach the greatest number of prospective applicants in the most expeditious fashion
- Organizations with no experience in hiring archivists or in supporting an archival program should consider using a knowledgeable consultant to help ensure a successful search

Advertising for archivists has become easier than ever, although writing advertisements still requires careful thought about the organization's needs. Most advertisements are now placed on the listservs, primarily the Archives and Archivists list, or on the World Wide Web; the Society of American Archivists posts advertisements on its "Online Employment Bulletin."[22] More specialized positions, such as those focused on visual materials or electronic records, might appear on the rapidly proliferating number of electronic discussion lists with an emphasis on archives (although most of these are also posted on the Archives and Archivists list as well). Basic information about the core group of these listservs can be found at SAA's Web site.[23]

The advantages of these electronic advertisements are obvious. Advertisements can be posted almost immediately and reach more potential applicants than was ever possible through the slower traditional print sources. When the archival community relied on print distribution, the posting of job positions could take one or two months, and it was often a guessing game as to where to print the advertisements. While university archivist positions were obvious advertisements for the *Chronicle of Higher Education*, it was more difficult to decide where to place advertisements for other kinds of positions. Many local archival programs or organizations hiring their first archivists often advertised in local and regional newspapers and printed business outlets, but this always lessened the breadth and depth of the applicant pool (unless the organization happened to be in a major urban area already supporting a community of archivists). The new networked society and profession has eliminated nearly all of the problems about timing, distribution, and reaching qualified applicants.

What has not changed at all is the difficulty of defining and describing the position and advertisement. The structure of archival job announcements has been relatively stable over the past two decades. These advertisements usually include general information about the institution, a description of position responsibilities, qualifications, clarification of any "preferred" qualifications, salary (although only about one-quarter to one-half provide any specific salary statements), closing dates for applications, expected hire dates, and, of course, application information about where to submit applications. Some elements are promotional in nature, such as the information provided about the institution. The other elements should be described more precisely, but being precise about educational requirements can be difficult given the range of educational backgrounds that prospective applicants might possess.

The key to writing a good archival job announcement (a good advertisement being defined as one that attracts a suitable pool of applicants) lies in the organization visualizing what kind of person it wants in the position while being open to a broader spectrum of applicants. Phrases like "dynamic and creative individual" indicate that such thinking has occurred. Beyond this important activity, there are other steps organizations can take to attract strong applicants and eventually hire the right individual for the position. First, the job responsibilities should be as specific as possible, indicating to whom this archivist reports and the number of paid and volunteer staff the archivist supervises. Second, if this position includes unique requirements (such as subject knowledge) or has special characteristics (such as responsibility for developing a new electronic records management program), these should be described clearly. Third, if there are particular opportunities for professional growth within the organization and if the organization is committed to having the archivist professionally involved, the advertisement should refer to these aspects of the job. Fourth, the salary ought to be specified (if there is room for negotiation mention this as well), at least within a certain range of low–high salary parameters. The higher the salary the better for attracting a large pool of qualified applicants; most organizations should review current job advertisements to determine salary ranges within their organizational setting and region (primarily to be able to offer competitive salaries).

The method of interviewing applicants is a process that must be carefully considered long before the advertisement is placed or the first applicant arrives. Some organizations set up elaborate series of group and individual interviews while others use a more informal process with one search committee. There is no right or wrong way to conduct interviews, unless the interview process does not allow the organization to discover what it needs to know about each applicant. If an organization is vitally concerned about the archivist's ability to make public appearances, then it should require each applicant to make a presentation about their view of archival work or why they are interested in this particular career opportunity. If an organization requires an archivist who can work on very technical problems using electronic information systems for recordkeeping, then it should make sure that the applicant is interviewed by other technically oriented and proficient staff. There should also be opportunities for flexibility within the interview process to accommodate the prospective archivist's questions (after all, this individual is interviewing the organization, too).

Using a Consultant

Organizations that have no experience in hiring archivists or in supporting archival programs, should consider hiring an archivist to help them work through the process. The consultant can be useful first in assisting the organization to evaluate the need for and nature of institutional archives. The consultant can also be helpful in writing the position advertisement, guiding the organization in where to post position announcements, structuring the interview process, helping to identify individuals to be brought in for interviews, and in making final decisions about who to hire. Having an outside, objective, and knowledgeable consultant can save the organization from making critical errors in what is obviously a very important process for developing institutional archives.

BASIC READINGS

Institutions interested in hiring archivists also can do a modest amount of homework. There are only a few basic books that will help an organization begin to approach hiring an archivist. Elizabeth Yakel's *Starting An Archives* (Metuchen, New Jersey: Scarecrow Press and the Society of American Archivists, 1994) and Gregory S. Hunter, *Developing and Maintaining Practical Archives: A How-To-Do-It Manual* (New York: Neal-

Schuman Publishers, Inc., 1996; 2nd edition, 2004) are the most basic primers on the fundamentals of an archives program. Judith Ellis, ed., *Keeping Archives* (Canberra, Australia: DW Thorpe in association with the Australian Society of Archivists, Inc., 1993) is an excellent one-volume textbook on archives. Richard J. Cox, *Managing Institutional Archives: Foundational Principles and Practices* (New York: Greenwood Press, 1992) is a thorough description of the elements of institutional archives programs. Some volumes focus on particular kinds of institutional archives, such as Nancy McCall and Lisa Mix, eds., *Designing Archival Programs to Advance Knowledge in the Health Fields* (Baltimore: The Johns Hopkins University Press, 1994); William J. Maher, *The Management of College and University Archives* (Metuchen, New Jersey: Scarecrow Press and the Society of American Archivists, 1992); and Bruce Dearstyne, *Managing Government Records and Information* (Prairie Village, KS: ARMA International, 1999). To get a feel for the history and nature of archives and archival programs, James M. O'Toole and Richard J. Cox, *Understanding Archives and Manuscripts*, 2nd ed. (Chicago: Society of American Archivists, 2005) is a good place to start.

CONCLUSION

I am most often asked what should be the salary for an archivist in a particular organization. Usually, this is a trick question, because what the inquirer really wants to know is what is the lowest salary they can pay. My response is always the same—you get what you pay for; in other words, if the organization believes that it is essential to have an archivist (for all the reasons enumerated in this chapter), it should set a salary that will attract the best person available and one that will keep the archivist happily working in the organization. The more important issue ought to be whether the institution can continue to administer its records, and the information found in these records, without an archivist. Once an organization reaches this point, it will make the proper decisions concerning matters like salary and type of individual to hire. Then, the organization will understand the importance of carefully considering what it needs to do in order to make the best decision in hiring an archivist.

ENDNOTES

1. "National Association of Government Archives and Records Administrators Statement of Preferred Qualifications for Directors of Large-Scale Government Records and Archival Programs." (January 1999) Available: http://www.nagara.org/news/02_04_99_news.html.
2. This can be found at http://www.archivists.org/prof-education/arprof/html.
3. Sue McKemmish, "Yesterday, Today and Tomorrow: A Continuum of Responsibility," available at http://www.sims.monash.edu.au/rcrg/publications/recordscontinuum/smckp2.html.
4. This statement is available at http://www.archivists.org/prof-education/arprof.html.
5. Yogesh Malhorta, "Knowledge Management for the New World of Business," available at http://www.brint.com/km/whatis.htm.
6. See the United States Environmental Protection Agency, *Glossary of Common Records Management Terms*, available at http://www.epa.gov/ngispgm3/nrmp/gloss/gloss01.htm.
7. Richard J. Cox, "Electronic Systems and Records Management in the Information Age: An Introduction," introduction to a special issue of the ASIS *Bulletin*, 23 (June/July 1997), available at http://www.asis.org/Bulletin/Jun-97/.
8. Terry Cook, *The Archival Appraisal of Records Containing Personal Information: A RAMP Study with Guidelines* (Paris, UNESCO, 1991). Available: http://www.unesco.org/webworld/ramp/html/r9103e/r9103e00.htm#Contents.
9. *Glossary of Common Records Management Terms*, available at http://www.epa.gov/ngispgm3/nrmp/gloss/gloss01.htm.
10. *Free Online Dictionary of Online Computing*, available at http://wombat.doc.ic.ac.uk/foldoc/index.html.
11. See, for example, Piers Cain, "Data Warehouses as Producers of Archival Records," *Journal of the Society of Archivists* 16, No. 2 (1995): 167–171.
12. This statement is found at http://lcweb.loc.gov/ead/.
13. Refer to the Privacy Rights Clearinghouse, for example, available at http://www.privacyrights.org/.
14. See Paul Conway, "The Relevance of Preservation in a Digital World" available at http://www.nedcc.org/plam3/tleaf55.htm.
15. See Kiwi Careers, available at http://www.careers.co.nz/jobs/11b_lib/j21730c.htm.
16. *SAA Directory of Archival Education in the United States and Canada, 1999-2000*, available at http://www.archivists.org/prof-education/dir_part1.html#archivalprofession.
17. This statement is at the New England Archivists Web site available at http://www.lib.umb.edu/newengarch/aboutArchives/index.html#saves.
18. The minutes of the meeting are available at http://www.hunterinformation.com/caf99.htm.

19.   All of these statements are taken from the SAA's current education directory at http://www.archivists.org/prof-education/dir_part2.html.
20.   These statements came from the Academy's Web site at http://www.certifiedarchivists.org/membaca.html.
21.   At the time of the original writing of this essay, these views came from my "Certification and Its Implications for the American Archival Profession: Changing Views, 1989 and 1996" located on my personal Web site. I subsequently expanded these comments in another essay published in 2002 and now chapter six of this book.
22.   This is available at http://www.archivists.org/employment/index.html.
23.   This is located at http://www.archivists.org/listservs/index.html.

2

Why Organizations Need Archival Consultants

INTRODUCTION

Consultants play an extremely important role in helping organizations reevaluate and rethink their priorities, objectives, and activities, but there has been little discussion about hiring consultants to advise about archives. This essay is intended to make up for this lack.

Years ago I ran a project that required hiring a number of consultants. One of these consultants was asked to make a public presentation, and he started his remarks with the admonition that a consultant was nothing more than a "dummy away from home." The substance of the joke was somewhat two-edged. It spoke to the fact that someone could look good out of his or her native habitat but not be listened to back home. Since then, as I have both consulted and hired consultants, I often have had reason to reflect on this definition. Sometimes, as I have consulted, I have felt like a dummy. Other times, I have wondered if I was involved in hiring a dummy.

Besides being a humorous perspective on a sometimes difficult process, the notion of a consultant as a nearly empty vessel is actually closer to why and when we hire people to work as consultants. The prospects for a consultant being successful often resides more in the process leading to the decision to hire a consultant and how his or her task is formulated rather than in the knowledge, experience, or interpersonal skills of the consultant.

The failure of a consultant has more to do with the hiring organization being dumb than anything the consultant might or might not do, say, or recommend. There are instances, primarily in the business world, where consultants have learned a lot, developed astute working principles, written books, become famous for inventing the latest buzzword, and ultimately commanded hefty speaking fees. These cases often have a major impact on how records are created, administered, and viewed by the organizations, as the reengineering and reinventing craze of a decade ago suggest, requiring archivists and records managers to be aware of what their bosses are reading, thinking, and desiring.[1]

CONSULTING EXPERIENCE

We have had general advice written about how libraries and archives find and hire archival and records management consultants,[2] but we had not had many discussions about records management programs hiring archival consultants. Given that there is no certification or licensing of individuals to qualify them as consultants or to guide organizations in the process of identifying and hiring a consultant, some basic common sense and principles about how to do this seems warranted.

The advice offered here is based largely on my own experience as a consultant or in hiring consultants (as well as in teaching about the basic administration of archives and records programs). Since judging the experiences of an individual is critical to determining whether to engage his or her services, a brief discussion of my work in this area follows. In reading this essay, one can assess how much credibility to assign to my advice based on what I bring to the table.

For over twenty years I have consulted, not as a full-time vocation but as an activity in addition to my other responsibilities either working as an archivist and records manager or, over the past decade, as an educator of future archivists and records managers. Why do I consult? Sometimes it is because the consulting activity represents an intriguing or challenging task. Sometimes I undertake a consulting assignment because someone asks me to do the project as a favor. Sometimes I seek a consulting project because it is a way for me to stay abreast of what is happening in the field (now that I am mostly in the classroom) with the possibility of building case-study material for use in the university. There is also, of course, the prospect of additional income, but it is rare that the financial reward has been incentive enough to spur me to go into an institution.

Like most consultants, I tend to specialize in certain dimensions of providing such advice. Mostly, I have focused on either the assessment of existing archives programs or in advising an organization about how it should administer its archival records. Occasionally, I have examined a particular archival function, such as appraisal. Often the use of my services has expanded during the consulting work since new issues, problems, and interests emerge as a consultation is carried out. It is rare, in fact, that my consulting experience has not turned out to be broader than expected. Organizations seeking advice about their archives seldom anticipate all the matters that they should consider; this is, of course, why the organization is seeking outside advice.

My consulting has cut across nearly every kind of organization. I have consulted in cultural organizations (such as museums and historic sites); government agencies (such as county and municipal governments, state archives and records management services, and regional authorities); educational institutions (such as music conservatories, universities and colleges, and private high schools); regional consortia; religious organizations (such as dioceses and monasteries); businesses (such as bank and financial organizations, architectural and engineering firms, and consulting services); and professional associations (such as in the medical and health-care industry). While these organizations generally have differing recordkeeping requirements and interests, their problems and needs are remarkably similar when it comes to the preservation and management of their archival records. Helping them define what archives and archival programs represent is almost a universal need throughout these organizations. Perceptions of archival programs are often incorrect, while practical problems are often the same. For this reason, consultants are often advocates or educators on behalf of archives and archival programs.

WHAT DO ARCHIVES CONSULTANTS DO?

The obvious answer to this question is that archival consultants provide advice and assistance in the care and management of an organization's archives. Australian archivist Judith Ellis notes that archival consultants are hired when there are none on staff, when additional expertise is needed, when external opinions or recommendations are needed (perhaps for political reasons), and when "dedicated" resources are needed for a person to take on a full-time project.[3] I have seen archival consultants assess existing programs in general, train current staff through workshops, analyze particular archival functions (appraisal, arrangement and description, preservation, reference and access, and public programs), make public presentations in order to provide a framework for building broader support and resources, and perform basic arrangement and description work. The range of potential archival consultation services is as enormously varied as are archival programs.

There are more basic aspects of what such consultants do. Well-known records management consultant John Phillips states, "Consultants add value to an organization that is, for some reason, beyond the capability of existing employees or contractors. This added value may arise from a number of consultant attributes, including content, expertise, knowledge, behavior, special skills, or contacts."[4] In some cases, an expert is hired to help the organization to determine what it needs to do in establishing an archival operation. In other cases, a consultant may work with present archivists to reevaluate some aspect of their services.

At their most fundamental level, consultants are about problem solving. Again, John Phillips provides this view: "What clients invariably need is to solve a problem—a business risk, a technology bottleneck, or a conceptual quagmire. The consultant's role is to solve that problem through possible combinations of analysis, report writing, presentations, team facilitation, or innovative perspective."[5] Most often in archival consulting, the problem is whether an organization should establish a program for its archival records or seek some other arrangement (such as depositing the records within an archival program collecting records within a region or a documenting a particular industry or topic). Because of challenges about the uses of or implications of technology for an archives program or in records systems, a common problem is trying to determine how an archives program could or should administer electronic records. The challenge with problem solving is the level of expectation that an organization possesses about what an archives consultant can do for them.

Archival programs often seem to run on the proverbial financial shoestring. As a result, there often are unrealistic expectations about what a consultant can do. Many times I have witnessed various staff of archival programs being antagonistic when they initially discuss possible costs with a potential archivist. Consultants are facilitators and sources of knowledge, offering their expertise for hire. They are there to evaluate a situation and to make recommendations, but it is ultimately the responsibility of the organization to implement the recommendations in a manner that is meaningful to their own corporate culture (in other words, it is their responsibility to make things work).

External advisors often have limitations in what they can learn about an organization in consulting work that may last only a few days or a few months. As a result, the consultants often will provide options and alternatives, or they will offer consulting over a longer term to monitor how an organization tries to make changes or start new programs. Any successful implementation of a new program or reengineering of an existing program depends on the program being a good fit with the institutional culture. It is impossible for an outsider to understand such a culture in a matter of a couple of days or even a couple of weeks. It is ultimately the organization that needs to adjust the consultant's recommendations to match the culture. If an organization is working constantly to do things on the cheap, the chances for success may be very limited. Following the advice of a consultant to create a new archivist position and then having the institution hire someone who is unqualified is not conducive to success.

It is often amazing to watch organizations work with consultants. A prominent archival institution once hired a public relations expert to deal with a problem: the archives' press releases were never picked by the media to become featured news stories. The archives hired a good public relations expert, sent her a stack of press releases for evaluation, and participated in a day-long meeting with her. The consultant tactfully explained that the press releases were too long, too dense, and too packed with professional jargon. The chief staff of the archives seemed more inclined to argue about this conclusion, and the institution ignored any advice to make changes in the substance of their press releases. The result was predictable: the archives press releases continued to be ignored.

WHAT IF OTHER CONSULTANTS WERE THERE BEFORE?

An interesting problem arises when a consultant discovers that other consultants have worked with the same organization on the identical issues a few years or more before. The present consultant should always ask if there have been other consultant reports and ask to be given copies of the report(s). If necessary, the consultant can specify that the names of these other consultants be redacted.

The purpose of examining such reports should always be to try and ascertain why the earlier efforts were unsuccessful and not to critique the efforts of previous consultants. Many years ago I was asked by a local government to evaluate its archives and records management needs, and I approached the state government archives, which I knew had had advisory services for local governments for many years. I was sent a thick file with nearly seventy-five years of contacts, advice, and descriptions of efforts. At first glance I wondered what I could offer that would be new. However, I learned a lot before ever visiting the local government about why a records program had not been established. This information was instrumental in enabling me to develop recommendations that were successful in starting a new program that has continued to this day.

SETTING REASONABLE EXPECTATIONS: FORMULATING QUESTIONS IN ADVANCE

The problem with intelligent and professional staff investing financial resources and time into a consulting process that seems doomed from the start most likely stems from a failure in formulating particular objectives for the consultant. Most often a consultant is hired to help bring about change. It is possible–(actually, it is likely)–that the desired change will require other more substantial changes, ranging from alterations in a cherished mission to the replacement of staff. If an organization is not interested in making changes, then the effort and money are wasted.

If we return to the general theme of "dumb and dumber," it is necessary to be honest about the process of hiring an archives consultant. The organization seeking to hire a consultant will often set forth basic requirements in a request for proposal (RFP), and the consultant will need to set forth certain questions for consideration. How well the organization can develop an RFP and how well the prospective consultant can present questions and issues to be explored will often determine the potential success of the consulting project.

Here are some of the kinds of questions a good consultant needs to ask to help an organization evaluate its existing archival program:

- What is the main mission of the records management and archives programs? Is this mission primarily to serve the organization and its ongoing administrative, legal, fiscal, and research needs, or particular research constituencies inside and outside of the organization, or both?

- Do the current budget, staffing, and administrative placement of the archives and records management operation support the present or desired mission of these programs? How well coordinated is the archives and records management program? Do these programs support the organization in documenting itself, as well as enabling it to meet legal, fiscal, and administrative needs?
- Could digitization projects and use of the World Wide Web eliminate the need for any physical restructuring of the organization's archives? Is there an adequate infrastructure (staff expertise and resources) to enable the organization to utilize the Web for administrative, research, training, and other purposes in an effective manner?
- How well known and regarded is the archives and records management program *within* the organization? Is it effective in meeting records management and archival objectives? How well known and regarded is the archives program by external researchers?
- Are the archives and records management staff given the opportunity to attend professional archives and records management conferences, workshops, and institutes? What is the nature of support given to this staff?

Here are some questions that a consultant should ask office workers and managers within an organization that is considering how to integrate an archives program within a records management operation:

- What are your key concerns in managing records within your office? Do you believe that the organization is providing adequate assistance to you in your efforts to manage records? What do you see as the organization's major strengths in managing its records? What are the major weaknesses or areas where improvement is needed?
- Are you primarily still working with paper-based records and records systems? What are your primary concerns about these kinds of records systems?
- What kinds of changes have you detected regarding the use of electronic systems in your office? Do you consider these electronic documents in the same manner as other more traditional records? Is the organization's technological infrastructure adequate for its present work and for continued operations in the next five to ten years?
- Do you know how to get help to resolve a records problem or to have a question answered about a records matter? How often have you needed such assistance in the past year?
- Have you had a reason to request records from the archives or to search for information in the archives? What kinds of assistance have you needed? Do you feel you need to know more about the archival program?
- If you could change anything about the present management of the organization's records what would it be? Why?
- Have you been unable to answer questions because of insufficient records? If so, describe these occurrences.

Consultants also need to ask careful questions of the staff currently working within an organization's archives and records management program. Some of these questions are:

- Do you believe that the organization has the right configuration of staff to support its records management and archival programs? If not, what are the most obvious weaknesses in the staff?
- Does the organization provide enough support for the continued training of its archives and records management staff? What are your major needs in training? What do you think the major priorities are to help strengthen the archives and records management staff in their regular work and responsibilities?
- Are there enough staff to perform the duties required to carry out the mission of the organization in regard to managing its records?
- Are the salaries and benefits adequate for attracting the best staff to work in the archives and records management programs?
- What is the best aspect of working for the organization? What is the least desirable aspect of working for the organization?
- How well connected to the archives and records management professions do you feel? Do you have acceptable access to the professional literature and standards?
- How do you feel about your working relationships with other organizational staff in assisting them to manage the institution's records? Describe the nature of any improvements that are needed.
- Do you have a sufficient technological infrastructure to support your work? If yes, what do you anticipate your future needs will be? If no, describe your most pressing technical needs?

A similar set of questions needs to be asked of the institution's managers regarding their records, including the following:

- Are the management lines within the organization clear and well articulated? Do people understand who is responsible for records management and archival decisions, policies, and procedures? Are all of the various units and key individuals connected via electronic mail for ease of administrative and other decision making and communication?
- Does the organization possess detailed policy and procedures manuals or guidelines to enable all of its units to understand how they should create, maintain, and dispose of records? Does the archives and records management programs provide adequate policy guidelines for matters like privacy and other access restrictions?
- Have the archives and records management programs developed and used workshops, institutes, and other venues for staff training about records matters? What is the present need for such training within the organization?
- What role should the organization's Web site play in offering advice and guidance in archives and records management work? Should it develop

a clearinghouse of information, with links to other useful Web sites and materials readily accessible to staff about archives and records management standards, methodologies, practices, and trends? What are the implications of such a Web site for staffing in the archives and records management program?

- Are the position descriptions up-to-date and suitable for the staffing of the archives and records management programs? How often are these position descriptions reevaluated? How are they reevaluated? Is there adequate staffing and adequate designation of the various archival and records management functions?
- Are the current salaries and benefits of the staff in the archives and records management programs adequate for attracting and holding individuals with the necessary knowledge, skills, and attitudes?

All of the above questions cover critical aspects of an archives and records management program within an organization. These are general questions meant to produce a profile of the archival operations. Often, however, a consultant is employed to examine one or more aspects of what constitutes the essential functions of an archives program. This may require more than one consultant since there are specialists within the archives field, and the organization may need such specialization to go more deeply into the problems and practices within such functions.

PROBING DEEPER INTO PARTICULAR ARCHIVAL FUNCTIONS: MORE QUESTIONS

An archives program generally consists of the functional areas of appraisal, arrangement and description, reference and access, preservation, and outreach. Each function requires specific questions tailored to the motives, means, and mechanisms of the functions, as outlined below:

Appraisal and Documentation

- How adequate is the organization's collecting or acquisition policy? Do the present archival holdings represent an adequate documentation of the organization? What are the particular strengths and weaknesses of the documentation, and how could any gaps best be addressed? How do the organization's archives and records management programs measure success in appraising, or acquiring, or documenting certain aspects of the organization?

- How does the organization determine when to seek to acquire an individual's personal papers? What are the relative space, staffing, and other resources involved in working with the organizational versus private papers? How do the various archival programs balance these very different responsibilities? Are there other archival repositories (either connected to the organization or completely separate from it) that collect or would wish to acquire such personal papers?
- What presently happens with the records of organizations that may have a particular connection to or role in the history of the organization? Does the present archival program actively seek out such records? Has the acquisition of the records of affiliated groups been the result of a deliberate documentary objective or the result of serendipitous circumstances?
- Does the organization have standard records management retention schedules? Do the records retention schedules provide adequate documentation about the nature of the records and the reasons for the appraisal decisions? Can these schedules be easily understood by staff within the organization who may not be well versed in records management and archival terminology and standards? Are the schedules current? How often are the schedules reevaluated?
- How does the organization deal with artifacts related to its history? Does the archives program have exhibit areas where these materials can be displayed? Is there adequate staffing to support such an operation? What are the implications for the storage and display of artifacts? Is there another institution connected with the organization that has a museum function or that could serve this purpose? How do the archives and records management programs advise the organization's staff and others about what to do with such artifacts?

Access and Use

- How often do various administrative units within the organization use the archives or ask for assistance in records management matters? How do the archives and records management staffs work with these units to inform them of relevant information found in records?
- What is the current usage of the archives by outside researchers? What kinds of statistics and information about archival use are being maintained by the archival operation? How often does the archives conduct evaluations of its reference services?
- Are the research facilities adequate for visiting researchers in terms of providing parking, suitable work space, computer connections, copying facilities, reference materials, and archival finding aids? Does the archival program regularly ask for feedback from researchers about the nature and quality of its reference services?
- What is the level of reference services provided over the Internet? Are staff of the archives programs subscribed to listservs in case researchers interested in the organization's records post questions and make inquir-

ies? Is the organization using these listservs and Web-based resources to promote its services and collections?

- Is the organization monitoring creative, important, or groundbreaking use of its records by external researchers?
- Is the archival program using accepted professional standards (machine-readable cataloging [MARC] format and Encoded Archival Description [EAD]) for describing its records? Are the programs reporting their holdings to the national bibliographic utilities (like Research Libraries Information Network [RLIN]) or providing finding aids on the World Wide Web for researchers to use?

Preservation

- Has there been an assessment of electronic records development and use? Are these newer technologies being adequately dealt with by the records management and archives programs? Do individuals within the organization understand that electronic mail, databases, and other digital materials may be records that should be managed using appropriate procedures and standards?
- What is the present condition of the archives storage areas? Do they provide appropriate environmental controls for archival records? Can these spaces be easily and economically retrofitted for appropriate archival storage? What would be the costs of converting these spaces? Are there better alternatives for securing adequate archival storage space?
- What is the present condition of the archival records? Has a conservation needs assessment been done? How often have such assessments been done?
- Does the organization have a professional conservator on its staff or access to a conservator or regional conservation center? How does it provide advice to administrative units about the creation and use of records so that archival materials are handled in appropriate and sensitive ways?
- Does the records management program use a commercial records center for the storage of its inactive records? Have the costs of using such a center been evaluated? Has the organization considered the advantages or disadvantages of using a commercial records center versus that of renovating and using its own facility (perhaps in a unified archives-records center operation)?
- How does the organization use microfilming for preservation purposes? How does it adhere to standards for such microfilming?
- Has the organization's archives considered digitization of certain of its key records series for use in making such records available over the Web?
- How is the organization dealing with rare and valuable printed materials that need conservation treatment?

Public Programs

- How do individuals find out about the archives or records management programs? Have the archival programs, especially, periodically ascertained why, how, or where the researchers come from?
- What kinds of publicity has the organization done to promote its archival programs? Is there a brief descriptive videotape of its operations? Have the archival and records management programs identified and used other video materials about archives and records management issues?
- Does the archival program have current descriptive brochures of its holdings and services that can be mailed or used at conferences and other general publicity venues?
- Do the archives and records management programs distribute a newsletter (print or electronic or both) about its services, activities, and other aspects to the various units within the organization?
- Does the organization's archival program have a sufficient public profile for individuals and organizations holding related records to know they could donate or deposit the records?
- Do the archival program's staff gather and maintain finding aids and other information materials on records related to the organization held in historical societies, public libraries, university special collections, and other repositories?
- What kind of relationship with the media does the organization have in regard to its archives? Have the archival programs been featured in newspaper, television, or radio reports?

WHERE DO ARCHIVAL CONSULTANTS COME FROM?

There is no one source to find a consultant to help assess an organization's archives program or to determine whether there should be an archives program. Word-of-mouth continues to be important in identifying individuals who can consult, but it is important to be able to evaluate the qualifications of such potential consultants. Some have practical notions of where consultants come from. Here is one view: the "consultant is probably someone you've known and worked with for years, loyal and competent, who has found himself prematurely 'downsized' or 'reengineered' or 'outsourced' out of a 'permanent' job and forced back out into the job market to earn a living any way he can—with consulting the perceived easiest option." This has happened a lot in the records management world: "many predict that with the dominance of new technologies and electronic record-keeping practices, many traditional records managers are bowing to the more deeply entrenched information systems managers and finding little room to coexist in the corporation. They are finding themselves expendable."[6]

This trend certainly suggests that there are many reasons why someone becomes a consultant. It does not indicate that everyone should, and it certainly provides little guidance as to why an organization should select a particular individual for its consulting needs. Organizations can examine resumes, ask for a list of references, and generally inquire about a potential consultant's expertise and reputation. There are other means to determine whether someone should be hired.

Archives consultants come from the ranks of practitioners, educators, and a small group who are full-time consultants. The matter of where the consultant comes from has far less to do with the notion of why someone's services are engaged and more to do with the knowledge, experience, and other qualities that are appropriate for the organization's needs. A well-known practitioner who has already been successful in his or her own organization might be an ideal choice if there is close similarity between the organizations. An educator who has been in the forefront of research about archives and the elements of what constitutes a successful institutional archives will be a good choice if the organization believes it needs innovative approaches or if the nature of the organization's leadership will respond more positively to someone of an academic ilk. Obviously, there are as many variables among those who call themselves consultants as there are among the organizations seeking their services.

CHOOSING AN ARCHIVES CONSULTANT

The first priority in choosing an archives consultant is finding one with the appropriate background and knowledge for meeting the objectives of the consulting project. This is not just a matter of choosing someone who seems qualified, but it is also a process of finding someone who has professional perspectives compatible to the organization seeking to use the consultant's services.

Not too long ago, I provided a statement of my own principles and convictions about approaching a particular consulting project. I described my fundamental working principles as follows:

- Records are valuable to an organization (and to society) for their evidence, accountability, and memory.

- Archivists and records managers are first and foremost experts on records and recordkeeping systems, and they are part of an array of records professionals.
- Organizations need to support records programs in which archival and records management functions are joined or, at the least, closely connected.
- Institutional archives are essential both to the organization and to society, and they have been underemphasized by both the archives and records management disciplines.
- Personal papers and organizational records share many common characteristics by virtue of being records, and the prospects of having one program administer both should not be a problem.
- Although electronic records systems are becoming more commonplace, most organizations have challenges to face in administering both electronic and paper records.
- Broad-based documentary objectives and cooperative acquisition programs can be effective means for identifying, preserving, and making available archival records.
- There is a discernible and distinct body of knowledge supporting the work of archivists and records managers.

None of these convictions would be surprising, because I have written extensively about them over the past decades. However, some of these are debated within the archival profession, and it is important that the consultant and the organization contemplating using the consultant's services be as candid about their views as possible. Otherwise, the prospects for a happy relationship and a successful consultation are remote.

IS MORE THAN ONE CONSULTANT NEEDED?

Many organizations assume that a single consultant is more than satisfactory for dealing with their archives. Often, one consultant is more than adequate. However, most organizations should expect that the consultant will advise them to employ other consultants for certain kinds of specialized areas, especially since it is often impossible for either the organization or the consultant to know for certain about everything that they will encounter before they commence the consulting project. Consulting work is, after all, first and foremost a data-gathering exercise, and all such exercises are likely to uncover hidden needs and result in some surprises.

Some organizations have recognized that their needs require them to employ more than one consultant. A decade ago I was involved in a consulting project in which a local government employed about a dozen consultants, each representing a different aspect of archival work. The consultants were brought together initially for a group meeting about the overall purpose of the project, then dispatched separately to examine different areas of the government archives program, and then brought back together to share the results of their work and to share thoughts about overall needs and priorities. Another consultant was hired to bring together all the various consultant reports into one summary report.

This project was a rich and valuable process, as much so for the consultants as for the government. For me it demonstrated how a few people look at the same situation and see completely different needs and solutions. The downside of this project was that it required a large expenditure of funds, and it produced so many valuable ideas as to make it a bit difficult to know exactly where to begin. For example, some consultants recommended replacing existing staff, others suggested re-training present staff, and others advised creating and filling new positions in an effort to work around problem employees. These are contradictory recommendations, but ultimately the government had to contend with its own rigid civil service requirements that made any of these solutions untenable.

WHAT SHOULD THE FINAL CONSULTING PRODUCT BE?

Good final reports are not only the result of hiring the right consultant. Organizations need to be specific in what they seek from the consultant, keeping in mind how the report will be used and who will read it. An organization might ask a consultant to prepare a more general, concise version of the longer report in order to make sure that busy executives who make the final decision about implementing the consultant's recommendations can read and understand the recommendations. The organization should also ask the consultant to provide advice about both internal and external requirements governing the institution's records, identify positive dimensions of the present organization's records management that can serve as a foundation, and offer a variety of options for how the archival records can be administered.

Many organizations assume that all that a consultant will do is to examine the records and interview records creators and custodians on site. This seems logical given both the nature of the consultancy and the fact that records and information are the lifeblood of any organization.

Records, the documentation of transactions carried out by a company or any organization in its normal course of business, provide evidence that a company uses to meet its administrative, fiscal, legal, and other requirements. Records help a company to be accountable to external regulatory bodies. They are also crucial for any organization's corporate memory.

Corporate memory is often crucial to helping an organization function in essential ways, from supporting corporate culture and staff morale to providing a means for understanding past decisions and current practices. So, for example, firms working in architecture, engineering, and environmental realms or some other heavily regulated occupations have to be aware of legal concerns generated by the Americans with Disabilities Act, national energy codes and standards such as the United States Department of Energy Building Standards, local standards for residential and commercial buildings, codes enacted by the Federal Emergency Management Agency and the U.S. Department of Housing and Urban Development, the U.S. Department of Energy's various codes and standards, as well as professional standards and best practices reflected by the American Institute of Architects and other professional associations. Such companies also need to comply with standards and codes related to their own offices, employees, and related internal activities. Many of these standards, codes, and best practices contain advice, guidelines, or absolute requirements for the management of records and other information sources.

The consultant will learn some information about such external regulations affecting records as interviews with staff are conducted. However, at times preparing a set of recommendations regarding an organization's archives requires research by the consultant best done away from the organization. This can lead to problems in the consultancy if time for this is not built into the negotiation about the project. An organization can avoid some of these problems if it employs an individual who is very knowledgeable about the company's business or by hiring two or more consultants who bring different required knowledge to the project. Most consultants build in time for such research and preparation of the report into their proposal.

Although most organizations that employ a consultant are asking for advice about a problem and a solution (an exercise that can be negative in results and tone), it is important for the consultant to remember that developing a solution requires building on some positive aspects of the organization, its staff, and its culture. I once consulted with a company with the worst administration of records that I had ever witnessed, but even there I discovered positive elements that were crucial to establishing new policies and practices for the management of its records. This organization demonstrated that it possessed a growing awareness of the need to manage its records (it had, obviously, hired a consultant). No one seemed opposed to the idea that records needed to be better managed in the company, and every unit seemed to be making some efforts to gain some control over records. This company was also taking steps in developing better company-wide communications with an internal newsletter, an intranet, and other means for individuals in various divisions to know what was going on in terms of projects, new technologies, and other topics, all supporting the more mature development of a company records and information resources management program.

The organization reflected a commitment to providing its staff with the best information sources to make its employees as up-to-date in their work as was possible, providing another critical element to a foundation in standardizing records practices. This company also had a quantity of records that was still manageable, with a sufficient corporate memory to assist in improving the management of records and information (the company was only a quarter of a century old, with individuals who had been there long enough to help unravel the mysteries of older projects, the company's history, and the company's noteworthy projects and successes), and the company had a strong focus on services to clients, which suggested they had maintained good records about the relationship between the company and its customers.

Most consulting projects end in a final report. Such reports can range from a letter of a few pages to extensive reports of thirty to fifty pages or more. Any report should consist of a detailed description of the consultant's findings, recommendations, consideration of various options when there are options, and potential partners and other resources. It is generally advisable for the consultant to arrange the recommendations in a plan of work of short-term (one to two years or less), mid-term (three to five years), and long-term (more than five years). Executive summaries are usually helpful to guide an organization in discerning the most salient points and advice.

A final report should show that a consultant has digested and assimilated data gained from site visits, interviews, and analysis of policies and procedures and other documentation, with careful annotation of the basis for the recommendations. The final report should also indicate when the consultant has sought the advice of other experts and what aspects of the report are being influenced by such sources. Print and electronic resources that have served as the basis for certain recommendations should be mentioned and the most important of such sources might be added to the final report as an appendix. The consultant should also identify key activities where other consultants, in future development work, might be required. Since archives and records management work is becoming increasingly complex and specialized, it is becoming more rare that one individual can provide the full range of advice being sought.

A final consultant's report also should include a variety of options. For an archives program, for example, options range from hiring an archivist and having an institutional archives, to placing the records in an existing archival repository, to entering into a cooperative arrangement with other similar organizations to manage their archival records. There are strengths and weaknesses to any of these options, but the relevance or value of these options depends on the organization's interests, resources, and culture. I have long been an advocate for the establishment of institutional archives, and I am not embarrassed to explain my reasons in a consulting situation. However, there have been instances where I have recommended that an institution's records be deposited in a nearby archives where they could be better used in a safer environment. Giving an organization such options will help them wrestle through the complexities of managing their records.

CRITICAL ASPECTS: ADVICE ABOUT GETTING STARTED AND OPTIONS

Archival consultants (or any consultants for that matter) are change agents. In one of the best essays on archival consulting, Virginia Stewart writes, "Archival consulting is the application of outside expertise to a situation demanding capabilities or resources that are not available within the organization. Consulting is a direct intervention in the operating processes of an organization with the expectation of change."[7] Consultants are hired not only to assess needs but to make recommendations for meeting such needs and solving problems. The most critical advice needs to come in the area of starting an archives program (or an archives and records management program).

Common advice almost always involves a few important actions.

An organization should start the process of establishing an institutional archives by establishing an internal advisory committee for implementing an archives program. An advisory committee should focus on key tasks such as determining the best administrative placement of an archives unit within the company, writing position descriptions for professional staff, establishing a working budget for starting the new unit with funds for equipment, software, office furniture, professional subscriptions, travel funds for staff development, and other such activities.

For an institutional archives to be successful, it must possess some particular attributes and play some important roles. These include establishing an organization-wide records management program; hiring a professional archivist; vesting the archives program with administrative authority; providing/locating a suitable archives facility; preparing a manual of policies and procedures for archives and records management; creating a Web site for publicizing the records program; and securing sufficient funds to support the ongoing functions of a records program. Each of these attributes and activities is described in more detail below.

Organization-wide Records Management Program

For an institutional archives to identify the most important records possessing continuing value to the organization, it must be part of or connected to a records management program. Records management programs focus on the administration of active records (still being used at the point of creation), but they enable organizations to carry out a variety of other important activities, as follows:

- develop a full picture of their records and needs for their management
- ensure that legal, fiscal, and administrative uses of the records are being accounted for
- identify records with archival value through the process of assigning time lengths for the maintenance of all records (called records schedules)
- advise on procedures for managing records in all offices
- keep all staff aware of legal, fiscal, or other changes that might affect the nature of records and recordkeeping systems

Professional Archivist

An institutional archivist must have the services of an individual educated about archival and records management work and the nature of records and recordkeeping systems. This individual oversees all aspects of the archives program, including

- appraising (identifying records with archival value)
- arranging and describing archival records
- handling reference requests
- making decisions about additional preservation needs of the records
- promoting the purpose and services of the archives

In the case of an institutional archives the archivist will be responsible for records management policies and procedures and for seeking manuscripts and other materials related to the organization from outside sources. The archivist also will need to serve as a clearinghouse of information about records matters for the organization, requiring him or her to:

- attend professional conferences
- stay current with professional literature and standards
- develop networks so that other experts may be consulted as to certain concerns regarding the organization's records (an example would be utilizing a conservator for the repair of certain archival records beyond the normal cleaning and storage)

Archivists usually enter the profession with a graduate degree in history or library and information science with an emphasis on archival studies.

Administrative Authority

The success of the archives program is very dependent on having sufficient authority within the organization. The archivist should not have to negotiate every aspect of work on archival or records issues, but it should be well known within the organization that this person is vested with authority to make decisions about all aspects of the management of records. Such authority usually requires two components. First, the archivist should have as direct a tie to the chief administrative officer as is possible. This means different things in different organizations, but the crucial concept here is that the archivist is able to seek advice and make decisions about records matters as quickly and easily as possible. Second, there should be an advisory group overseeing the work of the archivist and the archivist. Again, while the situation may vary from organization to organization, such a group is usually comprised of individuals who can deal with administrative, legal, fiscal, and research aspects of archives. Some organizations will have one or more experts from outside serving on the group, and the nature of these experts may vary as well with different organizations. This group obviously advises the archivist and usually has the authority to set records policy with the archivist's assistance.

Archives Facility

Every institutional archives program must have an adequate archival facility. Such a facility enables the storage of archival records and requires space for researchers and archival staff's work on the records. Storage space must allow for the maintenance of records in an area that has stable temperature and humidity controls and is free from dust, pollutants, insect, and vermin. The area must also have an adequate security and fire suppression system. The public research and staff work areas should be well lighted and wired for computer and other equipment. The archives facility should be accessible to people in the organization and the public, meaning that it should be nearby the primary working areas of the organization and provide adequate parking. There also need to be arrangements for handicapped accessibility. The facility should be clearly marked by signage and easy to find. Most institutional records programs also usually have contracts with commercial records centers for storage of inactive records that will be destroyed at some point without coming into the archives. The use of commercial records centers can save money and free up valuable storage and office space for the use of more important records and other functions. However, commercial records centers are only a viable option if the organization has a records management program with well-developed records retention schedules.

Policies and Procedures Handbook

All institutional archives programs produce policies and procedures handbooks. These handbooks cover all aspects of archival and records management work, and they generally include policies and procedures directed to individuals working within the organization, researchers who come to use archival materials, and volunteers and other staff who may work within the archives. Besides providing an opportunity for an institutional archives program to bring together existing professional standards, such policies and procedures handbooks cover the following:

- records retention schedules
- procedures for transfer of records to the archives
- access policies
- guidelines for arrangement and description practices
- researcher's rules and forms
- disaster-preparedness plan in case of emergency
- appraisal criteria and collection development policy

The nature of such handbooks will change as an institutional archives program is established and matures. Most programs, working with their advisory group, will identify and add new policies as circumstances warrant them.

Web site

With the advent of the Web, most archival programs have set up Web sites to reach a wider segment of the public and to make their services and holdings more accessible. These sites usually include the following information:

- location
- hours of operation
- mission
- nature of archival holdings
- special events

Some archives have made full-texts (digital reproductions) of important records available on the Web. Others have created educational packets for use in elementary, middle, and high school history and other classes. Some programs have created virtual exhibitions (sometimes based on real exhibitions held at their institutions) highlighting their archival materials. Not all institutional archives put up publicly accessible Web sites if their records are generally reserved for internal use only.

Sufficient Budget

The size of a budget for an institutional archives always will depend on the scale of the archival program. At the least, there needs to be:

- a full-time professional
- some support staff (at least a part-time secretary)
- a personal computer (with printer and scanner)

- funding for professional conferences and professional publications
- a discretionary budget for the purchase of software and other equipment as needed

DO ARCHIVES CONSULTANTS LOOK ONLY AT RECORDS?

There has been a lot of debate in recent years about whether the records professions have morphed into other information and knowledge disciplines. Some of this debate has been quite acrimonious, as we have seen with the Association of Records Managers and Administrators (ARMA) recent initiative in the area of "strategic information management." We can amass a wide range of views, from cynical to visionary, and never resolve just what archivists and records managers should be setting in their professional parameters. Organizations seeking consultants for archival issues may have no opinions or they may have strong (and sometimes wrong) perspectives. To a certain extent it makes little difference, since a consultant is likely to start at one point and uncover many other issues not thought of at the beginning of the project.

A consultant considering the needs for an institutional archives may wind up considering matters such as artifacts or libraries, since there are substantial parts of the archives held in the form of laboratory equipment or books and other published materials. In my own experience, for example, I have repeatedly been hired to look at the issues related to the organization's archival records and found myself needing to advocate for the establishment of a records management program. In another consulting effort I was engaged to make recommendations regarding reformatting, but I quickly became aware of other concerns and issues regarding the use and maintenance of the archival records that required a broader report on records. I wrote a report considering both solutions for general problems regarding the management of the archives and proposals regarding the reformatting of selected archives. Reformatting, whether accomplished through traditional approaches such as microfilm or through the use of newer digital technologies, must be decided upon and utilized within the context of records management needs and current records uses. There is no reason to focus on a small portion of the archival records for enhanced preservation or access if no provision is being made for overall administration of records.

WHAT WILL ALL THIS COST?

Costs for archival consultants, as with all consultants, can vary quite a lot. General consultants will range up to $1000 a day (and more) plus expenses for consulting, while specialized consultants in technology issues can cost even more. There is a perception that archival consultants who charge this much and more are over-charging for their services. The primary reasons for this perception are the lower salaries of certain groups of archival professionals and the limits of funding by federal agencies for consulting services that often go no higher than $350 a day. Another problem is that many people believe archival consultants are those hired on an hourly wage to do such work as arrangement and description of historical collections. The latter are not consultants but hired itinerant professionals.

Some of the most frustrating experiences I have had were in working with organizations that balk at consultants' fees *and* reasonable salaries for professional positions. There is the old adage that you get what you pay for, and trying to establish and run an archives program with little investment is hardly a good idea. Managing and protecting archival records is an expensive process, but that should be of little concern since these records are quite valuable both to society and to the organization.

Beyond the daily consulting fees, organizations will face a variety of decisions about how long to employ an archivist. I have done assessments of an organization's archives in a day with another day to write a report, but I generally believe that a three-to-five day consulting arrangement is best. Of course, the timing depends on how complex the organization is and what it is seeking to assess. However, all things being equal, an organization needs to think in terms of $3000 to $5000 for a useful consulting project to be done. It may be even more expensive since some organizations seek to engage the services of additional consultants or extend the contract of the original consultant to help in advertising and hiring an archivist or for continuing advice about the establishment of an archives program.

CONCLUSION

The success of a consulting arrangement rests on the long-term results. Most organizations make immediate gains in their knowledge about archives and archival programs, since this is what the organization was seeking. It is the responsibility of both the consultant and the organization (although ultimate responsibility always rests with the organization creating and holding the archives) to set reasonable benchmarks for measuring progress. Some organizations will decide to employ the services of an archives consultant either periodically or on a retainer to help evaluate what is being done in establishing an archives. But whatever the organization ultimately accomplishes will depend on how well it formulates its consulting objectives and on its ability to secure the services of a qualified consultant.

ENDNOTES

1. I originally wrote about this in my essay, "Archives and Archivists in the Twenty-First Century: What Will We Become?" *Archival Issues* 20, no. 2 (1995): 97–113, included in this volume in an updated form as chapter seven.
2. Karen Benedict, "The Records Management and Archives Consultant," in Edward D. Garten, ed., *Using Consultants in Libraries and Information Centers* (Westport, Connecticut: Greenwood Press, 1992), pp. 129–136, and Virginia Stewart, "Transactions in Archival Consulting," *Midwestern Archivist* 10, no. 2 (1985): 107–115.
3. Judith Ellis, "Consulting into Business Archives," *Archives & Manuscripts* 27 (November 1999): 16–25.
4. John T. Phillips, "Preparing to Be a RIM Consultant," *Information Management Journal* 34 (January 2000): 58.
5. Phillips, "Preparing to Be a RIM Consultant," 60.
6. Linda A. Farrell, "So You Want To Be A Consultant . . .," *Records Management Quarterly* 31 (January 1997): 21.
7. Stewart, "Transactions," p. 107.

3

How Organizations Define Archival Positions

INTRODUCTION

What should those being hired for an entry-level archives position know? What other attributes should they bring to their first job? These are obvious questions for those educators of prospective archivists and other records professionals who are responsible for developing and maintaining a curriculum for preparing people to do such work. These questions get to the heart of what higher education is seeking to do. Henry Roscovsky, in a practical orientation to how universities function, provides some purposes for a "liberal" education that also ought to be objectives for a "professional" education:

- An educated person must be able to think and write clearly and effectively.
- An educated person should have a critical appreciation of the ways in which we gain knowledge and understanding of the universe, of society, and of ourselves.
- An educated American, in the last quarter of this century, cannot be provincial in the sense of being ignorant of other cultures and other times.
- An educated person is expected to have some understanding of, and experience in thinking about, moral and ethical problems.
- Finally, an educated individual should have achieved depth in some field of knowledge.[1]

But the real issue is whether these kinds of qualities are actually being sought by organizations hiring entry-level archivists and other records professionals.

This issue is closely tied to another critical matter. How should an educator advise students on how and where to seek jobs in the archives and records professions? It is, at best, a dicey proposition. David Denby, in his return to the university that he recounts in his *Great Books*, captures this dilemma when he writes, "In 1965, I could afford to be in a funk; they could not [referring to students today]. Many of the students' older brothers, sisters, and friends may have had trouble finding a job. Gloomy talk of 'downward mobility' was in the air. The economy was changing rapidly: entire categories of work were vanishing. Even the highly educated were vulnerable, their jobs—their functions—disappearing in a fit of corporate 'downsizing.' An eighteenth-century writer rejecting the very idea of society may have seemed to be playing an irritating and malicious game, taunting the students just as they felt growing anxiety about finding a way *in*, finding a *job*."[2] Budding archivists and other records professionals are also uneasy about their ability to obtain that first position, especially as they use up their savings or borrow heavily to finance an education. Their attitudes may become hostile as they encounter archivists in the field who harbor less than positive thoughts about graduate and even continuing education.[3] The exercise for an educator in examining job descriptions is important because it can serve as a reality check, providing more concrete examples to ensure students that there are jobs out there and helping the educator to make sure that students are learning what they need in order to fill these positions.

The reasons why records are valued and the ways in which records are created and maintained are changing rapidly. Analyzing position advertisements provides relevant and current information not just to those in education but to all information management professionals who are responsible for hiring and who desire to understand the shifting trends affecting their own careers.

Since an important role for archival educators is to be involved in the profession as an agent of change (making sure that students are educated for careers not for short-term technicians' labor),[4] job advertisements must be viewed against recent evaluations of records and the technologies supporting them. It is critical for the field to know about what it needs in records professionals given the immense changes in recordkeeping and the increased visibility or focus on the accountability, evidence, and memory roles of records. These changing values are reflected in the highly publicized cases of the Swiss banks and Nazi gold, World War II and stolen art, the Heiner or "Shreddergate" case in Australia, increasing concerns about secrecy and access to public records, and a host of other related concerns.[5]

It is also critical to understand how these attributes have changed in the past two decades given the advent of new electronic recordkeeping technologies and given the immense changes in the professional literature (especially the efforts of the past decade to define records and recordkeeping systems)[6] and professional education.[7] We have shifted from mainframe to mini to personal to networked computing. We also have seen a new move back to the centrality of records and recordkeeping systems as the focus of archival work (although just how far this has spread has the archival or records management professions is uncertain).

What has not kept pace is the effort to define specific competencies for archival and records management work. The adoption more than a decade ago by the American archives community of individual certification (trying to define basic competencies), with the guiding statement that "Certified Archivists are practitioners who have demonstrated mastery of the knowledge and experience necessary for modern archival practice," seems like a good start until one looks more closely at the competencies, education, and practice intended to enable someone to gain these competencies. Upon closer examination, it seems unlikely that an individual can gain the competencies with such modest education and experience as is required for certification.[8] More importantly, these competencies may no longer be appropriate given the current marketplace.

National efforts in Canada and Australia to define competencies for records specialists in new electronic office environments have produced very different results. The Canadians have identified four job functions—systems designer, policy driver, retrieval expert, and advisor/coach with skills, knowledge, and abilities going much farther beyond what has normally been seen in job descriptions.[9] The Australian competencies are based on the Australian Standard in Records Management (AS 4390, published in February 1996) and include responsibilities such as designing, creating, and using systems that keep records; creating records and capturing them into recordkeeping systems; maintaining and managing records over time; and making records accessible.[10] While these competencies continue to be refined, they nevertheless start from different premises.

There are some hopeful signs: the growth of stronger, more comprehensive graduate education programs with a new focus on records and recordkeeping systems and a renewal of research by doctoral students on archives and records topics. These suggest changes in the manner in which the knowledge of archivists is being constructed (or reconstructed).

STUDYING JOB ADVERTISEMENTS

One way to determine what organizations are searching for when hiring archivists is to study job advertisements. The hypothesis of my original study was that entry-level job advertisements would, over a twenty-year period, reflect a significant shifting toward the new technologies and a knowledge of records and recordkeeping systems, instead of just archives and records management principles and practices (experience). A supplemental study extended the analysis through the year 2003, providing a run of almost thirty years of job advertisements. The study examined entry-level archivist positions, critical to all information management programs and suggestive of what other information management professionals may face in regard to changing organizational and societal requirements and needs. The study's findings should be instructive to all organizations employing information management professionals, regardless of whether their focus is on current records management, archives, or the converging of records into new fields such as knowledge management.

The study examined entry-level archivist position advertisements in 1976–77, 1986–87, and 1996–97, with the supplemental study covering 2001–03. The earliest job advertisements (1976–77) reflect the work of a reinvigorated Society of American Archivists, coming just as it started publishing a newsletter and as it was establishing itself as the prime route for advertising positions. The next group (1986–87) reflects SAA's subsequent solidification of itself as the primary professional outlet for position announcements, as well as the beginning of new professional standards governing archives and records management work. The late 1990s group provides an opportunity to determine the impact of the Academy of Certified Archivists and the emergence of stronger graduate and continuing education programs. The most recent group of advertisements provides additional opportunity to determine the impact of new technologies and changes in the field on requirements for hiring new archivists. The last two groups of advertisements (1996–97 and 2001–

03) were based on advertisements posted on the Archives and Archivists listserv. The time periods were sampled to provide a longer view of changes in job requirements and to cover a substantial period in information technology uses for archives and records management.

Why should archivists and other records professionals look at job advertisements now? For educators, continually reflecting on what should be taught and how to place students, this is part of an ongoing set of responsibilities. But what about others who identify themselves as records professionals? They are challenged by other information disciplines, as they stress information or knowledge, an emphasis weakening the importance of records as information sources because records primarily capture evidence. Then there is the rapidity of change in recordkeeping technologies, especially in systems such as document management systems that do not stress records but objects and which do not allow for the orderly management of records in whatever format. The growth in education programs in terms of number of faculty and comprehensiveness of curriculum provides more options for individuals interested in records professions as well as greater confusion about what such a career choice means or about the differences between these programs. These concerns justify considering job advertisements.

Job advertisements ought to help employers to attract the right people for records positions.[11] Employers, and the records community in general, need to have the best qualified and best prepared people going into the profession; but those people have to possess the right education and have to be interested in the right jobs. The field also needs people who can deal with change and recordkeeping technologies, not those who long for a static notion of records and recordkeeping systems. Records professionals need to be able to understand how a particular system has grown, changed, what it represents, where it may be going, and how to advise in its future development or replacement by another system—or its demise.

A study of changing notions of archivists and other records professionals in job advertisements may help us to understand our needs for future professionals in a more precise manner. This understanding can then be used to develop new or revise existing curriculum, to attract different kinds of students, and to advise organizations hiring records professionals about the kinds of qualities and qualifications these people should possess.

Archival and records management educators and the field should be looking for the most creative people they can find. For creativity to occur, according to Howard Gardner, "On the one hand, one must be sufficiently steeped in the findings and principles of the domain, or the chances that one will reinvent what has already been discovered are too pronounced. . . . As a complement, one must be willing to advance beyond the facts and even the conspectus of the domain, and dare to lay out a wholly new approach to the issues."[12] This most closely approximates the role for emerging graduate archives and records management education programs and for the graduates of these programs.

It is also crucial to examine job advertisements because we need to focus on knowledge instead of merely skills and attitudes (although the latter are important). Numerous comments on the importance of the knowledge of recordkeeping for archivists and records managers have been made through the years, but much of what passes for education is still training (teaching short-term skills) or apprenticeship (learning the particulars of work at a single work place).

More than twenty years ago, Frank Evans urged that the "archivist must master by study of the holdings themselves most of the administrative history and the subject content of archival holdings which are, by definition, unique. All archivists, however, need an understanding of how institutions and organizations, both public and private, originate and develop; of types and patterns of internal organization and functions; of recordkeeping and records systems past and present; and of the relationship of documentation in all of its forms to organizations and functions."[13] Evans incorporated records management into his notion of archives management and studies.[14] Have education programs supported Evans's commentary, or do they really focus on how to do certain archival functions with the assumption that they provide insights into aspects like organizations, recordkeeping systems, and recordkeeping functions?

THE CHALLENGES OF EXAMINING JOB ADVERTISEMENTS

There are limitations in looking at job advertisements. Sociologist Dorothy E. Smith notes that a "job description" is not an "account of an actual work process," but it orders the relations among a variety of organizational settings. "When actually hiring," she argues, "a job description functions as a schema ordering selective attention to an individual's qualifications and experience. . . . The standardization of job descriptions or methods of generating job descriptions across firms facilitates the functioning of extended labor-market relations: it is indeed integral to their organization."[15] This suggests, however, that there is still a crucial role for job advertisements in organizations; moreover, the similarity of job advertisement structure in archival advertisements (responsibilities, qualifications and education, preferred versus required experience, and salary) and in the content of the advertisements (especially in how educational requirements are described) suggests that these job advertisements, for better or worse, have come to reflect some consensus by the archival profession.

How job descriptions are used is another limitation. One human resources management specialist has suggested that managers often do not make full use of job descriptions because they believe that the descriptions can be too general, even if they are recognized as being quite valuable for activities such as designing jobs, recruiting, and orienting employees.[16] Still, even if flawed, job descriptions can be used in important ways for orientation and socialization.[17]

Given that a large percentage of North American and even foreign archives and records management jobs are now posted on the Archives and Archivists listserv (or other lists), we can perhaps suggest that these postings provide a kind of socialization and orientation to newly employed and budding archivists and records managers; certainly, students preparing for careers in the records professions are reading these advertisements as a means for preparing their own portfolios. Job advertisements and descriptions are crucial for delineating job duties and functions. Even with limitations regarding job objectives, performance evaluation, and abilities or personal attributes, job descriptions are important for stating the nature of duties or functions which are expected to be carried out.[18]

Another problem in evaluating job advertisements is that any critique of them depends on the individual's perspective and presumptions about the nature of the professional work being done. Records manager Ira Penn recently wrote a criticism of a records management job posting which is predicated on his notion that records management being subservient to that of archives is "completely backwards." He is concerned about how records schedules are put together, the nature of records creation, and the requirement for an MLS without the requirement for the Certified Archivist (CA) or Certified Records Manager (CRM) designation.[19] Admittedly, my own perspective is quite the opposite—that the nature of records work needs to be built around the record/recordkeeping system life cycle or continuum, requiring archives and records management functions to be tied together by a focus on records and recordkeeping systems. While I have not focused on records management positions, my own predilection is that archives and records management positions will become more similar due to the changing nature of records systems and the growing recognition of the importance of records.

RESEARCH ON JOB ADVERTISEMENTS AND POSITION DESCRIPTIONS

Like most aspects of archives, there is an uneven quantity and quality to research about the basic requirements for archival work. Twenty years ago, Peter Wosh noted the problems with the lack of standards and adherence to what standards did exist.[20] A brief essay in the Society of American Archivists newsletter about the same time provided a glimpse into what employers were looking for, including good writing and speaking skills (67 percent), the ability to get along with people (61 percent), good common sense (55 percent), the affinity for detail and accuracy (45 percent), a desire to learn and grow (42 percent), the love of hard work (18 percent), possessing well-defined goals (9 percent), having a determination to succeed (6 percent), having a talent for persuading or selling (3 percent), and demonstrating a sense of urgency (3 percent). This informal survey was based on ten qualities sought by administrators outside the archival profession and featured in a 1981 essay in the *New York Times* by William N. Yeomans. Archival administrators, in this survey, added three more qualities: responsibility (24 percent), initiative (21 percent), and good judgment (18 percent).[21]

Two months later, the same newsletter ran a brief description of what applicants thought were important qualities, developing the following set of qualities: good writing and speaking skills (89 percent); ability to get along with people (67 percent); good common sense (11 percent); affinity for detail and accuracy (78 percent); desire to grow and learn (33 percent); a love of hard work (22 percent); and a determination to succeed (11 percent).[22] These two surveys clearly suggested an orientation to personal attributes and attitudes rather than knowledge. It appears that this attitude is being challenged today, even though recent job advertisements still list most of these kinds of attributes and attitudes— almost as if they are inherent qualities that make one a good records professional. Records management positions are even more likely to be dominated by such personal characteristics since most entering into this part of the records professions are likely to have a lower minimal education, to be more dependent on experience, and to be dependent on the ability to move up an employment ladder—all emphasizing skills and attitudes more than knowledge.[23]

The Society of American Archivists also started then to conduct more systematic salary surveys, capturing some of the characteristics of basic qualities required for holding an archival position, although the last most comprehensive survey is now more than a decade old. A 1989 SAA "Salary" Survey provided some additional information on job characteristics if not requirements, updating the earlier 1979 and 1982 SAA surveys. It was found that there was an average salary of $31,967, versus $21,419 in 1982, versus $16,092 in 1979; half of all working full-time reported in 1989 earning more than $29,000. Typical responsibilities were also noted: in 1989, 28 percent indicated that they do a little of everything versus 37 percent in 1982, and 30 percent had administrative responsibility while only 23 percent did so in 1982. The 1989 survey also concluded that "with the exception of a 35 percent increase in reference specialists, there is virtually no change in the relative proportion of archivists who claim to specialize in particular archival activities." The education of archivists was shown to include 12.8 percent with bachelor's degree versus 18 percent in 1982; 18 percent have a doctorate, while 16 percent held such a degree in 1982. Two-thirds of the archivists responding to the 1989 survey have one or more masters degrees, with half of these holding a MLS degree or dual MLS/masters degree. Fully 60 percent of the archivists reporting had taken workshops or institutes, 52 percent had taken graduate courses, 44 percent had taken field experience or internship, and one-third had received in-house training.

According to the survey's author, Paul Conway, "It is probably premature to declare either the MLS or the single master's degree (in history?) as the de-facto standard educational 'ticket' for becoming an archivist" although "the findings call into question the viability of the concept of the history master's or the MLS as an entry-level degree. . . . Archivists new to the profession report significantly lower levels of education. Respondents without advanced degrees are just as likely to report having a particular functional speciality as those with advanced degrees. . . . Those with graduate archival education courses are just as likely to be generalists as specialists." According to the 1989 survey, "these findings suggest that people who consider themselves a part of the archival profession and who are sufficiently committed to join the profession's only national association simply start working in an archival repository and increase their educational experiences as they work their way up the ranks of the organization or gain additional years of experience."[24]

The nineties, perhaps because of the increasing influence of the computer on both recordkeeping systems and records professionals' management applications as well as the expansion of graduate archival education programs to include doctoral research, was a time of renewed interest in position descriptions and job advertisements. Some of the writing was decidedly impressionistic,[25] but other essays appeared that carefully sorted through the evidence of job advertisements to consider particular impacts such as the emergence of more systematic descriptive standards.[26]

More detailed studies have come from dissertation research. Alan D. Gabehart, for example, conducted a study on employers' qualifications for entry-level archivists that produced a number of interesting conclusions.[27] Gabehart discovered that "the choices of bachelor's degree and master's degree in library science dominated the selections for all types of institutions," with a preference for a double masters degree in history and library science over just an MLS and/or only a masters in history and for undergraduate degree history was preferred with second choice being library science.[28] Gabehart's study also found that "A bachelor's degree appears to satisfy the minimum educational qualifications for employment in institutions outside the college/university community. For an individual planning to pursue an archivist position as an employee of a college or university, a master's degree in library science would be advisable. To attain a higher level of employability and mobility within the archival profession, one should look to a master's degree in history, library science, or, preferably, both." Gabehart extrapolated that, "Regardless of the subject of the master's degree, it would appear that an individual would be more employable in the archives field with an undergraduate degree in history."[29] Other findings worth noting include the low interest in foreign language competency, the fairly weak concern for conservation training and computer automation training, and the lack of impact of individual certification as a requirement.[30] Perhaps the most difficult conclusion to grapple with is that most employers do not place a high premium on graduate archival education, with 48.5 percent indicating it would have some benefit and only 24.6 percent seeing it as essential.[31]

Other studies from this decade have used job advertisements as one source to note changes in professional responses to changing records technologies, such as in my own study on electronic records management noting the paucity of advertisements for working with these technologies.[32] This latter book did prompt one response, with specific reference to my use of job advertisements. Thomas Brown, a National Archives staff member, took umbrage at my reference to the weak entry-level qualifications of the United States National Archives as well as to the evaluation of posted job advertisements. He stated, "by limiting the sources to position descriptions and vacancy announcements for archivists, Cox's study omits consideration of many professional staff at an archival institution who are not archivists."[33] This is a relevant point, except that most archival programs do *not* hire such people due to size, professional attitudes, and other factors; even with the National Archives the job advertisements and descriptions seem particularly relevant given that institution's inability into the late 1990s to deal effectively with most electronic records (no matter how many kinds of records and information professionals it may be hiring).[34]

NEW FINDINGS FROM AN ANALYSIS OF JOB ADVERTISEMENTS

The importance of records to society, its organizations, and its citizens is too great not to understand more about the qualifications needed for hiring professionals to manage them. For this study, an entry-level position was defined as being any position requiring two or fewer years of experience or explicitly described as an entry-level position. Experience suggests that new graduates of education programs compete for these jobs. Defining an archives position does pose some problems, partly because of the legacy of the schism between archivists and records managers. I have included those positions that are advertised in the SAA employment service or posted on the Archives and Archivists listserv. I have excluded specifically conservation jobs because of the great differences in qualifications and responsibilities,[35] but included records management jobs if advertised via SAA or the listserv. Records management jobs do reflect a much greater diversity and range at this point, from senior records management positions to technical information analyst and database management positions to clerical and filing positions at a much lower level.[36] Yet there is a much closer relationship between archivists and records managers, historically as well as through certification.[37]

The methodology employed in this study is a simple tabulation of jobs advertised—looking at educational requirements, knowledge areas explicitly asked for, archival functions mentioned, skills explicitly required, regional locations, institutional type, position titles, salaries, and content for records/recordkeeping systems focus. No jobs were counted twice and both Internet and printed advertisements were used for the 1996–97 positions. An interesting aspect of this study was the discovery that the Internet has become *the* primary source for archives job postings; 87.8 percent (202 of 230) of the positions were posted on the Internet in 1996–97 (in 1976–77 there were 63 positions advertised in the SAA *Newsletter*, in 1986–87 129 positions, and in 1996–97, 230 positions) with only 24.8 percent (57 of 230) of the most recent advertisements printed exclusively in the SAA newsletter. Since SAA is now placing its job employment bulletin online, the Internet/World Wide Web will continue to dominate the announcements of job openings.[38] Does this skew the results? Possibly. Paul Gilster noted that "employers today frequently post job offerings on the Net, the notion being that those unequipped with the skills to acquire them don't possess the skills to fill the position anyway."[39] While this may not be the thinking behind the electronic posting of archives positions, it is possible that there has been an effect on the positions considered here. The advertisements for the last time segment, from September 1, 2001 through the end of 2003, consisting of 266 advertisements, were captured exclusively from the Archives and Archivists listserv.

The appropriate place to start is with the basic educational requirements needed for entry-level positions. While Gabehart had found the opportunity for organizations to hire individuals with only a college degree, my analysis reveals that only a small portion of the positions advertised seem open to such individuals. The slight increase in the portion over the two decades of the eighties and nineties is puzzling, but it may be a recognition of hiring individuals with more records management orientation who traditionally have held lower-level degrees— as the much greater diversity of subject majors perhaps also reflects (see Table One). The more recent decline in the value of an undergraduate degree may be recognition that graduate archival education, after several decades of substantial improvement, has been established as the main means of entering into the field.

What seems likely is that posted archivist positions requiring only an undergraduate degree relate to institutions, such as historical societies or historic sites, or particular kinds of positions, such as those stress-

Table One
Educational Requirements for Positions
Requiring BA/BS
1976–2003

Discipline	1976–77 N=7 (11.1%)	1986–87 N=17 (13.2%)	1996–97 N=37 (16.1%)	2001–03 N=28 (10.5%)
History	4	17	21	25
Social Sciences	0	1	8	0
Archives	1	6	5	21
Library & Information Science	0	1	8	11
Humanities	0	1	6	0
Political Science	1	6	5	2
Public Administration	0	1	5	2
Records Management	0	5	2	4
Miscellaneous Disciplines*	1	8	12	24

* The miscellaneous disciplines include the sciences, American studies, business administration, art, anthropology, and architecture. None of these disciplines is mentioned more than a few times in any given year. Although records management was not mentioned often, it was left as a separate category.

ing records and information resources management, drawing on organizational or professional traditions. A position in a municipal archives program included the following requirement: "Bachelors Degree Knowledge of records management theory and practices. Knowledge of Washington State Public Records statutes. "Positions in state government archives or state historical societies, for example, often will only require a bachelor's degree because of state civil service requirements, resulting in statements such as this: "Bachelor's degree required; Master's degree or post-bachelor's coursework/training in Archives Administration, Library Science, History, Museum Studies or Records Management preferred." While some organizations continue to advertise a baseline educational requirement of an undergraduate degree, the general consensus of practice in the field is for a masters degree.

The masters degree is the predominate degree requirement, with decided emphasis at this level on a library and information science degree. In an earlier version of this essay, I stated that there was a weakness in focus on archival education because of a decline in the number

Table Two
Educational Requirements for Entry-Level Positions
Requiring MA/MLS
1976–2003

Discipline	1976–77	1986–87	1996–97	2001–03
Library & Information Science	20 (31.7%)	88 (68.2%)	142 (61.7%)	181 (68.0%)
Archives	19 (30.2%)	73 (56.6%)	104 (45.2%)	115 (43.2%)
History	38 (60.3%)	63 (48.8%)	83 (36.1%)	87 (32.7%)
Miscellaneous Disciplines*	11	22	38	25

* The miscellaneous disciplines include the Humanities, social sciences, art, public health, political science, liberal arts, museum studies, American studies, education, photography, public administration, business, conservation/preservation, law, records management (mentioned once in 1976–77, four times in 1986–87, three times in 1996–97, and twenty-two times in 2001–03), anthropology, folklore, architectural history, cinema, literature, and ethnography. The numbers in this category represent the number of times the discipline is mentioned and not the total number of positions as with the other categories.

of positions requiring graduate education *in* archives (see Table Two); it remains surprising that explicit references to *archival* education have not shown a marked increase. There has been, along with the growth of interest in the library and information degrees, a definite decline in history as a requirement. Certification of archivists is nearly invisible as a requirement, appearing in only 11 of 230 advertisements in 1996–97 and 24 of 266 positions in 2001–03 and all listed "preferred" or "desired" instead of required. Although some might quibble that archival certification is largely a post-appointment process, the fact that the entry-level positions are used suggests that certification's impact has been marginal.[40]

Why, given the supposed improving and changing nature of education, is there a weakness in representation in archives education as a requirement for entry-level archivists? Could it be the traditional wide casting in educational backgrounds in order to attract the best and most applicants or could it be (for government, at least) the way human resources or civil service define positions and their requirements? Most positions advertised seem to include an educational requirement that is more litany of possibilities rather than educational standard. It is not unusual, indeed it is quite common, to find educational requirements such as follows: "Master's degree in archives administration, library science, information management, business administration, history, or other relevant field." Clearly, this does not represent the wishes of an employer for the kind of disciplinary knowledge; rather, such a statement suggests a concern to make sure that no qualified candidates might be eliminated and a lack of clarity about where and how archivists are educated. Could this weakness also be because there are no separate archives degrees in the United States, leaving open the possibility for any number of degrees?

Despite the growth in graduate education, the main knowledge area preferred is experience (fully two-thirds of the advertisements seek experience, a portion that has been steady for twenty years) with an emphasis on descriptive standards and computer applications knowledge or general computer literacy, other heavily experiential knowledge domains (see Table Three).[41] It is surprising that the stress on computer applications and literacy has remained fairly constant, given the growing concern with how to administer electronic records systems and preserve digital documents. The demand for special subject knowledge has remained constant, reflecting the many topically or geographically defined archives. Many positions require knowledge of a state, region, or discipline. These findings could be an aberration because of the way I defined an entry-level archivist position (two or fewer years of experience), but the stress in requirements for standards and computer applications is not. The consistent request for special subject knowledge is probably a reflection of the preponderance of academic origins of job postings or the heavily regional and topical orientations of so many archives and historical manuscripts repositories.[42] The experience requirement might also reflect a continuing uneasiness with graduate archival education.

What is more telling about educational requirements and knowledge areas is the manner in which job advertisements enumerate archival functions as part of the job responsibilities. The primary responsibility, to an overwhelming degree, is arrangement and description (see Table Four), and this has been the dominant responsibility in job advertisements for three decades. This may be the most conclusive finding: the archives profession thinks of an entry-level archivist as one who will arrange and describe records and do reference on the side. The management responsibility, appearing consistently with some decline in recent years, is most often to supervise technical staff, student interns, and volunteers in arrangement and description work.

Table Three
Knowledge Areas Sought in Entry-Level Job Advertisements
1976–2003

Knowledge Area	1976–77	1986–87	1996–97	2001–03
Descriptive Standards	0	28 (21.7%)	85 (37%)	100 (37.6%)
Special Subject	16 (25.4%)	41 (31.8%)	58 (25.2%)	69 (25.9%)
Computer Applications/Literacy	0	28 (21.7%)	96 (41.8%)	98 (36.8%)
Languages	5	16	24	15
Research Methods	0	8	22	10
Archival Experience	28 (44.4%)	82 (63.6%)	151 (65.7%)	169 (63.5%)
Electronic Records	0	0	13	18
Audio-Visual Applications	0	8	10	7

Table Four
Archival Functions Enumerated in
Entry-Level Position Advertisements,
1976–2003

Archival Function	1976–77	1986–87	1996–97	2001–03
Arrangement and Description	45 (71.4%)	112 (86.8%)	166 (72.7%)	199 (74.8%)
Reference	13 (20.6%)	67 (51.9%)	99 (43%)	110 (41.4%)
Conservation/Preservation	4 (6.3%)	29 (22.5%)	67 (29.1%)	67 (25.2%)
Appraisal	13 (20.6%)	56 (43.4%)	63 (27.4%)	66 (24.8%)
Management	14 (22.2%)	46 (35.7%)	77 (33.5%)	43 (16.2%)
Public Programs	8 (12.7%)	30 (23.3%)	50 (21.7%)	52 (19.5%)
Oral History	4	1	2	2
Records Management	4	14	26	49 (18.4%)

All of this supports the heavy reliance on experience as a knowledge area—archives want people who can come in and arrange and describe from the start. This also supports the growth in interest in wanting people with a knowledge of descriptive standards. This is troubling to me. Given the move to appraisal as an analytical exercise requiring a knowledge of records and recordkeeping systems as well as how organizations work and create records, why hasn't appraisal increased in importance? Has arrangement and description as an exercise changed substantially in practice over the past twenty years, *other* than by the use of standards because of the reliance on automation? What may be occurring is that archival description standards are relatively easy to mention specifically, and these standards are quite well known at all levels of the field. Statements such as "Knowledge of Anglo-American Cataloguing Rules (AACR2), Library of Congress subject headings, Machine Readable Cataloguing Record (MARC) formats, Online Computer Library Center (OCLC), and use of an online cataloging system," or "Relevant experience should include work with large collections of organizational records, Machine Readable Cataloguing Record-Archival and Manuscript Control format (MARC-AMC) cataloging and familiarity with Ended Archival Description (EAD)" are straightforward and unambiguous (as opposed to softer responsibilities such as appraisal or reference).

In the past decade there have been two substantial changes in the archival functions enumerated in the position advertisements. There has been a sizeable jump in the percentage of entry-level job advertisements mentioning records management as a responsibility (Table Four). In some cases, records management is simply listed as one of the archivist's responsibilities, such as ,"Develop and maintain records management program, including document retention schedules." In other cases, the archival position is almost exclusively for records management functions, such as one university posting for an "Archivist for Records Management," seeking "an archivist to administer and further develop its university-wide program to manage records in all formats in accordance with state guidelines and professional best practices." This suggests that archival and records management positions, in certain organizations, may be converging, although the more recent emphasis by records managers on information and knowledge management also indicates that the convergence may not go far enough.

The other recent substantial change is the advent of digitization as an archival function. In the mid-1990s advertisements digitization is not even mentioned (and I have not included it as part of Table Four because of this). In the most recent group of archival job advertisements, 38 of the advertisements (14.3%) mention digitization. Clearly, the decrease in costs associated with digitization and the increasing importance of the World Wide Web for publicizing and making available archival records partly accounts for the recent importance of digitization as an archival function. It is also the case that knowledge of digitization is quite important for archival arrangement and description work.

Phrases like, "Experience in EAD/Document Type Definition (DTD) encoding of finding aids, Web page design, digitization of materials and electronic access strongly preferred," suggest the connection between digitization and arrangement and description work. And since the Web has expanded the possibilities of public programming and access to archival holdings, position descriptions are featuring responsibility statements such as, "Provide access to primary source material through a variety of means including digitization, traveling kits and classroom visits."

The strong emphasis on organizational and communications skills (see Table Five) should come as no surprise, since they would seem to be a commonsensical element for any job advertisement. Archival work (and all records work), after all, requires the ability to write well, to compose brief descriptions of elaborate records systems, and to prepare memoranda, grant proposals, articles, and other such products. The lack of detail about such skills three decades ago may reflect that over the past thirty years job advertisements have gotten longer and more detailed, although it does not fully explain why the advertisements of the mid-1970s were consistent in not including such language.

An examination of advertisements from four kinds of institutions posting advertisements in each of three time periods (through 1997) reveals a growth from averages of 97.8 words to 163 words to 202.5 words in length. The posting of positions on the Internet may be the most recent reason for this, eliminating word limits or a cost per word that was evident in the print advertisements. The most recent job advertisements, pulled exclusively from the Internet, average 346 words.

The prevalence of posting information about such skills also reflects the need to include information that will diminish legal and human re-

Table Five
Predominate Skills in Entry-Level Position Advertisements, 1976–2003

Skill	1976–77	1986–87	1996–97	2001–03
Organizational and Communication	1	50 (38.8%)	112 (48.7%)	178 (66.9%)
Word Processing/Computer	0	16 (12.4%)	54 (23.5%)	27 (10.2%)
Interpersonal	0	27 (20.9%)	63 (27.4%)	167 (62.8%)
Physical	0	3 (2.3%)	26 (11.3%)	26 (9.8%)
Close Attention to Detail	0	5 (3.9%)	22 (9.6%)	50 (18.8%)

sources problems; how else do we account for the growth in the ability to pick up and move boxes (the "physical" skill category in Table Five) as more and more archivists must face working with electronic records? The emphasis on basic skills such as using word processing is certainly logical although diminishing most likely because it is an assumed skill. All of this may be the result of the American archives profession's inability to resolve the issue that there are different levels of archival work, favoring instead a more democratic or egalitarian approach to employment and professional status.

The geographic distribution of the job advertisements was something of a surprise, with a flattening out over the three decades (see Table Six). The smallest portion in the Southwest was not surprising, given its generally more sparse population. But the greater balance between the other regions suggests, again, that the posting of job advertisements on various listservs may have provided a greater democratization in the archives community; possibly, smaller repositories and archives programs now feel better able to post advertisements given the ease, speed, and low cost.

Another interesting finding is the concentration of entry-level positions in the university/college environment; there is virtually a one in two chance that is where the entry-level archivist will be hired (see Table Seven). The most compelling statistic is the continuing preponderance, by a substantial margin, of higher education as the employer of entry-level archivists. This poses some interesting speculations. Has this relationship been the reason why the old three-course archival education/apprenticeship programs (the consensus educational standard of the

Table Six
Regions of Entry-Level Job Advertisements,
1976–2003

Region	1976–77	1986–87	1996–97	2001–03
Southeast	12 (19%)	25 (19.4%)	48 (20.9%)	54 (20.3%)
Midwest	18 (28.6%)	29 (22.5%)	49 (21.3%)	34 (12.8%)
Northeast	9 (14.3%)	27 (20.9%)	28 (12.2%)	44 (16.5%)
West	8 (12.7%)	13 (10.1%)	37 (16.1%)	38 (14.3%)
Mid-Atlantic	14 (22.2%)	37 (28.7%)	46 (20%)	68 (25.6%)
Southwest	2 (3.2%)	5 (3.9%)	22 (9.6%)	24 (9.0%)

Table Seven
Repository Type Advertising for Entry-Level Archivists,
1976–2003

Repository Type	1976–77	1986–87	1996–97	2001–03
University/College	27 (42.9%)	59 (45.7%)	94 (40.9%)	95 (35.7%)
Historical Society	16 (25.4%)	15 (11.6%)	30 (13%)	34 (12.8%)
Institutional	7 (11.1%)	7 (5.4%)	21 (9.1%)	49 (18.4%)
State Archives/				
State Government	5 (7.9%)	10 (9.3%)	27 (11.7%)	30 (11.3%)
Other Repositories*	7	43	58	51

* Other repositories include public libraries, museums, religious institutions, medical programs, local and federal government, and specialized libraries.

1970s) have remained so embedded that these programs generate their own potential employees? Or is it merely ironic that a profession with essentially an academic orientation has dallied so long in developing graduate archival education programs? The only major change appears to be a recent jump in the portion of positions in institutional archives, such as corporate and civic organizations.

In contrast, the 1998 Cunningham records managers' salary survey shows nearly a quarter of the new positions were established in corporations, followed by government, utilities, and other similar organizations. The continuing small number of institutional archivists positions ought to be a great matter of concern to the archives community, although the recent growth might be a promising sign. The archival profession ought to stress nurturing new corporate and institutional archives programs, in addition to their traditional emphasis on collecting. Examining entry-level positions advertisements over these three decades reveals a decided lack of development in institutional archives.

The remarkable array of titles for archivist positions would, at first glance, reflect a profession that has not made up its collective mind about its identity (see Table Eight). Actually, it more likely reflects the diverse structure of the hiring organizations. If one works in a library, one is apt to have a librarian classification, whereas, if one labors in a cultural organization, a curatorial designation might be appropriate. There is a drop in curatorial designations. More importantly, in this wide array of job titles, records or information classifications represent a small portion of the positions available. Archivists, perhaps, have not been embraced as part of the information professions, despite the strengthening of archival education in library and information science schools. The continuing small number of records classifications continues to reflect, unfortunately, the schism between archivists and records managers. The recent spike in positions employing the title "archivist" might suggest the emergence of a more settled identity, but the evidence is not sufficient to confirm such a conclusion. The continued presence of specialized entry-level positions—with titles such as Descriptive Archivist, Special Formats Cataloguer, Photographic Archivist, Electronic Records Archivist, Business Archivist, and Field Archivist—suggest that nothing is settled.

The more disturbing finding concerns the average salary of entry-level archivists. Factoring in for inflation, we see a decided decline in salaries (see Table Nine for the salary ranges). The average salary of 1976–77 would be worth $32,844.07 in 2002; the 1986–87 average salary would be worth $31,150.72. As a result, based on the position advertisements mentioning salary there appears to be an average decline of 9.7 percent from the mid-1970s to the present.[43] Are salary matters improving? In the 2001–03 group of job advertisements, the salaries range from $19,000 to $49,000, with a real average of $35,213 (perhaps an encouraging sign). This may be the most telling and most problematic finding for the profession and for graduate programs. As Steven Brint, in his study on expertise, reports: "The claim to 'formal knowledge' in 'expertise' is one thing; being rewarded in relation to those claims is quite another."[44]

Table Eight
Position Titles for Entry-Level Archivists,
1976–2003

Position Title	1976–77	1986–87	1996–97	2001–03
Assistant Archivist or variation	13 (20.6%)	29 (22.5%)	45 (19.6%)	31 (11.7%)
Specialized Archives	15 (23.8%)	14 (10.9%)	38 (16.5%)	30 (11.3%)
Project Archivist	2 (3.2%)	21 (16.3%)	31 (13.5%)	54 (20.3%)
Librarian Classification	5 (7.9%)	22 (17.1%)	38 (16.5%)	22 (8.3%)
Archivist	17 (27%)	34 (26.4%)	39 (17%)	103 (38.7%)
Curatorial Classification	7 (11.1%)	7 (5.4%)	9 (3.9%)	5 (1.9%)
Records Classification	2 (3.2%)	8 (6.2%)	15 (6.5%)	16 (6.0%)
Information Classification	0	0	3 (1.3%)	0

What gives a profession or a professional "market advantage"? "These are," according to Brint, "in approximate order of importance: (1) the capacity of professions to organize in private or group practice; (2) for salaried professionals only, the industrial location in which members of the profession are predominately employed; (3) again, for salaried professionals, location in the 'industrial-corporate core' (or 'technostructure') within organizations; (4) legal and other sources of valuable task area monopolies; and (5) the gender composition of the occupation."[45] It is possible, of course, that the real source of these low salaries is that there is a greater quantity of smaller programs, such as local libraries and historical societies, with traditionally lower salaries reporting due to the ease of use of the Internet to post such positions.

There is virtually no explicit wording in any of these entry-level job advertisements for working with records and recordkeeping systems. Only six of the 1996–97 positions included some wording related to this and, of these, three could be rightly called records management positions. Very few positions contain any statements that suggest that archivists are experts on recordkeeping. Most statements are about the knowledge of archival and records management principles and statements, but what do these statements actually mean? The closest wording on records and recordkeeping systems knowledge includes the following from a 1996–97 advertisement for the Records Officer, University of Idaho, Divison of Finance and Administration, includes a "Good knowledge of records management and archival theory and practice, files management and records storage systems, privacy and access laws, federal and state regulations relating to records retention and disposition, and records management professional resources." But this might be little more than a typical description for a records management position.

An advertisement for an Archivist II: Webmaster, Ohio Historical Society, calls for a "Knowledge of the functional requirements of record keeping." This position includes responsibility for making electronic records available over the Web, and the wording is probably a general allusion to recent efforts by the Universities of Pittsburgh and British Columbia to develop recordkeeping functional requirements.

An advertisement for an Archivist, North Carolina Department of Cultural Resources, Archives and History, asks for "Considerable knowledge of supplies and equipment used in the creation and maintenance of records," which again might be typical phrasing for records management positions.

Table Nine
Salary for Entry-Level Archivists,
1976–2003

Salary	1976–77	1986–87	1996–97	2001–03
$7000–10,000	10	0	0	0
$10,000–13,000	29	0	0	0
$13,000–16,000	7	8	1	0
$16,000–19,000	0	31	18	1
$19,000–22,000	0	31	18	2
$22,000–25,000	0	17	17	6
$25,000–28,000	0	4	37	14
$28,000–31,000	0	0	35	23
$31,000–34,000	0	0	17	38
$34,000–37,000	0	0	5	28
$37,000–40,000	0	0	2	20
$40,000–43,000	0	0	0	13
$43,000 and above	0	0	0	8

An advertisement for a Government Records Specialist, Minnesota Historical Society, seeks an individual with "Knowledge of and experience with electronic records," a typical wording for the advertisements with allusions to electronic records (still, it is difficult to determine the degree of records and recordkeeping systems really being required).

An advertisement for a position with the Massachusetts Historical Records Advisory Board calls for applicants with "Demonstrable knowledge or experience in records management, electronic records management, or documentation activities," again, with some uncertainty about what this implies in terms of knowledge of records and recordkeeping systems.

An advertisement for a Records Analyst, Utah State Archives, sought someone with "Advanced skills in analyzing agency operations and identifying solutions to records management problems." While this is probably a statement used for typical records management work, it at least includes an analytical component one would expect to see more frequently in any archives and records work.

There are more such descriptions in the 2001–03 job advertisements, mainly because there is a stronger emphasis on records management as an archival function and considerably more described about electronic records management than in earlier years.

CONCLUSION

As stated above, the hypothesis for this study was that entry-level job advertisements would, over more than a twenty-year period, reflect a significant shift to new technologies and to knowledge of records and records keeping systems instead of just archives and records management principles and practices (experience). The findings, however, disprove this hypothesis. While there has been growth in the demand for experience with computer applications and computer literacy, this growth is tied to the prevailing archival arrangement and description function. There is no discernible evidence of a shift to knowledge of records and recordkeeping systems as the focus for entry-level archivists.

There are a number of speculations worth making in light of the above findings. First, it seems that the archives profession is tied to traditional scholarly users (still mostly academic historians or other academically based scholars) and content-based practice, not knowledge areas (as a means of providing better access to the highly selective sense of potential users of archives). Second, the shift to library and information science seems to have maintained emphases of traditional archival functions, especially classification and bibliographic standards. Third, despite the decided changes in graduate and continuing education, the predilection when hiring entry-level archivists is to consider experience at least as important as education. Fourth, despite a growth in graduate archival education programs, there have been no substantial changes in knowledge or skills areas over the past few decades. The archival profession seems oriented to its basic or rudimentary practice, processing backlogs, and distrust of what it sees as theoretical or conceptual approaches (even though the growing complexity of records systems suggests the need for such approaches).

Some concerns ought to emerge from these kinds of speculative assessments. Educators need to ask some obvious questions: Are we teaching the right things? Are we preparing students for the right jobs? It is probably the case that the majority of graduate archives education programs are tied to marketing their graduates to traditional settings, primarily because of the fact that most of the educators have come out of these settings, have strong connections still, and are attracting people interested in these traditional settings.

A number of educators have the feeling (we are only beginning to collect data on this) that some of their graduates are either leaving traditionally defined archives positions after a few years or, increasingly, not accepting these kinds of positions to begin with. This may portend a crisis for the archives profession, or it may strengthen the profession to meet its mission to an unprecedented degree if people accepting non-archives or non-records management positions assume roles of potentially greater influence in gaining resources and respect for the administration of records. Or it may reflect a growing trend by individuals to pursue multiple careers in a lifetime, a case that still suggests educators need to adjust curriculum and training approaches.

But, what about the possibility that many important records jobs are being taken over by other professionals? Other commentators have seen this with the explosion of information jobs. Blaise Cronin, for example, states that we live in a "world of libraries-without-walls and distributed information systems, where disciplinary pedigree and professional affiliation matter less than perceived competence and adaptability." He adds that "The portmanteau labels of 'librarian' and 'information specialist' have splintered dramatically to reflect the pluralistic character of the marketplace."[46]

The current trendy focus on knowledge management—supposedly melding together technology, information, operations in new ways—also is seen as including records management. The idea is that this person, the knowledge manager, will know where the organization's research and other expertise are located.[47]

Then there is the problem of outsourcing. The idea of outsourcing often involves the notion that seemingly routine records management tasks are ripe for removal from organizational responsibilities. Jobs like human resources can be outsourced because so much of the time on these tasks is spent on routine administrative tasks—the four main areas with potential for outsourcing are (1) benefits design and administration; (2) information systems and record keeping; (3) employee services like retirement counseling and relocation; and (4) health and safety.[48]

Given such challenges, one might hope that graduate archival education has taken the lead in at least beginning to redefine what constitutes the qualifications for entry-level archival work. However, it seems that graduate education might merely reflect ideas first formed about graduate education two generations ago. The SAA *Education Directory*'s inclusion of philosophy statements is telling; with 38 U.S.-based programs included in the directory (at the time of the study—the number constantly shifts), 18 have no statement, 7 define their role within a broader history function, 4 merely offer a description of what is offered, 5 include a statement emphasizing archives career-oriented objectives, and only 4 include some sort of records-centered approach.[49] The focus of graduate programs needs to be on equipping individuals to become records and recordkeeping experts, in a way that enables them to manage records regardless of technology, organizational type, or institutional mission. Yet, the nature of job advertisements suggests that the archival field has been static. The rapidly changing nature of records systems and organizational records creators suggests that we need more change to remain relevant, helpful, and well versed with records, their warrants, values, and significance. Similar research studies focusing on other related disciplines (e.g., records management, corporate librarianship) need to be undertaken. Not only could such research tatter cherished assumptions, but it might also provide the firm data to lead those fields in new directions.

ENDNOTES

1. Henry Rosovsky, *The University: An Owner's Manual* (New York: W. W. Norton, 1990), pp. 105–107.
2. David Denby, *Great Books: My Adventures with Homer, Rousseau, Woolf, and Other Indestructible Writers of the Western World* (New York: Simon and Schuster, 1996), p. 285.
3. I have found that I must sometimes counsel students who encounter other students and experienced archivists who are negative about formal graduate archival education. For example, a student from my program, with multiple archives courses, can be put into a work situation where they are laboring side by side with other students or archivists who have but one introductory course or no formal education at all. This can cause friction, but students can learn a lot by figuring out how to cope in these circumstances.
4. This is certainly how I view the education of archivists. The purpose of graduate education, even as situated in professional schools, is to provide a basis for knowledge that serves as a foundation for additional continuing education. Continuing education is primarily intended to serve as a means for imparting particular skills and to expand the knowledge base. I have written extensively about archival education, but the essay most pertinent to this discussion is my "Continuing Education and Spe-

cial Collections Professionals: The Need for Rethinking," *Rare Books & Manuscripts Librarianship* 10, no. 2 (1995): 78–96.

5. There are many books about these and other cases, but for a convenient summary see Richard J. Cox and David A. Wallace, eds., *Archives and the Public Good: Accountability and Records in Modern Society* (Westport, Conn.: Quorum Books, 2002).

6. The writing is extensive about this, but for my perspective on this see *Managing Records as Evidence and Information* (Westport, Conn.: Quorum Books, 2001).

7. Although there is no convenient current history of American archival education, it is relatively easy to grasp the kinds of changes I mean. The 1977 Society of American Archivists graduate education guidelines provided for just two courses and a practicum. The 1994 SAA guidelines called for a move to a full-fledged masters degree in archival studies. The other dramatic change can be seen in the proliferation of graduate educators. Twenty years ago there were only one or two full-time educators in North America, now there is an array of programs supporting two or more full-time educators with a growing number of doctoral students conducting research in archival subjects.

8. At the time of my study, students could meet the requirements if they were graduates of a Masters program with 9 semester hours or 12 quarter hours of graduate archival education, but they cannot be certified until having one year of professional experience. Yet, consider the general knowledge areas: the "impact of social, cultural, economic, political, and technological factors on the evolutions and characteristics of documents and their management"; the "origins, development, and definitions of archival concepts, terms, principles, and methods"; the "development of archival institutions and programs in society"; the "similarities and differences between the nature and administration of archives and manuscripts"; the "physical characteristics of documents and how these characteristics influence the value, acquisition, preservation, and use of documents"; "archival methods and practices appropriate for different media such as electronic, microform, paper, photographic, cartographic, etc."; the "standards and accepted professional practices that apply to archival work, including their rationale and implications"; the "concept of the life cycle of records"; the "relationship between accepted professional policies and practices and institutional applications of these policies and practices"; the "core archival functions of appraisal, accessioning, arrangement, description, preservation, reference, and public programs and how these relate to each other and influence the administration of documents"; the "different institutional settings in which archival programs may exist and the implications of placement within a particular institution"; and the "practices and objectives of such disciplines as records management, information resources management, librarianship, information science, museuology, and oral history and the ways in which they relate to and differ from the administration of archives." This is found in the *Handbook for Archival Certification: Including the Official Role Delineation, Study Guide,*

and Reading List (Albany: Academy of Certified Archivists, 1998) at http://www.uwm.edu/Library/arch/aca/handbk.htm. Can such competencies really be gained via such a modest amount of education and experience? Are these competencies really still that relevant for the *modern* records professional in the twenty-first century? For my own, updated, views about the certification movement, see Chapter 5 in this volume.

9. The knowledge includes business functions and activities of government institutions; current information management and information technology concepts and practices; "generally accepted record keeping practices"; and emerging technologies. The skills include communication, presentation, and coaching. The abilities include analyze and conceptualize; "translate ideas into structure"; and "develop creative solutions." See *Preliminary Study on the Core Competencies of the Future Records Specialist* ([Ottawa]: Information Management Standards and Practices Division, National Archives of Canada, June 1996).

10. 1997 Australian National Records and Archives Competency Standards.

11. Charles R. Schultz, "Personality Types of Archivists," *Provenance* 14 (1996): 15–35.

12. Howard Gardner, *Creating Minds: An Anatomy of Creativity Seen Through the Lives of Freud, Einstein, Picasso, Stravinsky, Eliot, Graham, and Gandhi* (New York: Basic Books. 1993), p. 113.

13. Frank B. Evans, "Postappointment Archival Training: A Proposed Solution for a Basic Problem," *American Archivist* 40 (January 1977): 72–73.

14. Frank B. Evans, "Archivists and Records Managers: Variations on a Theme," *American Archivist* 30 (January 1967): 45–58.

15. Dorothy E. Smith, "Textually Mediated Social Organization," *International Social Science Journal* 36, no. 1 (1984): 59–75 (quotes pp. 66–67). See also Dorothy E. Smith, "The Social Construction of Documentary Reality," *Sociological Inquiry* 44, no. 4 (1974): 257–268.

16. Philip C. Grant, "Why Job Descriptions Are Not Used More," *Supervision* 59 (April 1998): 10–13.

17. M. Ronald Buckly, Donald B. Fedor, Shawn M. Carraher, Dwight D. Frink, and David Marvin, "The Ethical Imperative to Provide Recruits Realistic Job Previews," *Journal of Managerial Issues* 9 (Winter 1997): 468–484.

18. Philip C. Grant, "Job Descriptions: What's Missing," *Industrial Management* 39 (November/December 1997): 9–13.

19. Ira A. Penn, "Wanted: Records Manager: No Experience Necessary," *Records Management Quarterly* 30 (July 1996): 16-19.

20. Peter J. Wosh, "Creating a Semiprofessional Profession: Archivists View Themselves," *Georgia Archive* 10 (Fall 1982): 1–13.

21. "The Ideal Archivist: What Employers Look For," SAA *Newsletter* (January 1982): 9.

22. "What Employers Look For: The Applicant's View," SAA *Newsletter* (March 1982): 16.

23. An analysis of what 67 companies in 12 U.S. cities did in hiring and using records employees revealed a low level of education: "Over 80% of the respondents indicated that no more than 1 out of 4 records employees

had records management education in high school, business college, or community college" and "over 75% of the respondents reported that no more than 1 out of 4 had records classes in a 4-year college" (p. 47). There was also a wide range of job titles and wide range of salaries, as reported by Barbara A. Christensen, "Responsibilities and Training of Records Employees," *Records Management Quarterly* 16 (January 1982): 40–47. This certainly has produced unease by records managers about their education, as reflected in Robert V. Williams, "Records Management Education: An IRM Perspective," *Records Management Quarterly* 21 (October 1987): 36–40, 54. At this time, Williams notes that "formal records management education is dominated by the office administration/secretarial approach" (p. 37).

24. Paul Conway, "Membership Survey Results," SAA *Newsletter* (January 1992): 3, 9.

25. David J. Murrah, "Employer Expectations for Archivists: A Review of a 'Hybrid Profession,'" *Journal of Library Administration* 11, nos. 3 and 4 (1990): 165–174.

26. Donald DeWitt, "The Impact of the MARC AMC Format on Archival Education and Employment During the 1980s," *Midwestern Archivist* 16, no. 2 (1991): 73–85.

27. Alan D. Gabehart, "Qualifications Desired by Employers for Entry-Level Archivists in the United States," *American Archivist* 55 (Summer 1992): 420–439, based on 1991 dissertation of same title done at Texas Tech University.

28. Gabehart, "Qualifications Desired," p. 428.

29. Gabehart, "Qualifications Desired," p. 437.

30. Gabehart, "Qualifications Desired"—For foreign languages, 83.6 percent stated that there was no such requirement (p. 432); for training in archives conservation, 27.5 percent saw this as of some importance (p. 433); for training in computer automation, 28.1 percent deemed it "fairly important" (p. 433); for the effect of certification on hiring, 5.1 percent saw this as a potential employment requirement (p. 434).

31. Gabehart, "Qualifications Desired," p. 435.

32. Richard J. Cox, *The First Generation of Electronic Records Archivists in the United States: A Study in Professionalization* (New York: Haworth Press, 1994).

33. Thomas Elton Brown, "Myth or Reality: Is There a Generation Gap Among Electronic Records Archivists?" *Archivaria* 41 (Spring 1996): 239.

34. See my response to the Brown essay, published in *Archivaria* 42 (Fall 1996): 4–5, more fully explaining my views about his article. For the National Archives, refer to David A. Wallace, "The Public's Use of Federal Recordkeeping Statutes to Shape Federal Information Policy: A Study of the Profs Case," Ph.D. dissertation, University of Pittsburgh, 1997.

35. Conservation positions are really more like technicians' positions, with a bench-like mentality towards individual document repair and treatment. These positions require, in my estimation, more training than education, more technical knowledge than knowledge about records and archives,

and require working under the direction of archivists and/or preservation administrators with a broader mission in mind.

36.   Look at the Association of Records Managers and Administrators job
hotline page at http://www.arma.org/hq/jobsmain.html. Some of these
differences are evident in Raymond K. Cunningham, Jr., "Handbook for
Records Management Careers" at http://www.staff.uiuc.edu/
~rcunning/job.htm (dated 1997). Cunningham acknowledges that records
management came from archives, but that "records managers today are
unlike librarians or archivists in that they are: (1) better paid and, (2) they
tend to move to better jobs more often." He notes the "slow pace of archival work to the faster pace of records management." Cunningham
argues that the masters degree is best now, over the undergraduate degree. He favors a move away from the MLS—"I have seen records management jobs requiring a masters in library science, generally by
educational institutions or records management programs administered
by a library. Hiring policies by libraries are narrow and generally done
by administrators knowing little about records management, believing it
to be an appendage of librarianship. The same is unfortunately true of
some in the archives profession." He then provides advice on building
careers. "With such a broad range of job descriptions, experience is easier
to obtain than in many other professions. You can build a career several
ways; by chance, flowing from job to job; by lateral movement, moving
from allied field to allied field; and by progression, from clerk, to assistant records manager, and to records manager." Cunningham's salary
survey also shows the diversity with titles from clerk to supervisor to
technician to administrator, manager, and director included; see at http:/
/www.staff.uiuc.edu/~rcunning/results.htm. Cunningham's results,
while very informally collected and not very systematic, reflect some
generally valid information that connects well with my conclusions: Archives Assistant average salary $24,000; 70.2 percent have MA, MLS, MBA,
or MS. (See his posting to Archives and Archivists Listserv on May 9,
1998).

37.   The CRM suggests a close relationship to archives management. The
Institute of Certified Records Managers (ICRM) was established in 1975,
with the primary responsibility to develop and administer a program for
professional certification of records managers. Its six-part exam: management principles and the records management program; records creation and use; records systems, storage and retrieval; records appraisal,
retention, protection and disposition; equipment, supplies and technology; case studies. See http://www.arma.org/hq/crminfo.htm. People
are eligible to take the examination based on a combination of education
and experience, where a bachelors degree is basic although 11 years experience would allow one with no college education to take the exam.

38.   It is impossible to track, however, the number of local institutions that
post entry-level job announcements only in local newspapers, other local
print sources, or via word-of-mouth. My sense is that many local institutions do operate in this fashion. Since many of these organizations do

this because of a lack of awareness of professional qualifications, educational programs, and national standards, if these announcements could be evaluated I suspect we would discover a weakening of the basic attributes profiled in this study.

39. Paul Gilster, *Digital Literacy* (New York: John Wiley and Sons, Inc., 1997), p. 13.
40. Certification is more fully discussed in Chapter 5 of this volume.
41. This is what DeWitt, "The Impact of the MARC AMC Format," was suggesting at an early point in time.
42. Most archives and historical records repositories have a geographic orientation, a point I argued in my *Documenting Localities: A Practical Model for American Archivists and Manuscripts Curators* (Metuchen: Scarecrow Press and Society of American Archivists, 1996).
43. The comparative salaries were calculated using the "Inflation Calculator" by S. Morgan Friedman at http://www.westegg.com/inflation/.
44. Steven Brint, *In An Age of Experts: The Changing Role of Professionals in Politics and Public Life* (Princeton: Princeton University Press, 1994), p. 66.
45. Brint, *In An Age of Experts*, p. 67.
46. Blaise Cronin, Michael Stiffler, and Dorothy Day, "The Emergent Market for Information Professionals: Educational Opportunities and Implications," *Library Trends* 42 (Fall 1993): 257–276 (quotes pp. 258, 263).
47. Peggy Watt, "Knowing It All," *Network World* 14 (August 18, 1997): 17–18.
48. Thomas A. Stewart, "Taking on the Last Bureaucracy," *Fortune* 133 (January 15, 1996): 105–108. See also Sandra E. O'Connell, "Outsourcing: A Technology-based Decision," *HRMagazine* 40 (February 1995): 35–39.
49. The four programs with a records-centered philosophy include the University of Michigan, SUNY–Albany, University of Pittsburgh, and the University of Wisconsin–Milwaukee. The Education Directory is at http://www.archivists.org.

4

Why Records Professionals Need to Explain Themselves

INTRODUCTION

In recent years, records have been in the news as the focal points of the stories rather than as background or interesting subplot more than any records manager or archivist might have expected. On November 1, 2001, President Bush signed an executive order transforming the process by which the records of former presidents would be opened for scholarly and other use. This order set off a spate of newspaper and newsmagazine editorials expressing worry about a new emphasis on government secrecy and reduced accountability of the federal government to its citizenry. Most of the discussions reflected a reasonably short-sighted view of how presidential records had been administered, but offered little or no reflection about the role of the National Archives and Records Administration (NARA). A few months later, the controversy about Enron's collapse and the federal government investigation into this business disaster brought with it revelations that the company's auditors, Arthur Andersen, destroyed (inappropriately it seems) records related to its work for Enron. In this case, some additional media coverage speculated about how corporate records were managed, but it would be difficult to argue that the role of records professionals, or even the significance of records management, were made any clearer to the public or policy makers.

Professional listservs followed these events with interest, confusion, controversy, and a vast array of opinions. Without describing all the ideas presented, it is safe to state that there were very conflicting opinions on the lists. Some posters argued that these were political issues and not matters that archivists or records managers should worry about or take public stances on. Others were convinced that the main professional associations, the SAA and the ARMA, should become much more energetic, both in lobbying for how these public controversies should be resolved and in making such advocacy a greater priority for their resources than what they would normally allocate funds, staff and volunteer time, and workshops and conferences to support.

Public awareness of records issues by records professionals is certainly greater now than it has been in the past. Archivists and records managers can track legal cases, legislative initiatives, news stories, and other public events concerning records and their management more easily than ever before, thanks to the World Wide Web, 24-hour television news channels, and other media coverage. Yet, we can consistently detect in the news coverage stereotypical images of records and their custodians—archivists and records managers might wonder whether they can ever position themselves to affect public policy, funding, and understanding of what they do and why it is important. It is obvious that records professionals are still working at a fairly superficial level when they enter the public forum. This is not due to the fact that we have not tried, especially in a variety of campaigns, educational programs, and other initiatives going back two or three decades. What is the problem, then? Unfortunately, archivists, records managers, and other records professionals—and their allies—have failed to develop a sustained presence in the immense field of public scholarship supporting and influencing public opinion and policy. While records professionals can take solace that they are trying to make public statements about important records issues more often, they have a long way to go to grab a niche in public scholarship.

In this chapter, I discuss the nature of public scholarship, its implications for and importance to archivists and records managers, my personal forays into this realm of writing as a sort of case study about public scholarship in archives and records management, and what records professionals need to do in order to achieve more success in public scholarship. Archivists and records managers need to position themselves to expound their views on important issues with records implications that surface in the news. Just as importantly, they need to create a sustained presence that builds a stronger public understanding of why records are important. With this presence, when events occur involving records, the media know where to turn for advice, and greater sensitivity about the nature of records and their systems will result.

Breaking news, like the Bush executive order and the Enron collapse, tend to catch both the media and records professionals unawares. In these stories, the manner in which our presidential records have been managed and the way large corporations and their auditing firms work seems to be a more mysterious than understood process. For too long corporate and government recordkeeping has been handled by the media as stereotypical hallmarks of bloated bureaucracies, and for just as long archivists and records managers have been timid about trying to influence public opinion and policy makers. If archivists and records managers believe records are important, then they need to proclaim that message.

WHAT IS PUBLIC SCHOLARSHIP?

There are a number of ways by which we can define the notion of public scholarship. In the most cynical manner, we can consider it to be a reaction to an arcane academic scholarship; arcane in one sense that such a scholarship is only addressed to a very small group of other like-minded scholars, or arcane in another sense in that it is not easily understood, or even relevant to the public. Richard Posner's study on public intellectuals, a book that becomes another trashing of academics and the university, argues that the decline of individuals writing for the informed public is a result of the rise of the university and the creation of many academics discovering a public voice.[1]

According to Posner, the decline is due to the fact that many of these academics often make public judgments quickly and without the benefit of allowing time and space to develop between the events and their evaluation. These academics further complicate matters by moving outside their normal areas of knowledge into processes stressing the influence of the media and emphasizing celebrity.

This perspective has been challenged. Rick Perlstein, in an op-ed essay, argued that Posner's thesis was more of the same old "blame game" and that the real problem was the eroding publishing venues:

"The intellectuals are there; the public need not feel starved; we need no more jeremiads. What today's public intellectuals need are publishers, and maybe a few publicists, too."[2] If publishing outlooks are declining for such individuals, what does this mean for archivists and records managers who need to reach the public?

While there is much that is useful in Posner's assessment of what public intellectuals do and how they function, his study misses the point for records professionals who are affected heavily by public opinion, policy, and resources. Archivists and records managers must learn how to make their voice heard in ways that provide clear views about their mandate, importance, and needs. In our present networked information age, the opportunities for doing this are considerably improved, provided we develop mechanisms, incentives, and resources for taking advantage of such opportunities. In fact, given the small number of academics (those who are on teaching faculties) in the records professions, Posner's alarms are mostly irrelevant. What is more pertinent is his description of the increased opportunities for individuals to practice public scholarship: "With hundreds of television channels to fill, with the Internet a growing medium for the communication of news and opinion, and with newspapers becoming ever more like magazines in an effort to maintain readership in the face of the lore of continuously updated news on television and over the Internet, the opportunity cost to the media of providing a platform for public intellectuals has shrunk."[3] One would also think that with regular news stories featuring records, we would see more records professionals appearing in the media. That has not happened.

We often define public scholarship by what it is not. This distinction between an individual writing for the educated public or for a small, often-closed world of scholars manifests itself in different venues. An English professor ruminating about the nature of acknowledgments in academic life describes how these sections of books seem to have expanded remarkably in recent decades. Why? He speculates, "Ambitious younger scholars must avoid such missteps. An author may compile a prestigious genealogy and gush over comrades, but the text remains his responsibility. Having passed years in the stacks, in the office hours, on the conference circuit, he now commits himself to print and stands or falls alone. The book will be lucky to sell 500 non-library copies, but it will be fodder for hiring committees, tenure reviews and panel organizers. The public will ignore it, and neo-conservatives may ridicule it, but in academe it will have a coterie reading."[4] More cynically, this assessment of the acknowledgments function suggests that it flourishes because "academia, especially the humanities, is increasingly isolated from the public sphere. Despite a few high-profile scholars who have crossed over, humanities discourse is virtually illegible to lay readers. . . . Here is where the Acknowledgments pages come in. They take up the job that readers are supposed to do: validating the book."[5]

In the world of books directed at records professionals, we have much the same problem. Generally, unless these books have a very practical "how-to" approach, they tend to be ignored, and it is rare that such books are read very far outside of the various segments of the records professions. Moreover, despite the fact that we have a much greater number of books, from practical manuals to research studies, it still appears that they are not often read as widely as they should be within the places where archivists and records managers work. It is rare, for example, that any of the listservs frequented by archivists and records managers discuss publications of any kind. Indeed, it sometimes seems that the orientation of most working records professionals is to experience and practice, rather than to any kind of knowledge that might be codified or forwarded in monographs, manuals, technical reports, and professional journals. This may be one reason why it is so difficult for records managers and archivists to present their case in the wider world of public scholarship. Most records professionals have little experience in writing and presenting their case in such a way, and others who are already involved in academic and public scholarship rarely pay attention to the writings of archivists and records managers.

Another more mundane manner in which to discuss public scholarship is to consider the differences between trade, university, and professional publications. As opposed to the smaller runs of university press titles, trade publications are generally intended to appeal to the "educated general reader" and are supposed to sell thousands of copies and reach a larger audience. University presses like the notion of trade books, not just because there is the incentive of larger sales, but because these books can help the presses' authors better package their scholarly ideas as well as build a more public profile for the presses themselves.[6] While Posner may worry that what is being packaged here is often poor scholarship in that these scholars might feel necessary to break free of their normal academic checks and balances in order to engage the educated lay public (expanding their arguments too far beyond their data or knowledge and revealing poor judgment in social prediction or application), this is not a problem for archivists and records managers.

Records professionals face the opposite problem. Trade presses publish books that feature interesting stories about and lessons from records that often become the topics for the media (such as the intense debate about the validity of IBM's role in the Holocaust, or the use of historical evidence in subsequent research about the Holocaust, or even something as seemingly mundane as the theft of historical maps from archival repositories.[7] However, archivists and records managers seem unsure about how to capitalize on such discussions and media attention.

A more helpful manner by which to consider public scholarship is merely to suggest that it is writing intended to engage or influence the public and policy makers in specific and meaningful ways. Richard Posner loses track of this important mission by focusing on what he sees as needy academics in search of an audience or fame and fortune, but it would be difficult for professionals like archivists or records managers to miss such an important quest. Scholars ensconced in the academy often seem to have given this aim up, seeking perhaps to influence a few other scholars or perhaps their students, already a captive, if not always receptive, audience. Stephen Carter, the Yale law professor who has written a number of important books about American religion and politics, commenced one of his books in this fashion: "Testing one's scholarly ideas through repeated presentations to learned but skeptical audiences is an important part of academic tradition, but one that is rapidly disappearing, as more and more scholars share their ideas, if at all, only with those who are likely to agree with them."[8] This seems to support the earlier cited notion of the changing uses of acknowledgment pages. Faculty sitting in positions in professional schools also have their form of a public, although their world of scholarship is often more tenuous. They walk an uneasy balance between their university world and that of professions demanding graduates with practical skills that often seem to have little to do with scholarship of any sort. However, these professionals often have to deal much more forthrightly with public issues, leading one to assume that they would have developed the connections, skills, and interests in building a public literature. Some fields have, others have not. The records professions have a very receptive audience at this point, but they also have a very long way to go in positioning themselves to take advantage of it.

There have been examples of where archivists and records managers have tried to institutionalize public scholarship and managed to confuse the issue even more. One can glance back in time over the past quarter of a century and consider the rise, fall, and stabilization of an entity called public history. This field, or orientation, can be considered part of public scholarship depending on how one might view it, or whether one is a cynic or realist. As enrollments dropped and the decline in placement of students from graduate history program materialized, these programs scurried to find new ways of righting the ship. Many developed tracks or specializations in something called public history, where their students were either being prepared to seek positions in non-academic positions, such as archives, museums, libraries, government, and even records management, or where they could utilize their history skills in analysis for public policy and related applications. The range of definitions encompassed non-academic history practice, history in public policy, and the engagement of the public in historical issues or historical perspectives on current concerns and debates.

Out of this public history movement have come some positive signs and indicators of a reengagement of historians with the public. If one examines bestseller lists and the titles being released by trade publishers, the public seems quite immersed in the past. Whether this has something to do with professional historians and a change of approach and audience, at least by some of them, or more to do with the work of individuals from outside of the academic circles, like documentary filmmaker Ken Burns, is debatable.

Nonetheless, it is clear that there is opportunity for records professionals to engage in the public forum, since there are so many books being published not just about historical topics encompassing the importance of documents, but also about information, the Internet, the future of the printed book, and libraries and museums. The public attention to Nicholson Baker's diatribe about the librarian's apparent disdain of paper—partly generated because of Baker's stature as a novelist and essayist and partly due to his sensational conspiracy theorizing—also extends to the role of the archivist and records manager. As a result, there is opportunity for response by records professionals who can improve the public perception of their mission and the nature and importance of records.[9]

THE PUBLIC SCHOLARSHIP TRACK RECORD OF INFORMATION PROFESSIONALS

At one point, I published a brief study on how effective the faculty of North American library and information science schools were in publishing in leading public opinion journals and news magazines.[10] My premise was rather simple. It was clear that many of the topics being featured in these publications—such as the use of information technology in schools, knowledge about computer technology, and growing concerns about personal privacy and government secrecy—were also precisely the kinds of topics being taught in these graduate schools. Moreover, the faculty members were often focused on the role of information professionals in public policy and in helping students understand the broader social implications of information, information technology, and the information professions.

A review of the most influential print outlets on public policy makers reveals a remarkable interest in information technology and related issues suggesting that the faculty of library and information science schools could find a welcome home in writing for these publications. Looking at nineteen public forum periodicals through the 1990s, I discovered that they published slightly over seven hundred articles on Information Age issues. Stories about information technology issues—from new developments to fears and implications of the uses of the technology—are the most common topics for such publications. A predominant emphasis of articles is on the complicated and constantly changing matters of privacy, access, copyright, and intellectual property. Issues of censorship and free speech, many concerning the implications of computers and the Internet, are also a regular part of the diet of articles provided by these journals.

It is not only information technology providing the mainstay of Information Age-oriented articles in these journals. There is a healthy array of writings on reading, books, and literacy. Some of this writing is in direct reaction to the challenge by computers and the World Wide Web, such as articles on the future of the printed book, but much of it is just a reflection of the interest of these journals and their readers in such matters. One can also discover a good quantity of articles on libraries and their place in society as well as on archives and records issues. Looked at in this way, it seems that a library and information science faculty member (including one who is teaching about archives and records management) could build an entire course based on the popular writings found in these journals. Looked at in another fashion, it is clear that individuals regularly reading such periodicals are being normally exposed to the critical issues we face in the Information Age, and about which library and information science faculty would be expected to teach and research. Even if one were to read these periodicals with a stress on the ones concentrated on politics (such as the *American Spectator*) literary topics (such as *Harper's*), or of a more academic persuasion (such as *Daedalus*), it seems evident that one would have continuing exposure to writings on archives, information technology, censorship, books, libraries, and access.

A closer look at the nature of the essays published in these journals reveals the affinity of these publications to topics that library and information science faculty are interested in. The end of the Cold War and the sudden opening of Iron Curtain records brought a remarkable rise in writing about archives and records issues. New revelations about espionage have been a favorite topic. But there have also been stories about more complicated matters, such as the continuing issue of access to the Nixon Watergate tape recordings and recordkeeping and Holocaust victims' assets. Reflecting the so-called Culture Wars has been an intensity of writing—from all perspectives—about school textbook censorship and censorship in general. Also figuring prominently, of course, were articles on the contested notion of a literary canon and the purpose and nature of reading. Not unexpectedly there has been a vast amount of writing about the idea of an information "highway," access, security, and personal privacy. The negative or positive aspects of computers on all elements of society has been a consistent topic, including the impact on the economy, the future of publishing, copyright and the ownership of ideas, and education. Finally, writings about libraries have included some remarkably interesting essays, demonstrating the continuing resilience of books, print, and, of course, libraries.

Given the affinity of these journals for publishing such articles, one would expect to see submissions from the faculty or graduates of schools of library and information science. This is a logical conclusion, given the number of these schools that support over two thousand faculty and hundreds of research agendas related to the topics of the articles being published. However, we find a dramatically different result. There are virtually no faculty published from these schools and precious few working in libraries or archives. While over a quarter of the articles published in these periodicals come from academics, not a single author had a current affiliation with a school of library and information science. One conclusion might be that these journals are more open to established writers, or support freelance writers, editors, and journalists accustomed to writing in the appropriate manner and on timely topics for these publications. However, a good quarter of the authors are academics, suggesting that these journals would be open to publishing by faculty from library and information science schools, assuming they can write well on current issues with an absence of professional jargon.

What can we make of this total absence of library and information science faculty? Besides the obvious, that perhaps these individuals are simply not interested in publishing in such venues as *Atlantic Monthly* or the *New Yorker*, we need to look elsewhere for an explanation. It is very possible that publishing in such journals has proved not to be worth the effort. Publishing in *Harper's* or *Commentary* would certainly count little, if at all, for tenure or even promotion for these faculty, yet other faculty from other disciplines publish successfully in these journals and in the trade press, reaching into the public forum to contend with controversial issues.

One must also consider the effort involved. Moving from an academic venue to a more popular one requires more than just recasting lecture notes or revising research data. You have to write differently, if not considerably better. Library and information science faculty, while writing on many of the same topics reflected in these journals, also seem inclined to write only for fellow specialists and with the freedom of writing without the worry of whether they are read. We must lament the lost opportunities to do many things, ranging from presenting important views in broader forums to building a stronger profile for the important roles played by library and information science schools and the information professionals they are educating. Is it any wonder that library and information science schools are often deemed unworthy for being at a university by critics of modern higher education? Or, that the public often seems unaware of professionals like librarians and archivists?

In this study, I looked only at the faculty in library and information science schools. If we expand our focus to include archivists, records managers, and others who count themselves as part of or somehow connected to the records professions, we can be even more disappointed. The thousands of working archivists and records managers are not involved in public scholarship. This could be because they are too busy with other responsibilities, work in environments where they would not be expected or encouraged (possibly even punished if they did) to write essays or position statements about public policy matters affecting records, or because they simply lack the skills or inclination to try their hand at publishing in public forum journals, newspaper op-ed pages, or in e-journals with wider readership. Such reasons seem acceptable, until one realizes just how often records make the daily news and how frequently there are opportunities to comment on the state of archives or records management for the public and policy makers.

RECORDS AND ARCHIVES IN THE NEWS: A SNAPSHOT

Thanks to the regular reports to the archives and records management listservs by Peter Kurilecz, we can see that records are a regular staple of the news media. A typical weekend (January 11–13, 2002) of news stories provides a glimpse into the possibilities for records professionals to comment more publicly about their professions and the significance of records. There were stories about interesting or unique archival collections (such as the Eddie Rickenbacker papers at Auburn University), efforts to preserve early sound recordings, the nature of holdings of county government archives, inappropriate destruction of records by Arthur Anderson related to the Enron collapse, laws impacting access to government records on all levels, controversies about the use by various government officials of electronic mail and how they manage (or don't manage) this mail, problems with irradiated mail causing damage to its contents and revealing the many challenges with trying to increase security in the post-9/11 world, the implementation of new computer systems to manage local government records, the controversy over historian Stephen Ambrose's plagiarism in his popular histories, the auctioning of records and artifacts related to the early oil industry in Pennsylvania, and the creation of "cybercourts" using "digital record-keeping, videoconferencing, digital presentation devices and other high-tech tools" to speed up certain kinds of trials. In these stories we can see nearly every aspect of both managing records and the importance of records to society.

Even the titles of these articles seem to invite comment by records professionals. "Did Enron's auditors think they had something to hide?" suggests a rethinking of how records managers work with auditors. "Florence [Alabama] council won't ask why, but will ask who wants records," throws up many questions about how and why citizens expect access to their local government's records. "News media threaten Utah governor with lawsuit over e-mails," demonstrates that the challenges of e-mail are not restricted to technical problems but also to other issues related to control and prerogative. "Panel urges access to public data," concerns a report by a judicial advisory panel to urge public access to court records via computer from remote locations, opening up the issues regarding just what public access to government records should entail. "Protecting Indian trust records creates suspicious roadblock," concerning problems with hackers mucking about in the Interior Department's Web site, suggests the increasing problems of offering records access over the World Wide Web. "Plaquemines courthouse burns; many files saved," reveals that the traditional threats to records are still prominent, and suggests the need for greater attention to disaster preparedness at its most basic level.

These titles seem to mimic the titles of conference sessions, workshops, and professional articles. It is easy to see that there is nothing odd or foreign to records professionals in these news stories and that some, like the Enron controversy, shout for attention and responses by archivists and records managers. The possibilities for greater involvement in the public forum by records professionals seem unlimited.

THE POSSIBILITIES FOR PUBLIC SCHOLARSHIP BY RECORDS PROFESSIONALS: EXAMPLES

In the past, archivists and records managers have discussed public programs such as efforts encompassing exhibitions in their repositories, press releases issued to the media, and other forms of events that garner public attention. More recently, we have seen progress by the leading professional associations, the SAA and the ARMA, in issuing statements aimed at persuading public opinion about important events or continuing issues related to the creation, use, and maintenance of government and other records. At the SAA Web site (www.archivists.org) in late January 2002, for example, there were position statements on the Bush Executive Order 13233 (including a letter from SAA President Steve Henson originally published in the *Washington Post* and a "call to action"), an SAA response to proposed changes in the National Archives and Records Administration rules for electronic recordkeeping, and a position paper on copyright. The call to action is particularly interesting with its very strong statement: "The archival and public information implications aspects of this order are profound, being contrary to established archival principles and standards, being inconsistent with existing statutory law, and, most important, being at odds with the principles of open access to information upon which our country is founded."

While ARMA seemed to be more reticent about such public stances, there is evidence at its Web site (www.arma.org) that it also is working to take stands. For example, there was a call for input regarding the proposed changes by NARA in electronic recordkeeping: "ARMA International is accepting comments on the National Archives and Records Administration's [NARA's] Report on Current Recordkeeping Practices within the Federal Government. Comments will be compiled for drafting of a position statement from ARMA." In the Enron case, ARMA also did something rather unprecedented by making a public statement about the activities of the auditing company. In a letter dated January 18, 2002 addressed to *Business Week*, ARMA Executive Director Peter R. Hermann suggested that there may have been Arthur Andersen employee violations of the "established" procedures for the "administration of client engagement information" and indicating that there are "established best practices and records management standards that provide necessary guidance on how to organize, retain, and destroy records," also noting that "it is critical in today's business environment that organizations embrace these practices."[11]

While these public stances are critically important, they are only a sideline to what I see as the more important role of public scholarship. Public scholarship is necessary for strengthening both the profile of records professionals and their mission and work and for creating the milieu in which the public statements from groups such as ARMA and SAA have a greater chance for sympathetic hearings. At present, the statements of the professional associations, while important and representing a promising change of perspective on influencing policy and the public forum, seem to be rather isolated efforts to portray the importance of records and records professionals in society, governments, and organizations. Indeed, the need for records professionals who can respond quickly to breaking cases seems more critical in light of cases like Enron, since the professional associations—by necessity and by tradition—take longer to issue public statements in such situations, if they issue them at all.

Arthur Andersen's release in mid-January 2002 of a set of "internal communications" in an attempt to "explain the role of one of its lawyers in the destruction of thousands of documents by the firm's auditors at Enron just four days before the energy trading company announced a huge reduction in its net worth in October," seemed to pose precisely the kinds of questions that any records manager should be able to answer. The major accounting firm also released copies of its 1999 and 2000 document retention policies reflecting a policy on maintaining only final forms of records, but indicating that "in cases of threatened litigation, no related information will be destroyed." The policy, however, blocks records destruction only after a subpoena is served, and in the Enron case this had not happened.[12] In a bizarre twist of events, Enron stuff began appearing quickly on eBay, the online auction house, with the highest prices seeming to go for "internal company documents such as Enron's Risk Management Manual."[13] What is needed is for a sustained effort to reach the public and policy makers with the message about the importance of administering records. As I related above in my analysis of public forum periodicals, I detect that archivists and records managers have not done this very well, although they can relax in the sense that many others are writing about records issues, though not necessarily representing the perspectives of these professionals.

There are other means of capturing public attention, such as with the use of video documentaries, but here we have been surprised in rather unpleasant ways. Laurel Thatcher Ulrich's study of Martha Ballard, a Maine midwife in the late eighteenth century and early nineteenth century, was not only a gripping portrait of life on the frontier, but it was also a captivating account of diary writing in the period, with many implications for the importance of personal and official recordkeeping in our era.[14] The American Experience film shown on television in the late 1990s is a remarkable window into this frontier life *and* recordkeeping, a collaboration between two filmmakers and the historian to "craft an innovative film that combines dramatic scenes of Martha Ballard's life with interviews of Ulrich at work as historian, mapping out the relationships and events recorded in the diary and making the connections that reveal the realities of Ballard's life and the complex web of relationships within her community."[15]

Even more impressive is the sustained documentary work of Ken Burns. There are few who are not familiar with Ken Burns's documentaries, which air on public television and made him a celebrity with the breakthrough success of his *The Civil War* series in 1990. Burns has long been preoccupied with his role as a historian and his relationship to the professional academic history community. He has been especially focused on his heavy use of archival photographs and other materials, especially his manner in blending textual and visual sources into forming a "chorus of voices" drawing on archival records. A recent study of Burns' documentary work describes one of the keys to understanding Burns's success with many of the archival sources as being his ability to treat still images, including manuscript material such as official records and diaries, as motion photography: "the effect of this collage of techniques is to create the illusion that the viewer is being transported back in time, literally finding the emotional connection with the people and events of America's past."[16] This is a rare skill, although many other documentary filmmakers have copied and adapted the technique to their own work, and it is a skill that needs to be carried into the archives world in presenting their holdings to the public.

Dramatic readings from documents, the camera leisurely scrolling over a photograph or lithograph, and distinctive voices assuming roles of well-known and obscure historical documents all make these documentaries true films with both entertainment and educational value. While for the avid reader of history or the frequent visitor to a museum, library, or archives these films can't replace the real experience, they provide remarkable surrogates for many other people who do not regularly pursue such objectives. While Burns has been criticized by many historians and other scholars for his use of documentary materials, his ability to tell stories drawing on the visual representations of these sources has certainly enhanced the public image of archives and other documents and archivists and other records professionals. The list of credits, rolling the name of one archives after another, adds authority to the truth or validity of interpretation of Burns's films, much as footnotes attest to a work being scholarly and based on substantial research. It is not hard to imagine why any archivist might expect some new researchers to visit their archives the next day, or even have some new kinds of questions posed as a result of the public's imagination being kindled by Burns's provocative storytelling.

There is no question that the filmmaking of a Ken Burns or of those who transformed the Ulrich scholarly study into such a moving glimpse into the harsh life on the early American frontier is part of a public scholarship. And there are those among the librarians and archivists who might argue that we have done this quite effectively as well. In the early 1990s, filmmaker Terry Sanders released a film called *Slow Fires: On the Preservation of the Human Record*, followed in 1998 by *Into the Future: On the Preservation of Knowledge in the Electronic Age*, both unqualified successes in focusing public attention on the need for renewed commitment to the preservation of both paper and digital records and other sources.[17] But then along came Nicholson Baker who called *Slow Fires* part of the "incessant" propaganda by librarians and preservation administrators who have deceived the public into believing that paper becomes brittle and turns to dust.

The preservation community thought it had done a good job with films like *Slow Fires* and *Into the Future,* both sponsored by the Council on Library and Information Resources. The films raised public awareness about the threat of the technologies used in the creation of the documentary sources to the content of books, various print media, and electronic sources. Nicholson Baker perceived the films as part of a massive, misguided propaganda effort on the part of librarians and archivists. They are certainly a mix of propaganda and education, because they are public relations devices. The films were produced in order to grab public attention and to persuade policy makers to think about library and archives preservation matters. These films may seem misguided due to their zealous messages because they were designed to win political and monetary support. Baker assesses the early 1990s film *Slow Fires* in this fashion: "It would be a better film if what it was saying happened to be truth and not head-slapping exaggeration—then its use of crisis language . . . would have some justification."[18] The same applies, of course, to determining just how exaggerated the claims made by Baker in *Double Fold* and elsewhere may be. My engagement with Nicholson Baker brings me to some interesting insights about the nature of public scholarship.

A NEAR MISS: MY YEAR WITH TERRORISTS

The trials and tribulations of trying to engage in public scholarship can best be conveyed by my experiences in my own efforts. For the past twelve years I have been convinced of the need for records professionals to be more engaged in public relations, sustained advocacy, and public scholarship that can help get the message out in a more informed and broader fashion to build a foundation for how and what we communicate. Having spent most of my thirty years in the field writing for other archivists and records managers, along with a considerable amount of writing for librarians, historians, and others who are on the fringes of records work and need to understand more about what we do, it seemed to me to be logical to try to expand into the public forum.

Students often ask me very pointed questions about how to affect change, solve emerging and different kinds of problems in our field, and how to manage records programs in difficult organizational (and societal settings) in which archivists and records managers or their missions are not fully comprehended. I have found myself often offering advice that does not correspond to anything that I needed to do when I worked as an archivist or records manager. Likewise, as I re-read my essay on public scholarship and accountability and as I write this essay, I feel a sense of wrestling with what I have tried to do in my own professional career to break through and write about records management or archival work far outside of the field.

I have had some minor successes, publishing in journals like *American Libraries* and *The Multicultural Review*, journals with a more popular twist but still with some reasonably well-defined audiences that do not approach the size or nature of the audience for an article in a journal like *Harper's* or *Atlantic Monthly*.[19] My writings in these outlets have tended to fall not too far outside of the archives and records management yard, but still reached new audiences about such issues as the future of the printed book, appraising controversial records, and preserving the sources of librarianship.

More success has come with my publications in a peer-reviewed e-journal, *First Monday*, about topics like the controversy over the publication of traditional print documentary editions, the diversity of writings about the nature and future of the so-called Information Age, and issues of authority concerning how archivists were approaching the challenges caused by the management of electronic records systems.[20] E-journals represent a whole new possibility for those interested in reaching broader audiences with greater speed than through traditional print journals. *First Monday* describes itself as one of the "first peer-reviewed journals on the Internet, solely devoted to the Internet" and says that it is "an experiment in electronic publishing, exploring the possibilities of communicating in this Internet medium."[21]

It has been more recently, however, that my experience with public scholarship has picked up, providing some twists and turns that have prepared me to continue to push in this direction and that provide, I believe, some lessons with such writing and publishing. I can only characterize this as my year with terrorists, not merely in the guise of those making the news who are committed to the destruction of America (although my year has included this as well as it was in 2001), but extending the meaning to include those who are attacking the values and purposes of managing records and archives.

Most of one year was involved in debating, both in person and in print, one Nicholson Baker, a self-described library activist. Commencing with public critiques of weeding book collections at the San Francisco Public Library, then moving to slams on the destruction of old card catalogues, and finally taking aim at what he sees as librarians' (and archivists by implication) attack on paper in favor of microfilm and now digitization, Baker has earned considerable public attention with his writings, especially his book *Double Fold*. Part of the attention has been lavished on Baker because of his reputation as a novelist and essayist, but he also tells interesting stories in compelling ways. When his article on the destruction of original newspapers appeared in the *New Yorker*, with what appeared to be broad overstatements and serious misunderstanding of what librarians and archivists do, I responded with a lengthy essay in the e-journal *First Monday*.[22]

My response led to a series of other requested reviews of Baker's book,[23] a debate with Mr. Baker at Simmons Graduate School of Library and Information Science in May 2001, and the preparation of my own book-length response.[24] I also was invited to give a number of talks at various library and archives conferences, although my concern continues about how little response has been forthcoming from the archives and library communities about a book that paints them as villains or, at the least, terribly misguided people.

One of my main themes in these talks and my writings about Baker and his writings, interviews, book talks, and bookstore appearances has been that this book is of little use to the library and archives communities if it is not responded to in a careful and thoughtful fashion. My sense was that Baker cared much about libraries and their mission, and that he had written *Double Fold* in an effort to engage librarians and all other professionals involved in the management of our print and archival heritage. This soon turned out to be a mistaken assumption. Shortly after responding to the copyeditor's work on my book-length response, I received a letter from Mr. Baker's publisher, Random House, indicating that I did not have permission to quote from his book. So much for honest dialogue. And so much for my first lesson in public scholarship. Despite however vociferous and even mean-spirited academics might be in their own professional discourse, they are still committed to debate as a means of expanding knowledge. The publisher of Nicholson Baker does not propose to engage in debate, but it is interested in attacking and selling books—a sad commentary on modern publishers. As matters proceeded, personal contact with Baker led to his interceding on my behalf to see that I had permission to quote from his book, restoring my confidence that Baker's main intent was to raise public consciousness about what he perceived to be serious flaws in the work of preserving books and other documents.[25]

My next effort in public scholarship was generated by watching the news coverage of the horrific attacks on the World Trade Center and Pentagon on September 11, 2001. With the obvious destruction of so many paper records and electronic information systems, I soon found myself reflecting on the implications of the attacks and their aftermath for the education of future records professionals and other information professionals. I began discussions with my faculty colleagues, running the gamut from traditional library work to remarkably cutting-edge research on the technical infrastructure of our modern Information Age. Through a series of lunch meetings and other discussions we shared ideas about the implications for our own research and teaching. I agreed to take the lead in writing an article on this topic and we submitted again to the e-journal *First Monday* in order to guarantee timely publication.

The article considered every aspect of library and information science education that we could cover in a single essay.[26] The essay explored the implications for library and information science schools educating the next generation of information professionals, especially about how to reflect on the aftermath of the attacks for basic aspects of teaching, research, and curriculum design in library and information science schools. We examined disaster preparedness and recovery, knowledge management, workplace design and location, technology and the human dimension, ethics and information policy, information security, information economics, memorializing and documenting the terrorist attacks, the role of the Internet, and preservation.

When the essay appeared in early December 2001, a few messages appeared on various listservs indicating the article's existence. We expected some spirited discussion, and none occurred, perhaps because the essay's timing was at the end of academic terms and just before the extended holiday break. Whatever the causes were for the poor reception of the essay—and I would be the first to admit that perhaps the real reception may come down the road via print journals and professional conferences—it was another lesson learned about public scholarship. Despite Richard Posner's laments that often the new breed of public intellectuals seem to be chasing current news, our effort to engage the library and information science community, and hopefully some portion of the public, in our connection to breaking news events representing the lead story in every news broadcast 24 hours a day, seven days a week, seemed to fall flat. The primary benefits of the exercise were a momentary bringing together of a very diverse faculty at our school and as background for a doctoral seminar I was teaching in the Winter 2002 term on the implications of the events for information professionals. Even my own school's faculty quickly lost interest, and I went my own way in writing a brief volume reflecting on the implications of the September 11 tragedy for the records and information professions.[27]

The next effort in public scholarship of this past year was to comment more publicly on President Bush's Executive Order 13233, transforming the methods by which the release of former president's records would be handled. Over the previous year before this order was signed, I had been working on an article trying to provide a more critical examination of the presidential library system. When the president signed the order my essay was in the final stage for publication in the *Government Information Quarterly*.[28] In my essay I tried to balance views expressed by those working in the libraries and from those on the outside using these libraries in order to assess whether they were still working as they should (or if they ever worked as promised) more than 60 years after their inception.

Issued in the name of national security and supposedly explaining a better mechanism for releasing the records of former chief executives, the order seems only to complicate procedures while doing little that enhances security concerns already addressed by the earlier Presidential Records Act. The new order presents a straightforward series of steps. After the "Archivist receives a request for access to Presidential records," the "Archivist shall provide notice to the former President and the incumbent President and, as soon as practicable, shall provide the former President and the incumbent President copies of any records that the former President and the incumbent President request to review." The "former President shall review those records as expeditiously as possible, and for no longer than 90 days for requests that are not unduly burdensome." The "former President shall indicate to the Archivist whether the former President requests withholding of or authorizes access to any privileged records." The "incumbent President or his designee may also review the records in question, or may utilize whatever other procedures the incumbent President deems appropriate to decide whether to concur in the former President's decision to request withholding of or authorize access to the records." The order then presents the procedures to be used in the various options that might result with such reviews.[29]

What this means is that now *both* a former and a current president need to agree about the release of records, even though issues such as national security were already covered in the present process for opening presidential records. The president's aides defended the order as being merely procedural. With the new executive order, both ex-presidents and sitting presidents can review and block the release of records, justified by President Bush as being in conformity with the older Supreme Court ruling but adding, say its critics, another layer of possibility in withholding records from the public and researchers.

When President Bush signed his executive order clarifying the process of reviewing the records of former presidents, a chorus of boos resounded across the country. Editorials popped up everywhere. The *Los Angeles Times* entitled its editorial a "Dark Oval Office" and said that the executive order was a "recipe for inaction and endless legal wrangling," suggesting that the "decree is not about protecting troops or homeland security. Rather, the administration's sweeping refusal to release any documents from the Reagan era suggests a secrecy fetish." The *Courier & Press* entitled its editorial "Keeping Secrets" and urged that the order be dropped, noting that "there has been no indication that the former presidents or their archivists have had a problem with the act" and this newspaper adopted the cynical view that the order appeared because of the "many Bush appointees" who "served in the Reagan administration." The *Salt Lake Tribune* called the order an "attack . . . on history itself."[30]

Scores of articles and editorials such as these appeared across the nation. Many of them focused on the most obvious conclusion, that the current President Bush was trying to protect his father as well as his aides who had worked in the previous Bush and Reagan administrations. Eric Alterman, writing in *The Nation*, made this connection: "The obvious target of the new law is the Reagan papers. For the past nine months, Reagan's people have refused—with the Bush administration's backing—to release more than 68,000 pages they owe the nation under the 1978 law. The Bush administration is filled with Reagan-era retreads whose questionable actions might leave them vulnerable to criticism and/or ridicule. Among these are Elliott Abrams, John Negroponte, Otto Reich as well as Colin Powell, budget director Mitch Daniels, Jr. and Chief of Staff Andrew Card. And then there's the matter of Reagan's vice president, who, like Abrams et al., lied about his awareness of the commission of Iran/*contra* crimes."[31]

As I have already alluded to in this essay, records professionals responded to this, with the SAA and its president taking the lead. SAA also united with the Public Citizen Litigation Group to challenge the order, setting a path for more litigation against the executive order and the National Archives. What seemed so odd to me in all of these reactions and subsequent activities was the strange manner in which the existing procedures for managing presidential records were described or alluded to in the criticism of the new executive order. Nearly every article or editorial about the new executive order wistfully looked back on the success of the reigning law governing presidential records. In fact, there were many problems never successfully resolved with any of the traditions, laws, and the library system, and this seemed to me like the perfect opportunity to step forth with an essay.

Friend or foe of the new executive order, all seemed to miss that the real problem in the administration of presidential records rests in a tradition based on an array of privilege, compromise, mistakes, and ill-founded objectives. A hint at this occurred in Archivist John Carlin's testimony about the new executive order in which he rather complacently reviewed the history and background of the Presidential library system. In reviewing the system, Carlin noted that the Presidential Records Act "established Government control over presidential records while codifying and preserving some of the basic practices that long existed with respect to the papers that Presidents had donated to the National Archives (dating back to President Hoover)."[32] Prior to this act, presidential records, through the Carter administration, were "controlled by the terms of the deeds of gift by which the former Presidents donated their records to the National Archives. Each of these deeds has provisions outlining categories of records that may be withheld from public access for some period of time. All of them seek to protect information that could harm national security, invade personal privacy, or cause embarrassment or harassment. Some also seek to protect documents involving confidential communications directly with the President."

These earlier arrangements gave "independent authority and discretion to process and open the papers, with very limited involvement by the former President or representative" with the exception of a board whose "principal concern was with respect to the President's personal and family matters, and, in most cases, they disbanded after a short period of time." After this Carlin described how public access to these records is provided, noting the various restrictions and limitations, mostly complaining how Freedom of Information Act requests generally slow down archival processing of the records. Nowhere in this statement does the archivist directly comment on the new executive order, and it is hard to discern by his commentary whether he is in agreement, disagreement, or simply constrained to accept the provisions of the new double-permission process.

As the *Chronicle of Higher Education* was running regular articles on this new executive order, I penned and submitted a brief essay to this important publication outlining the historical background and all of the difficulties and unresolved issues of the presidential library system. The essay was politely rejected. This brought back memories of my efforts to publish the original version of what became my *Government Information Quarterly* essay in a venue like *Harper's* or *Atlantic Monthly*, also leading to rejection.

In his new book, Richard Posner has written about how successful public intellectuals are often the result of accident or some sort of celebrity (leading to, in Posner's view, the unfortunate situation of experts in one field writing about other disciplines), and my own lesson learned is how matters of expertise often do not matter as much as the public profile of the individual. What such experiences suggest, of course, is how far we still have to go, beyond mere press releases, professional associations' position papers, and media coverage (the latter of which is always unpredictable), in building better understanding about the importance of records and the professionals managing them. Photographs of Enron officials shredding their records after investigations have started deserved responses involving full and carefully worded assessments of why and how records ought to be administered in our society. And as the investigations about Enron tried to be extended to the White House, the new executive order about the papers of former presidents seems even more chilling.

PROFESSIONAL INFRASTRUCTURES

There are a number of possible initiatives that need to be taken by the archives and records management communities, and the list that follows is only a beginning point for discussion and reflection. Archivists and records managers need to do the following:

1. *Incorporate within their educational (pre-appointment) programs and existing continuing education operations a stronger emphasis on the skills needed for some individuals to engage in public scholarship.*
   Historian Patricia Nelson Limerick, who has been engaged in reaching the public about the history of the American West, argues that the traditional education of historians has been designed to weaken preparing one to become a public scholar.[33] The education and training of records

professionals is even more problematic with its focus on practical matters. Professional associations need to expand what they do in the education of archivists and records professionals.

2. *Institute within archives and records management programs incentives and structures (including release time) for individuals to assume responsibility for writing about archives and records management issues (devoid of professional jargon and difficult to understand insider allusions) that can educate the public and policy makers.*

    Some archives and records management programs have become more adept at utilizing the services of public relations experts to market their services. Records professionals need to expand this to a broader public forum.

3. *Develop a single Web-based resource of critical sources (press releases, position papers, news links) that will support activity into the public scholarship realm and that can track current stories with important ramifications for records matters.*

    At the moment, records professionals have some individuals (Peter Kurilecz comes to mind) who are making efforts to do this. Archivists and records managers need to harness the power of the Web to support themselves, not just to stay aware of records and archives in the news, but to provide support for records professionals to make and influence the news coverage.

4. *Encourage the professional associations to help identify and contact people essential to providing links to important public forum publications and putting individuals who can write about such matters in contact with these people.*

    SAA President Steve Hensen's candid discussion of how he came to publish his op-ed essay in the *Washington Post* about the executive order 13233 is a tale of making media contacts.[34] His story shows what can be done, especially through the leadership of the main, national professional associations.

Such steps represent a beginning for helping archivists and records managers to become visible in public scholarship. Whatever progress is made here will help all segments of the records professions.

CONCLUSION

Some day, we will see some records professionals engaged in the public forum, writing articles and books intended to reach a broader audience. There have been some positive signs that this is likely to happen, most noticeably as professional associations regularly issue statements on matters of public policy and interest. The one thing we can count on for sure is that there is not going to be any decline in the daily news coverage of events, crises, and controversies with implications about the administration of records. Archivists and records managers will continue to have ample opportunities to go public, and they have an important message to communicate.

ENDNOTES

1. Richard A. Posner, *Public Intellectuals: A Study of Decline* (Cambridge, MA: Harvard University Press, 2001); for a counterpoint to a decline in public scholarship by academics, see Anthony Grafton, "The Public Intellectual and the American University," *American Scholar* 70 (Autumn 2001): 41–54.

2. Rick Perlstein, "Thinkers in Need of Publishers," *New York Times*, January 22, 2002, p. A23.

3. Posner, *Public Intellectuals*, p. 61.

4. Mark Bauerlein, "A Thanking Task: What Acknowledgements Pages Say About Academic Life," *Times Literary Supplement*, November 9, 2001, pp. 16–17.

5. Bauerlein, "A Thanking Task," p. 17.

6. Peter J. Dougherty, "Trade Books Can Be Scholarly, Too," *Chronicle of Higher Education*, 23 November 2001, available at http://chronicle.com/weekly/v48/i13/13b02001.htm, accessed November 19, 2001.

7. Edwin Black, *IBM and the Holocaust: The Strategic Alliance Between Nazi Germany and America's Most Powerful Corporation* (New York: Crown, 2001); Richard J. Evans, *Lying About Hitler: History, Holocaust, and the David Irving Trial* (New York: Basic Books, 2001); Miles Harvey, *The Island of Lost Maps: A True Story of Cartographic Crime* (New York: Random House, 2000).

8. Stephen L. Carter, *God's Name in Vain: The Wrongs and Rights of Religion in Politics* (New York: Basic Books, 2000), p. ix.

9. Nicholson Baker, *Double Fold: Libraries and the Assault on Paper* (New York: Random House, 2001).

10. Richard J. Cox, "Accountability, Public Scholarship, and Library, Information, and Archival Science Educators," *Journal of Education for Library and Information Science* 41 (Spring 2000): 94–105.

11. The letter was originally posted on the ARMA Web site.

12. David Cay Johnston, "Firm Releases Messages on Handling Documents," *New York Times*, January 15, 2002.

13. Ann Williams, "Internal Memos Turn Into Collectors' Items," *The Straits Times*, January 19, 2002.

14. Laurel Thatcher Ulrich, *A Midwife's Tale: The Life of Martha Ballard, Based on Her Diary*, 1785-1812 (New York: Vintage Books, 1990).

15. See the description of the film and teaching materials at http://www.pbs.org/wgbh/amex/midwife/.

16. Gary R. Edgerton, *Ken Burns's America* (New York: Palgrave Press, 2001), p. 44.

17. For additional information about these films, go to http://www.clir.org/pubs/film/film.html#slow.

18. Baker, *Double Fold*, pp. 186–187.
19. Richard J. Cox, "Debating the Future of the Book," *American Libraries* 28 (February 1997): 52–55; with Jane Greenberg and Cynthia Porter, "Access Denied: The Discarding of Library History," *American Libraries* 29 (April 1998): 57–61; and "Archival Anchorites: Building Public Memory in the Era of the Culture Wars," *Multicultural Review*, 7 (June 1998): 52–60.
20. Richard J. Cox, "Messrs. Washington, Jefferson, and Gates: Quarelling about the Preservation of the Documentary Heritage of the United States." *First Monday* (August 1997), available at http://www.firstmonday.dk/issues/issue2_8/cox/index.html; "Drawing Sea Serpents: The Publishing Wars on Personal Computing and the Information Age." *First Monday* (May 1998), available at http://www.firstmonday.dk/issues/issue2_8/cox/index.html; "Declarations, Independence, and Text in the Information Age," *First Monday* 4 (June 1999), available at http://www.firstmonday.dk/issues/issue4_6/rjcox/index.html; and "Searching for Authority: Archivists and Electronic Records in the New World At the Fin-de-Siécle," *First Monday* (January 2000), available at http://www.firstmonday.dk/issues/issue5_1/cox/index.html.
21. See the description of the journal at http://www.firstmonday.dk/idea.html#idea.
22. Richard J. Cox, "The Great Newspaper Caper: Backlash in the Digital Age," *First Monday* 5 (December 4, 2000) available at http://www.firstmonday.dk/issues/issue5_12/cox/. This was written in response to Nicholson Baker, "Deadline: The Author's Desperate Bid to Save America's Past," *New Yorker*, 24 July 2000, pp. 42–61.
23. Richard J. Cox, "Don't Fold Up: Responding to Nicholson Baker's *Double Fold*," *Archival Outlook* (May/June 2001): 8–14; and "Review Article: Nicholson Baker, *Double Fold: Libraries and the Assault on Paper*," *Archival Science*, 1 (2001): 183–217.
24. Richard J. Cox, *Vandals in the Stacks? A Response to Nicholson Baker's Assault on Libraries* (Westport, Conn.: Greenwood Press, 2002).
25. I wrote about this experience in my "Unfair Use: Advice to Unwitting Authors," *Journal of Scholarly Publishing* 34 (October 2002): 31–42.
26. Richard J. Cox, with Mary K. Biagini, Toni Carbo, Tony Debons, Ellen Detlefsen, Jose Marie Griffiths, Don King, David Robins, Richard Thompson, Chris Tomer, and Martin Weiss, "The Day the World Changed: Implications for Archival, Library, and Information Science Education," *First Monday* 6 (December 3, 2001), available at http:/www.firstmonday.dk/issues/issue6_12/cox/.
27. Richard J. Cox, *Flowers After the Funeral: Reflections on the Post-9/11 Digital Age* (Metuchen, N.J.: Scarecrow Press, 2003).
28. Richard J. Cox, "America's Pyramids: Presidents and Their Libraries," *Government Information Quarterly* 19, no. 1 (2002): 45–75.
29. The order was available at http://www.fas.org/sgp/11/ep-pra.html, accessed November 13, 2001.
30. "A Dark Oval Office," *Los Angeles Times*, November 6, 2001, originally accessed online November 8, 2001; Marie Cocco, "We Can Only Guess

What Secrets Bush Is Keeping," *Salt Lake Tribune*, November 20, 2001, originally accessed online November 23, 2001; and "Keeping Secrets," *Courier & Press*, November 6, 2001, originally accessed November 8, 2001.

31. Eric Alterman, "Freedom Is History (And Vice Versa)," *The Nation*, December 10, 2001, originally accessed online November 23, 2001.

32. "Statement by John W. Carlin, Archivist of the United States, to the Subcommittee on Government Efficiency, Financial Management, and Intergovernmental Relations of the Committee on Government Reform, House of Representatives, Congress of the United States, On the Implementation and Effectiveness of the Presidential Records Act of 1978," November 6, 2001, available at http://www.archives.gov/presidential_libraries/presidential_records/archivists-statement.html.

33. Patricia Nelson Limerick, *Something in the Soil: Legacies and Reckonings in the New West* (New York: W. W. Norton, 2000), pp. 339–340.

34. Steven Hensen, "The Saga of Executive Order 13233," *Archival Outlook* (January/February 2002): 3, 15.

5

Archival Credentials and Professional Identity

INTRODUCTION

What makes someone an archivist or a records manager? You would think you could go up to someone working in an archives or records center and get a succinct and useful definition. Think again. Archivists and records managers have been debating about who they are for the past century. To make things more complicated, these debates have had different nuances and contexts in various nations. And this has not just been an internal professional debate, however engaging or emotional this debate might be for records professionals. Records, including those designated as archives, have become matters for both media and policy makers' attention. Society needs to know that there is a profession of archivists and records managers, and it needs to know how to distinguish them from historians and information scientists or museum curators and librarians. This is not an easy task. What some might dismiss as over enthusiastic navel-gazing is, in fact, a process with implications far beyond the bounds of the discipline of archives administration.

Profession, *professional*, and *professionalism* have not always been words referred to very kindly in our egalitarian age. For many, these terms smack of elitism, medieval guilds, and secret handshakes. Whatever attitudes might be expressed about professionals and professionalism, we live in an age of professionals. Robert Fogel, Nobel Laureate in Economics, notes, "throughout most of American history, the professional class constituted a small minority, generally less than 3 or 4 percent, of the labor force."[1] Influenced by the expansion of higher education and immense changes in technology, "professional occupations in 1997 accounted for about 33 percent of the labor force."[2]

While certain professions grow and new ones emerge, some the result of new technologies (think of Webmaster as one example), there continues to be a steady stream of criticism and concern expressed about what these professions mean and what they do for (or to) us. Lawyers are often berated, and physicians criticized for their interest in money; even the professional clergy are now often sneered at by both the public and social commentators. Archivists and records managers might not be on this list only because they are invisible to most! I do not, obviously, share the sentiments expressed by many against professions (although I do have deep reservations about some elements of the legal profession and about all who claim to be "professional" politicians).

THE WRONG PARADIGM? SELLING OURSELVES

Some of these same anti-professionalism sentiments can be found in the ranks of records professionals. One problem with the matter of professional identity, at least in North America, has been that archivists and records managers have leaned in the egalitarian direction of wanting to be inconclusive and, at least until recent years, sought to attract association members at all costs. How could anyone argue with this? If substantial services are included in the membership fee, new members will be attracted, revenue will increase, more services can be provided, and the records professions will be all the stronger.

I contend that this is, in fact, the *wrong* model and that the primary purpose of any professional association is *not* to include all the professionals. The purposes of a professional association are to promote and protect professional standards and the professional mission, and these aims can often be in conflict with "selling" a professional association. The first fallacy of such arguments is the leap from an emphasis on equating paying dues and professionalism to offering particular kinds of services to attract members.

Professionals ought to belong to their professional association because they *are* professionals. Being a professional is not limited to being paid to do certain activities associated with a particular discipline, nor is it restricted to working in a certain type of institution. In other words, being an archivist does not mean being paid to do archival work or working in an archives, but rather it means mastering archival principles and knowledge, having met certain educational and employment standards, and carrying out work that has been entrusted to the archivist by their institution and society.

The same is true for a records manager. Since professional associations exist to maintain certain professional standards—the essence of what it means to be a professional—individuals should be members of their national association no matter what they might think of its services. In a sense, such a view of professionals, as mere joiners, reflects the kind of anti-professional sentiment we see all around us, especially the stereotypes of professionals portrayed by the media as petty and mindless bureaucrats.

The nature of services described here is also extremely problematic and, in fact, if adhered to, undermines the very foundation of what the Association of Canadian Archivists (ACA) or the SAA or any association of archivists or records managers should be doing as professional associations. Such associations often want to reach all records professionals, whether they are members or not. If this means simply that membership materials are distributed so that no one misses what these associations are doing, then I have little to argue with this, but more is implied (such as suggesting that all individuals working as record professionals, regardless of education, experience, or knowledge, have an equal place at the table).

Where do we cross the line from individual responsibility of the professional to removing the responsibility? Is a professional association an umbilical cord for the individual who cannot function independently as a professional? Such attitudes seem to confirm that many within the discipline do not think of any records work as constituting professional practice, a sentiment they might vehemently deny in words but do not deny in practice.

At issue is the motivation. Archivists and records managers often portray themselves (not necessarily on purpose) as too busy to read, to think, or to stay current with their field. What is missing, of course, is the responsibility any professional must have for his or her discipline, critical to the societal mandate that a profession possesses or claims to have.

But wanting a professional association to reach out is very different from focusing on a profession's social relevancy. Often, the primary objective becomes getting every records professional to join a professional association. There are two problems with this statement. First, is it the *ultimate* goal? Isn't the real objective the establishment of standards coupled with advocacy for the use of these standards in behalf of the fulfillment of the mission? Second, *what* is a professional? Is a professional anyone who is paid to work as an archivist or calls him- or herself an archivist? If such adherence covers the latter, then we are heading in the right direction, but if the objective is simply snaring another dues-paying member, then this is an incredibly short-sighted objective.

Why does a professional association, like the ACA or SAA, or the ARMA have to be an advocate in our society? Controversies and issues concerning records are extremely common. They require us to have professional associations bold enough to be outspoken advocates for the preservation, identification, and use of records, not to be too internally focused on providing services that professional archivists and records managers themselves should be equipped to do.

Rather than publishing print versions of essential or important electronic communications for those archivists without access to those information systems, we should insist that every professional archivist gain access to such systems and that our attention be devoted to the larger public forum in building support for the archival mission. Given that all institutions and most individuals are shifting to the use of electronic recordkeeping systems, the suggestion that many archivists will not have access to computers is to admit that they cannot cope with basic, modern recordkeeping methods.

Why does a professional association, like ARMA, ACA, or SAA, have to wrestle with the definition of what it means to be a professional? We have been doing this for generations, it seems, but this is particularly relevant when we read calls for more inclusive membership of archival and records management practitioners. While there is a decided need for any professional to understand that he or she has a responsibility to their employer and to society, there is a counterpart notion that being a professional means having command of a certain knowledge that others do not. Institutions hiring archivists and records managers, and individuals donating archival records to repositories, assume archivists possess some basic competencies. Before we embark on reaching out to bring in every individual who thinks of him—or herself as an archivist or some kind of records professional, we need to realize that not everyone commands this knowledge or deserves the title of professional.

There are, of course, two dangers with struggling over the notion of the professional archivist or records manager. The first is that we become elitist, restrictive, and too constraining in our concept, and that we make no effort to assist all involved in archival work to raise their standards. The second danger is, however, just as real. We may become too inclusive, accepting anyone into the fold, and become so preoccupied with keeping them that we support professional associations that stand for almost nothing. The lowest common denominator rules. Association leaders will make decisions to keep the largest numbers happy, rather than do what is needed in order to ensure that our documentary heritage is managed. It is this, I believe, that has been the larger problem facing our associations.

The one argument with which I concur concerns the importance of voluntarism and commitment to working for a non-profit association. Rather than dreaming up such schemes as recognizing volunteers, however, records professionals should strenuously consider what the purpose of the association is and why they need such commitment. This is *not* about selling something. Rather, this is about working for stronger professional standards, monitoring the activities of government and other leaders regarding the care of archival and all records, and laboring to create better public understanding about why records are essential to our society. Building up ARMA, ACA, or SAA should come through efforts that support the profession, and not just through services that make members feel good or think that they are getting their money's worth.

Being a professional archivist, or records manager means being a member of the national professional association. Such membership is a professional responsibility. I would waste little time in trying to persuade someone who cannot understand that ARMA, ACA, or SAA is a good buy. I suspect that some individuals will stay members for only a brief time anyway, because they do not really understand the essence of what it means to be a professional. The notion of belonging to a modern profession can only occur *if* we understand the members of our profession to be those who possess good educational backgrounds, have mastered the essential professional knowledge, are keeping up with the expanding professional knowledge, and who use that knowledge in the appropriate fashion to preserve and manage archival records.

ARCHIVISTS, RECORDS MANAGERS, AND AUTONOMY

The notion of professional inclusiveness is not unique to North America. Dutch archivist Theo Thomassen draws on the sociology of professions to suggest that a professional is part of a "group of people with the same occupation, who dominate a specific intervention field, who do this on the basis of the exclusive mastery of scientific discipline underlying this discipline and who deliver specific services to society that are recognized as positively affecting public welfare." Thomassen elaborates on each of these aspects or attributes of a profession. And he comes back to the notion of professional autonomy, building off of a particular body of knowledge that is distinct and "not an auxiliary science" of either history or information science. Here, Thomassen creates a notion that is very different from what I commented on above: "An independent profession runs its own business. It gathers individual professionals together in an independent association of some kind. It controls the entrance to the profession, by enforcing entrance requirements, formulated mainly in terms of competencies in the scientific discipline involved." He continues: "The real measure for the independence of a profession, however, is the degree in which it is capable of imposing its own definitions of professional reality and its own standards and values both to its own members and to society as a whole."[3] This is more complicated than merely paying for membership in a professional association, and it is certainly much different from mounting a membership campaign.

I agree completely with Thomassen. In the mid-1980s, I wrote an essay also enumerating the characteristics of a profession. I argued with my colleagues that we needed to think about and correct our weak links so that we would possess sufficient *power* in society and in our organizations to fulfill the important responsibilities of managing the documentary heritage for the benefit of our global citizens.[4] Five years later I commented on this essay, but in the 1990 essay I used the work of the sociologist Andrew Abbott, who was intrigued by how disciplines often competed with each other.

The point, again, was that a group, like archivists, need to understand that they are in a contest that requires them to be astute about how they manage and strengthen themselves for the competition.[5] With the present emphasis on information and increasingly slippery definitions of "documents,"[6] it is even more imperative that archivists focus on what makes them unique than what I describe over a decade ago. In

America, archivists do not like to think about power or to give any indication that they might be elitist.

What is most interesting to me are the recommendations that I made in these earlier essays, involving an accreditation program for archival repositories, the strengthening of graduate education, and the individual certification of archivists. I have changed my mind about such matters. When I originally suggested this three-prong mechanism to strengthen the American archival profession, there was little evidence of much happening in *any* of these components. The debate about individual certification was raging, but the vehemence of the conversations did not suggest that this might happen. Graduate archival education remained largely unchanged, with the exception that a few full-time regular faculty in archival studies had joined universities, but no one envisioned much growth in graduate courses, faculty members, or number of programs. Finally, although there had been some work on identifying and clarifying the elements of archival programs, no one was advocating that this be ratcheted up to include accrediting the repositories. Of these, individual certification leaped to the fore, and it became, to the surprise of many, institutionalized. Graduate archival education began a growth spurt as well. The result was a set of additional factors dividing an already fragmented archives profession.

AN ACADEMY FOR AUTONOMY?

In 1987, the governing council of the Society of American Archivists voted to establish a certification process—starting with a "grandparenting" process whereby individuals could qualify on the basis of an application delineating experience, education, and other qualifications and then moving to an independent body whereby individuals qualified as the result of an examination. In 1989, the Academy of Certified Archivists was established, and it exists today. I was a proponent of the notion of individual certification of archivists, and I was a member of the SAA Council that approved the formation of the Academy. I was also among the initial group of archivists to be certified, and I ran (unsuccessfully) for president of the Academy in 1990. In the years since then, I have changed my position on certification, primarily because of what the Academy has not accomplished and due to the strengthening of graduate archival education.

The Academy of Certified Archivists seems to be a healthy organization. Its Web site (www.certifiedarchivists.org/) is upbeat and provides information about what an archivist is and why certification is useful, including the impact of certification on the field and how employers are using certification for hiring. The Academy's homepage enumerates many positive reasons why individuals seek certification, including "to validate their education, experience, and skills"; "to better prepare themselves for a highly competitive job market"; "to demonstrate their self-confidence, professional commitment, and personal initiative"; "for the personal satisfaction of comparing their knowledge and skills to a consensus national standard"; to serve "as an example to newer archivists of the importance of professional involvement, maintaining an interest in profession-wide concerns, and contributing to the development of the profession as a whole"; and "to show support for graduate archival education and professional archival standards."[7] The Academy's Web site provides information about how to become certified and news about the organization, with little data about certification's impact. Indeed, only a small portion of the profession is certified (perhaps eight hundred individuals just a few years ago, which certainly is less than ten (maybe five) percent of those who work as archivists in the United States). If they are the elite of the field, and if the Academy is a force in professional standards and practice, the size might be irrelevant. Despite the Academy's claim at the outset of its Web site that it "promotes fundamental standards of professional archival practice" and "lead[s] by defining the knowledge and abilities necessary to be an archivist," there is little evidence of such roles.

I was originally sympathetic to the certification of individual archivists. I am publicly on record for supporting the process, both in some of my writings[8] and by virtue of being on the SAA Council that courageously, or foolishly, voted for certification. What may not be so clear, however, is why I (and others) supported certification. Discussions about certification tended to be couched too heavily in black and white terms, polarizing around some basic issues. Some argued against certification, for example, by saying it is not as good as strengthening graduate archival education programs or by contending that it is impossible to develop an examination process because we have an insufficient knowledge base.[9]

I hope you can follow what has happened here, the tendency to move quickly to *either-or* scenarios. What was lost is that individual certification can be merely part of an overall effort to strengthen the profession *and* the management of archival records. I have *never* argued, for example, that individual certification is *all* archivists should do, or that it is the *best* that they can do. Rather, I have consistently seen individual certification as merely the *first* step, by reason of historical accident and convenience, of a broad agenda of change that includes the possibility of institutional accreditation, development of more stringent standards, and the strengthening of archival education.

Back in 1989 I predicted that certification would be eventually adopted by a significant portion of archival employers and seen by practicing or prospective archivists as a desirable credential. Thus far I have been proved wrong. I believed then that the certification examination would help the profession to codify its core knowledge. There is no question that a basic knowledge is an essential component of any profession. This is the criterion that distinguishes one profession from another and is, as well, the feature that provides a profession the ability to negotiate its relative position and influence in society.[10] Without question archivists have a diversity of views about their knowledge, ranging from low to high opinions and arguments for strengthening it through research, codification of standard practice, and other means. In most basic archival functions there is a considerable amount of knowledge that can be classified as both practice-based and theoretical. What the archival profession has seemed to lack, however, is some incentive to bring that knowledge into a more usable body of archival theory and practice.

While the Academy of Certified Archivists has put most of its energies into forming and administering an examination, there is little evidence that its work has influenced or broadened the knowledge of the discipline (or, for that matter, enhanced the profession's societal profile). It has not publicized very effectively the nature and extent of this knowledge, nor has it sought to work with the educators or the SAA Committee on Education and Professional Development to seek ways to promote a deeper understanding of the extent and content of archival studies. (Yes, some educators have been involved but this is far more limited than what I have in mind.)

I originally believed that the certification examination would promote the fuller development of graduate archival education programs. Some disagreed because this is exactly the opposite of what has generally been argued. At the earliest stages of establishing certification, there was interest in allowing the graduates of certain "entitled" programs to sit immediately for the examination. I thought then that this would provide an excellent tool for graduate archival educators to use to strengthen their programs, expanding well beyond the old three-course sequence then considered to be the norm for these programs. Now, the occasional odd discussion on the Archives and Archivists listserv affirms that *some* educators are teaching their students to take the certification examination, a considerable step backwards in the profession's efforts to consolidate its knowledge and establish its identity.

Although the Academy eventually adopted the notion that graduates of archival education programs could sit immediately for the examination and later endorsed more comprehensive SAA education guidelines, it contributed little to strengthening graduate archival education. In fact, the Academy has continued to be seen as an alternative to the higher education of archivists, suggesting that the core of archival work is practice-based. In its own workshops (which sounded like venues for learning how to pass the examination), the Academy minimized its effectiveness as an advocate for a well-rounded education of archivists. My view remains that archival science or administration (it makes little difference what terminology is used here to connote the body of knowledge) is a complex set of interdisciplinary principles and concepts that need to be applied to an increasingly complex environment of recordkeeping regimes and records creators. An archivist's ability to function depends on what he learns from a solid educational foundation and a lifelong commitment to learning via continuing education and reading across many disciplines.

A decade and a half ago, I also believed that the certification examination would provide a measure of quality of education programs and repositories, recognizing that this as a long-term potential implication for the profession. Assuming that the examination would move from adequate to excellent, the passing or failing graduates of specific programs might tell us something about the quality of students being attracted to these programs and the profession. Anything we learned would be valuable, I thought, since we knew precious little about such things at that time, despite a half-century of educating individuals to work as archivists.[11]

I also viewed certification as one means by which to define or at least identify an archivist. Why won't this also tell us something about the quality of archival repositories? Two published institutional self-studies have both attested to the need for programs to have "at least one person who possesses, through training and experience, professional competence in archives management."[12] At the same time, the archival community has not done very well in defining what an archivist is and who can fill an archival position. Obviously, certification seemed to be one potential measure. Why not say that each archival repository must have one *certified* archivist? To those who argued that certification does not equal competence, I can only respond that, while being aware of the problem, it is a greater problem of having *no* definition or criteria at all. I thought it was only one more reason for the archival profession to back certification and to guarantee its success.

Here I now have mixed sentiments. I have certainly changed my mind that we can use passing the certification examination as an evaluation of graduate archival education programs. I believe this for two reasons. Since the beginning of the Academy and its emphasis on the examination, there has been little effort between the Academy and the educators to have the examination reflect state-of-the-art teaching about archival science and practice. Furthermore, an examination focused on practice is not likely to be a good evaluator of graduate education based on advancing practice.

The role of a graduate archival educator is to *change* the discipline, strengthening its practice and knowledge, not *only* to reflect current or traditional practice. If anything, the failure of graduates taking the certification examination might be the better indicator of the more substantial graduate archival education programs, in that these graduates would see the nuances or vagaries of multiple-choice examination questions. For example, my own students study the limitations of Schellenberg's evidence-information paradigm for appraisal purposes so that they can both evaluate newer concepts and consider what kinds of additional appraisal approaches are needed. I wonder how they might answer questions related to this old model.

Using the process of certification to place knowledgeable archivists in archival and historical records programs is a more complex problem. For many small, poorly funded programs, the hiring of a certified archivist could be a significant improvement, even at the most basic, rudimentary level of development of the process. If such hiring occurred, there would be at least the acceptance of a common language and some core principles and practices. However, it may be that certification can only function at this level, a sort of technician's rather than professional's position. Graduate archival education programs, at least the more comprehensive ones, may be moving away from placing their graduates in small historical societies, public libraries, historic sites, and the like in favor of placing graduates in larger programs and organizations—such as corporations that need to develop institutional archives—and even in non-archival positions such as information policy and software engineering, to ensure that the archival perspective is considered in the future development of recordkeeping systems.

Sixteen years ago, I also believed that the certification examination would promote activities in other key areas to strengthen the profession. Here, I am going beyond basic knowledge to matters like ethics, standards, and publication of and access to textbooks and other literature that are essential to the well-being of the profession. All I am suggesting here is that the continual process of keeping the certification examination up-to-date will help to identify such needs and, hopefully, lead to activities that intend to meet these needs.

It is no secret, for example, that we still lack a decent, comprehensive, single volume introductory textbook on archival administration, the history of the field, or of records and recordkeeping systems.[13] I hope one or more archivists will be prompted to rise to the occasion to produce such volumes because of the need and growing market for basic courses that prepare individuals to sit for the examination. Just as importantly, the certification examination should lead to more serious efforts to rectify the poor access that we presently have to archival literature.[14]

Now you will notice that I did not add to the list of implications that the examination will make archivists *feel* better about being archivists. Bill Maher's suggestion, in his interesting essay on certification, that "in the end, the process may be more important as a means for the profession to improve its self-image from its public image"[15] might be true; only time will tell, but it is hardly worth worrying about. My experience keeps me convinced that archivists and records managers will always worry about such things and that this is a condition probably endemic to any profession.

I have backed away from the need for emphasizing the development of a "comprehensive single volume introductory textbook" in favor of more systematic research about archival practice and principles and more writing about archival issues for non-archivists. But this is a minor point. The problem is that the Academy has not looked beyond the examination and recertification to consider larger issues. Certification leaders have argued that the Academy should be doing more than focusing on the certification exam. That sounds promising, but the Academy also continues to focus on marketing the credential. Other than helping the smallest and weakest archival programs (which might not even be able to afford certified archivists), it is difficult to see how the Academy will help a profession that needs to deal with information technology, political issues, ethical dilemmas, and policy concerns.

I also believed, in the earliest years of the certification discussions and the establishment of the Academy, that the certification examination would force the archival profession to think about something different from the status quo or lowest common denominator. For a very long time archivists have been extremely generous in their viewpoints regarding who can be an archivist, the kinds of institution that can function as archival repositories, and who can teach archives.

The certification examination served notice, I thought, that archivists were changing their minds about such things. Giving an examination suggested that the chaff would be separated from the wheat; in other words, that there are some criteria about who can practice as archivists and who should be hired to work as such. A glance at archival employment notices suggests such a wide range of notions about what an archivist is and does and such poorly defined conceptions of archival knowledge, skills, and attitudes as to allow almost anyone to meet the criteria. The certification examination suggests there is a difference between an archivist and a non-archivist, a distinction archivists have always been willing to support and defend.

If anything, the Academy of Certified Archivists has acted as if its main concern has been with getting as many archivists certified as possible and keeping them certified. The recertification plan as adopted makes it difficult for anyone not to be recertified, and supporting comments about the plan betray a lowest common denominator viewpoint. Continued employment, attendance at a few conferences, and a modicum of professional activity will get anyone recertified. There is no real stress on archival knowledge. An archivist is defined as someone who works in an archives or who is employed as an archivist, not by what he or she knows about archives.

At the beginning of the development of the certification examination, I believed that it would legally protect individual archivists, archival employers, and the archival profession. Again, Maher suggested that there is concern about the legal implications of certification.[16] An informal review of archival certification by a labor lawyer I know suggested, on the other hand, that the archival profession has been "at risk" due to its lack of qualifications for employment of archivists.[17] This does not suggest that archivists discuss the possibility of lawsuits, but it appears that certification gives them a better ground for defending who they hire and how they evaluate their work.

Given the modest impact certification has had on employment, there are few legal concerns at this time. I have not changed my views about this matter, but I remain concerned about what would be contested. Are archivists protecting a very low level of archival work or a true knowledge of archival work? Doing the former is not likely to advance the profession very far; in fact, it could hurt the continued development of an archival science with a focus on theory, methodology, *and* practice.

I also believed that the adoption of certification, the development and use of the certification examination, and the formation of the Academy of Certified Archivists marked the end of one period of archival development and the beginning of another age. The American archival profession has been the beneficiary of significant milestones throughout its history: the founding of the first government archives in 1901, the start of the Conference of Archivists in 1909, the establishment of the National Archives in 1934 and the Society of American Archivists in 1936, and the release of the report of the SAA Committee on the Seventies in 1972.

One archival commentator has called the eighties the "age of archival analysis" by virtue of its emphasis on self-assessment and planning.[18] Perhaps the 1986 report of the SAA Goals and Priorities Task Force is another one of those milestones. I also suggested that 1989, the year of the formation of Academy of Certified Archivists and the first certification examination, marked the end of the age of archival analysis and, perhaps, the beginning of the "age of archival action." It seemed that archivists were now ready to take some bolder steps. Personally, I had hoped that accreditation of graduate programs and archival institutions and stronger standards in all areas would be additional steps that archivists could take in the nineties and beyond.

I now believe that the 1989 formation of the Academy and the 1993 SAA endorsement of the Masters of Archival Studies guidelines together provide a benchmark delineating the separation of the discipline between technicians and professionals (although SAA has now backed off from endorsing a specific masters degree in the field, bowing to the reality that no university in the United States after a decade had adopted such a degree). I do not believe this is necessarily bad. What will continue to be a problem is the Academy's insistence that its credential is the preeminent one. It can only be preeminent if it is based squarely on a comprehensive graduate education degree, and if it is promoted through an aggressive campaign in increasing public understanding of archives—ensuring that archives is part of information policy initiatives and implementations, and influencing information technology development and software engineering.

HAS ANYTHING REALLY CHANGED? DEBATING CERTIFICATION IN CYBERSPACE

One might wonder what certification has resolved, given how it is discussed in the field and its impact on how archival positions are described and advertised. One discussion about certification on the Archives and Archivists discussion list commenced on October 9, 2001, when someone innocently posted a message inquiring "what the arguments/opposition are against certification and the Academy of Certified Archivists?" This person was concerned because at present "ANYONE can call themselves an archivist. And our salaries and status in organizational charts usually reflect that."[19]

That alone suggested some issues about the efficacy of certification. Over the course of two weeks, twenty-five individuals carried out a debate on the discussion list, expressing mixed opinions about certification's utility, the nature of educational requirements for becoming an archivist, the ability of an examination to evaluate knowledge about archival work, and even what distinguishes someone as an archivist from other professionals. Two months later, nearly the same debate (I refrained from using excerpts from that debate for this reason) occurred again, with virtually the same range of differing views, and that discussion continued on for about a month as well. Indeed, the question of the validity of certification as a professional credential recurs every few months, generating considerable heat, but not always sufficient light, about the importance of it within the archival profession.

As is typical of this often highly charged discussion list, responses to the question appeared all over the landscape. Some were ambivalent about certification. One respondent speculated that he was "indifferent to negative regarding the certification program, because I think it has accomplished few of its stated objectives," but thought that it "may have helped improve the standards of archival educational programs to some extent."[20] There were also testimonials from some who were certified and had allowed their certification to lapse because they discovered "no tangible benefits" and little impact on position requirements, concluding "certification is an individual choice" and depends on one's personal circumstances.[21]

Others thought that certification could help them or their employer develop better standards. One individual noted, "I recently was asked to take the certification exam by my employer in an effort to standardize and raise the professional standard at our institution. I agreed to take the exam for those reasons alone—because our institution does not re-quire a masters degree—and I thought the standardization of certifica-tion would help the entire agency."[22]

Credibility in organizations seems to be of importance for some. One commentator believing that a "few letters after your name helps when decisions are being made."[23] Other commentators wondered if employers understood what being a certified archivist meant, and they were skeptical about the impact on salary: "paying a lot of money out of pocket to have the privilege of adding two letters after my name and announcing that I belong to an elite group of successful test takers."[24] Another thought that the purpose of the "CA" is to "give employers the indication that the holder is a member of a well-qualified group/profes-sion," but since the commentator had "never seen a job posting that said 'CA only' there was little indication that it was having an impact.[25]

Others engaged in this discussion argued clearly their preference for more formalized education, stating, "I worry that the archives com-munity is focusing too much attention on this test, and not enough on formal education. As it stands now, I feel that programs offering archi-val education classes are essential, but they are not receiving the respect they deserve. The education can—and is—being replaced with a test. I also worry that people who are hiring archivists (people who are not familiar with the field) rely only on certification rather than education and breadth and depth of experience."[26] Others simply stated that this was not necessarily a debate between certification and education.[27]

Some respondents were much more hostile: "I have never changed my opinion that the certified archivists exam is basically worthless and a waste of money. Other 'serious' professions would never substitute an exam for educational credentials and suggest that the exam is equiva-lent to academic study."[28] While a leader of the Academy of Certified Archivists corrected the sentiment that the certification examination is a "substitute for, or as the equivalent of, graduate study" by noting that the masters degree is a "basic requirement for taking the archival certifi-cation examination" and "can only be waived by a vote of the full Acad-emy board,"[29] the fact remains that many continue to view certification (drawing on knowledge derived primarily from professional experience) as the primary professional credential rather than education.[30]

A number of respondents believed that certification provided "an alternative to establish credentials outside of a degreed program."[31] In fact, the discussion of certification also revealed some deep-seated ani-mosity about education. One individual believed that "archival education has long consisted of a number of kingdoms and fiefdoms none of which is willing to be told what to do or how it is to be done. Each one had its own agenda and felt that it was the only one who knew how to do things right." This individual continued to question what has occurred in archival education, characterizing graduate education as something outside of the control of professional archivists, an assessment that is somewhat exaggerated since many professional archivists have been involved in the development of such education from its beginning. What is critical here is that this individual, along with others, believes that because of such matters, the "only option was to offer certification of individual archivists" and that somehow certification and education were working at cross-purposes.[32] For some, education and being a professional were not at all related: "I believe that one would have a very hard time arguing that each and every course required for that "graduate professional degree" is also required for one to be considered a "professional" archivist," worrying about "academic elitism."[33]

Other respondents supported certification because it provides "some type of professional identity. Unless we, as archivists, set ourselves apart in some way, we will never achieve professional and financial recognition. Certification is one way to do that."[34] Another sounded off, "We need to provide a benchmark for excellence that is recognized outside our profession."[35] The public profile of certification seemed to be undermined by internal professional confusion about some very basic matters. Many commentators readily acknowledge that we still don't have "agreement on how to determine what makes someone an archivist. But for now certification and a masters degree with archival coursework is what many in the archival profession consider the benchmark."[36] But others worry about the public impact of certification, one individual noting that a "CA wouldn't impress my management because they think archivists and librarians are the same thing . . . ." "Who are we trying to convince? I don't think the rest of the world gives a rat's arse. We seem to be the only ones wrapped up in the glory of certification."[37]

Some are pursuing the certification designation as a means of "job security?: "Do you find it in the organization employing you or in the wider job market? It is easy to oppose certification sitting in academia but if you are relying on the job market to employ you in the private sector, you may very well need it. . . . Get on the career track that will make you desired rather than taking the lottery approach to jobs. The CA is just a part of the overall professional development picture."[38]

Another argued that certification helps employers because they "rarely have the time to review an individual's portfolio, [and] professional certifications are easily verified and speeds along the process. When applying for positions employers usually see only a one to two page resume. The listing of certifications on a resume will generally (not always) put an individual in the stack that will receive further consideration. . . . Certification is a door opener."[39] At the heart of such concerns were worries about what was there to assist someone marketing themselves as an archivist. Others noted that the problem was that "There are no degrees granted in Archival Studies in the USA" and "certification is the only Archives-specific credential available. . . ."[40] Others worried that there is dissension within the field about matters like graduate education and that there needed to be "an internal standard that would have the benefit of being recognized/understandable/identifiable to those outside the field."[41]

Others expressed doubt about the certification examination and archival knowledge. One individual, identifying himself as *not* certified, confessed that "when I'm seeking to fill a position at this archives I would rather have someone with an MLS, to understand the technology needed, and a MA in history to understand the work we do. When the exam can test not only on how to memorize a limited amount of theory on how to file things, but also a person's ability to work in the subject matter of the archives where they hope to work (in my case, history) then I will consider it worth taking and considering."[42]

Some worry about whether an examination can "capture and test all the duties of an archivist."[43] Another pointed to problems with the certification examination as being reflective of the larger problems "between a technical and scientific education as compared to a broad humanities education. Tests are very well suited to the 'left brain' learner. In the humanities, however, we more often have to produce a product to show our competencies."[44] One respondent explained that he had taken five courses as part of a graduate program, "so I resent the idea that people in the field think I need to pay yet another sum of money to prove that I am competent. . . . There are many other professions where a degree is accepted as proof of competence."[45]

After more than a decade of work by the Academy of Certified Archivists, discussions about individual certification and the certification examination seem to be more a forum for all the continuing angst about whether archivists constitute a profession and possess any societal mandate for calling themselves one. This continues to be most dramatically highlighted in job advertisements, not only because they usually say little about certification, but also because the description of qualifications remains awkward, unwieldy, and often confusing if not amusing.

HAS ANYTHING REALLY CHANGED? CERTIFICATION AND JOBS

Some years ago I did an analysis of entry-level archivists positions in the United States over a twenty-year period, extending through 1997. I discovered that archival certification was nearly invisible as a requirement, with only 11 of 230 advertisements in 1996–97 mentioning it and all describing certification as "preferred" or "desired" instead of required.[46] Some might argue that this is only eight years after the establishment of the Academy and hardly sufficient time for its true impact to be felt within the field and certainly within society. However, more recent advertisements, from September 2001 through April 2002, suggested little change. Of 107 positions advertised, only 5 included any reference to the certification status, about the same rate as what was occurring five years ago. And none of these positions require a designation as a certified archivist.[47]

It is clear that the Academy of Certified Archivists has had little impact on the employment of archivists, but this is not the more serious issue in my estimation. The problem is that the job advertisements continue to display a wild and wooly array of educational and other qualifications that can perplex or discourage even the hardiest of souls. Most advertisements for archivists include a wide range of educational backgrounds, guaranteed to make one dizzy. A standard advertisement reads, "Master's degree in archives administration, library science, information management, business administration, history, or other relevant field." Another specifies these qualifications: "Must hold a Bachelor's degree with experience in archives and/or cataloging. A Master's degree is preferred. Possible degrees include MLS degree, Master's in Archival or Museum studies, Information Science, Preservation and Conservation." Another prospective employer asks for a "Graduate degree in archival/library/information science, humanities, or social sciences or equivalent professional archives or records management experience."[48]

After a decade and a half since the formation of the Academy of Certified Archivists, more than a quarter of a century after the Society of American Archivists issued its first graduate education guidelines, nearly three-quarters of a century after SAA's establishment, and more than a century after the beginning of the modern archives profession in the United States, the records community *still* have a hard time describing the qualifications of an archivist. What has gone wrong? And why could we not have learned from others? Our colleagues, records managers, have had an even longer experience with much the same results. The number of certified records managers (CRMs), part of an older certification process dating back to 1975, has also constituted only a small portion of the entire records management community. Michael Pemberton argues, "The specific—and documented—value of the CRM in terms of professional status, income, employability, and career mobility has yet to be established."[49]

HAS ANYTHING REALLY CHANGED? CERTIFICATION AND EDUCATION

The Academy of Certified Archivists continues to be aggressive in how it views its role in the profession. In 2001 Academy President Patrick Quinn commented on the varying nature of education programs within the profession and countered with this: "The fact remains that no matter what employment qualifying degree an archivist has, the only objective, empirically verifiable measure of an archivist's competence is the certification examination offered by the Academy of Certified Archivists. . . . No matter what advanced degree an entry-level archivist may possess, such degrees are not *prima facie* evidence of archival competence, nor do they ensure that archivists will not rest on their qualifying degree credentials for the rest of their careers."[50]

Perhaps we can go further and say that weakness of graduate archival education *requires* something like certification to be in place. There are two problems with this. One is the fact that certification has not been much of a success except in sustaining an Academy of Certified Archivists, as I have just discussed. The other is the fact that graduate archival education *has* shown remarkable growth over the past two decades.

When I entered the field in the early 1970s, there were very few programs where one could gain anything resembling an education. Mostly, you could go somewhere and take a couple of courses, work in an archives for academic credit (with very mixed results), and work with faculty who were practitioners, but only adjuncts, with little influence in their academic departments. But in the last 16 years we have had an explosion of regular, tenure stream faculty appointments; the development of some programs with multiple faculty appointments; and the emergence of very intense specializations within library and information science programs and history departments.[51] Although things look much more promising, my reflection on the wording in job advertisements suggests that it is still far too little.

As I have been stressing for some 16 years, the American archival community's *first* need in developing a stronger sense of itself and a higher profile in the public is establishing a separate masters degree in archival studies. I first wrote and advocated this more than a decade ago.[52] My sense of the need has only intensified, although I am not optimistic that this will ever happen. Mostly, it has intensified in the sense that I do not believe we need just any kind of masters degree, but ones that have strong perspective on records, records systems, evidence, accountability, corporate and societal memory, and other such matters.[53] This has also intensified in the sense that one of the archives community's most critical needs is raising up a new corps of archives faculty equipped with doctorates, research interests and publications, firm understanding of the nature of records and their importance in society, and the skills to mentor students and negotiate with the profession itself.[54]

We also have the extra challenge of the increasing number of public controversies, political incidents, and other events capturing the media attention that concern records and that require us, the records professionals, to know what we are about and what we stand for. At the same time, we are seeing substantial elements of the spectrum of records professionals seemingly abandoning records as their focus. In the United States, individuals within the Association of Records Managers and Administrators promoting something called "strategic information management" actually see this new approach as something liberating them from the tedious tasks associated with the administration of records.[55] Fortunately, however tedious they may be to handle, records are *important*.

Despite how archivists who are transfixed on credentials like certification might view such matters, it is clear that certification has sent mixed signals about the *basis* for archival knowledge. Certification is focused more on knowledge gained from practice; and while *all* proponents of archival education incorporate a strong weighting of practical assignments, applied research, and practice in archives, most educators also recognize that such practice is most meaningful when built on a knowledge of records, the principles that frame archival knowledge, and the ability to look beyond the walls of one archival operation to understand the societal, organizational, and other contexts of the archives, its mission, and its holdings. From my perspective, education is not the same as training and it is certainly not the same as apprenticeship. The core of being a *professional* archivist is *knowing* about records and archives, and that knowledge is gained by study, reflection, discussion, and the other components that constitute education.

Certification, a true credential, although based on an examination supposedly testing knowledge, both suggests that the knowledge is somewhat limited and opens the possibility that educational programs and continuing workshops will teach towards taking and passing the examination (as happens in other fields). Indeed, the Academy's *Handbook* tells us that the examination is a "practice-based" examination, deriving "directly from the practice and experience of professionals in the field." And even though the *Handbook* argues that this "pragmatic base presupposes a solid and growing theoretical component and written body of knowledge," it is obvious that the Academy endorses a model of the archivist as someone who *does* rather than someone who *knows*.[56]

The problem here is that even the suggested reading list is mostly basic manuals and handbooks in their own right, implying that if theory or more systematic methodology is involved, it is several levels away from what is going on with this examination. New models and approaches, debates about assumptions and current practice, tensions between different schools of thought about archival work, and other such elements that add richness, texture, and even pleasure to what archivists do are all missing in the interest of being able to test about *basic* practice.

The certification examination and the overall process have not had the success possibly because they represented little more than hanging a certificate on the wall and initials after a name. Being a certified archivist does not enhance the public's understanding of an archivist; far from it.

CONCLUSION

Proponents of certification see it as essential for improving the public image of archivists or records managers. Yet, there are a multitude of reasons why this might not make sense, primarily whether this has happened in other fields that have adopted certification. John Berry, commenting on the recent debate within librarianship about a post-MLS degree certification, candidly stated: "I'm not sure certification will deliver the improved status or image its proponents claim it will. I was shocked to realize that I know absolutely nothing about the level or currency of the certification of my accountant, lawyer, doctor, cardiac specialist, plumber, auto mechanic, or any other professional whose services I use. My perception of them is unaltered by their certification or lack of it and that includes my librarian. If my librarian were certified, I probably would never know. So much for improved image and status."[57]

Well, that may be true. But the real issue here might be that such certification really doesn't *mean* anything. Archivists and other records professionals have to be firm believers in a societal mission that is not just waiting about for historians and other researchers to visit them. They have to deal with all the challenges about the creation, maintenance, and preservation of records for a wide array of reasons supporting society, its organizations, citizens, and scholars. This necessitates, of course, that archivists have a public profile (meaning they are not just in their stacks) and that public persona requires that they know something.

Knowledge is the essence of records administration, not empty credentials. For credentials to be meaningful, they must be built on a knowledge base, and once the American archival and records management communities establish their first real, separate degree, this will truly begin to happen. Michael Pemberton, in his discussion of professional issues facing records managers and drawing on the sociological analyses of professions, enumerated the critical aspects of a profession as being: "abstract and practical knowledge," "social relevance," a "code of ethics," "education," "professional culture," "autonomy," a "sense of commitment," and "client service."[58] Having participated in debates about professionalism for well over twenty years, I am more convinced than ever that knowledge of records and recordkeeping systems and about what distinguishes certain records as being archival in nature is what we need to emphasize. The kinds of public profile that adherents to credentials like a CA or CRM designation seem to want will emanate from knowledge and its application for the good of society.

ENDNOTES

1. Robert William Fogel, *The Fourth Great Awakening & the Future of Egalitarianism* (Chicago: University of Chicago Press, 2000), p. 67.
2. Fogel, *The Fourth Great Awakening*, p. 72.
3. Theo Thomassen, "Archivists Between Knowledge and Power: On the Independence and Autonomy of Archival Science and the Archival Profession," 1999, available at http://www.archiefschool.nl/bibliotheck/pub.htm#ove.
4. Richard J. Cox, "Professionalism and Archivists in the United States," *American Archivist* 49 (Summer 1986): 229–247.
5. Richard J. Cox, "Professionalism and Archivists Revisited: A Review Essay," *Midwestern Archivist* 15, no. 2 (1990): 5–15.
6. See, for example, David M. Levy, *Scrolling Forward: Making Sense of Documents in the Digital Age* (New York: Arcade Publishing, 2001).
7. These reasons are stated at http://www.certifiedarchivists.org/html/whycert.html.
8. My support of certification comes as a result of my strong belief that the archival mission is important to society and that for this mission to be met requires the archival profession (composed of individual archivists and archival repositories) to have a prominent public profile that results from standards, a specific knowledge base, and identifiable educational programs. For a comprehensive statement of my views, see my *American Archival Analysis: The Recent Development of the Archival Profession in the United States* (Metuchen, NJ: Scarecrow Press, Inc., 1990).
9. John W. Roberts, "Archival Theory: Much Ado About Shelving," *American Archivist* 50 (Winter 1987): 66–74; William J. Maher, "Contexts for Understanding Certification: Opening Pandora's Box?," *American Archivist* 51 (Fall 1988): 408–427.
10. Eliot Freidson, *Professional Powers: A Study of the Institutionalization of Formal Knowledge* (Chicago: University of Chicago Press, 1986).
11. We don't know much about the kinds of students we attract, the placement of such students, what archival employers desire, and so forth. See Cox, *American Archival Analysis*, Chapter 6.
12. Paul H. McCarthy, ed., *Archives Assessment and Planning Workbook* (Chicago: Society of American Archivists, 1989), p. 25 and Richard J. Cox and Judy Hohmann, *Strengthening New York's Historical Records Programs: A Self-Study Guide* (Albany: New York State Archives and Records Administration, 1988), 23–25.
13. Richard J. Cox, "Textbooks, Archival Education, and the Archival Profession: A Review Essay," *Public Historian* 12 (Spring 1990): 73-81 and "The Failure or Future of American Archival History: A Somewhat Unorthodox View," *Libraries & Culture* 35 (Winter 2000): 141-154.
14. Malivina B. Bechor, "Bibliographic Access to Archival Literature," *American Archivist* 50 (Spring 1987), 243–247; Victoria Irons Walch, *Information Resources for Archivists and Records Administrators: A Report and Recom-*

mendations (Albany, New York: National Association of Government Archives and Record Administrators, 1987). Some of these problems have been rectified because of listserv discussion lists and World Wide Web sites, but the fact that there is no single bibliographic utility that archivists can go to for access to their literature continues to be a challenge.

15. William J. Maher, "Contexts for Understanding Professional Certification," 426.

16. *Ibid.*, 417–419.

17. Unpublished paper written by Ron Gilardi in 1989 for a course taught at the University of Pittsburgh School of Library and Information Science.

18. Bruce Dearstyne, "Archival and Public History: Issues, Problems, and Prospects—An Introduction," *Public Historian* 8 (Summer 1986), 6–7.

19. Respondent 1, October 9, 2001. I have kept each individual's identity private.

20. Respondent 2, October 9, 2001.

21. Respondent 3, October 10, 2001.

22. Respondent 4, October 9, 2001.

23. Respondent 5, October 10, 2001.

24. Respondent 6, October 10, 2001.

25. Respondent 7, October 19, 2001.

26. Respondent 4, October 9, 2001.

27. Respondent 8, October 10, 2001.

28. Respondent 9, October 10, 2001.

29. Respondent 10, October 19, 2001.

30. In a later posting, in a more detailed explanation of the relationship between certification and education, one of the Academy's leaders (the same individual) argued that certification is not a substitute for education: "From its inception, archival certification was intended and designed to foster archival education and complement graduate degree programs. The Academy's support of archival education is so strong that, except in rare cases, a graduate degree is required to take the exam." This individual also related that "Among the Academy's elected positions, archival educators have been represented at a far higher degree than in the general archival population. For example, the founding president of the Academy was an archival educator, and of the Academy's eleven presidents, five have been archival educators. Strengthening support for graduate archival education was one reason the Academy was founded, and it informs and motivates every Academy program and discussion." Respondent 10, November 27, 2001.

31. Respondent 11, October 9, 2001.

32. Respondent 12, October 10, 2001.

33. Respondent 11, October 19, 2001.

34. Respondent 13, October 10, 2001.

35. Respondent 5, October 23, 2001.

36. Respondent 14, October 20, 2001.

37. Respondent 15, October 19, 2001.

38. Respondent 16, October 22, 2001.

39. Respondent 17, October 24, 2001.
40. Respondent 18, October 24, 2001.
41. Respondent 5, October 24 2001.
42. Respondent 19, October 22 2001.
43. Respondent 20, October 22, 2001.
44. Respondent 21, October 24, 2001.
45. Respondent 22, October 24, 2001.
46. Richard J. Cox, "Employing Records Professionals in the Information Age: A Research Study," *Information Management Journal* 34 (January 2000): 18–33. An expanded version is Chapter 4 of this volume, also indicating that certification has not become a factor in such position advertisements.
47. One position requires an "ALA-accredited MLS degree or ACA certification as professional archivist, or an equivalent combination of education and experience in an archival repository." Another advertisement states that the "successful candidate will have a Master's degree in U.S. History, American Studies, or Library Science with an emphasis in archives administration, or ACA certification and formal experience in an archival institution." Another "requires specialized graduate-level coursework in archives management" but would "prefer" a "Masters in Library/ Information Science and three years experience in archives, records management and/or other information settings." Also "preferred" is the "Certified Archivist (CA) and/or Certified Records Manager (CRM) certification." One notice is a bit vague, requiring an "ALA-accredited Master of Library Science (MLS) and archival coursework; or Master of Archival Studies (MAS); or masters degree in other appropriate field and the Certificate of Archival Studies (CAS)." Since there is no MAS degree at present in the United States and the reference to certification is a bit different, it seems that this prospective employer might have been hedging his or her bets.
48. One can find more and more elaborate educational qualifications statements, suggesting the problem of both the absence of an archives degree and the failure of certification. Another job posting includes the following qualifications section: "MLS from an accredited institution with coursework and formal training in archival theory and practice. A Masters degree in another academic discipline with archives and manuscripts training or certification with experience in processing archival collections will receive consideration." Then there is this set of qualifications: "Candidates should have a master's degree in library science, history, or related discipline with degree concentration in archival studies or supplemented by archival courses, seminars, or practica." And finally, there is an advertisement with the following: "An ALA-accredited MLS with graduate level training in archival administration beyond the introductory course level, or an M.A. degree in history with graduate level training in archival administration beyond the introductory course level (candidates with an ALA-accredited MLS or an M.A. degree in history may substitute for the graduate level training in archival administration any relevant experience and a demonstrable knowledge of archival ar-

rangement and description), or an M.A. degree in archival administration."

49. J. Michael Pemberton, "Records Management: Confronting Our Professional Issues," *Records Management Journal* 8 (December 1998): 14. For typical reasons why individuals are urged to become CRM's, see Kenneth A. Megill, "Professional Development and the CRM," *The One-Person Library: A Newsletter for Librarians and Management* 13 (April 1997): 4–6 and Donald B. Schewe, "Why Become a CRM?" *Records Management Quarterly* 32 (January 1998): 53–54, 56–57, 66.

50. Patrick Quinn, "The Academy of Certified Archivists and the Accreditation of Archival Education Programs," *ACA News*, issue 41 (July 2001): 4, 6.

51. See Richard J. Cox with Elizabeth Yakel, David Wallace, Jeannette Bastian, and Jennifer Marshall, "Archival Education in North American Library and Information Science Schools: A Status Report," *Library Quarterly* 71 (April 2001): 141–194. A shorter version of this was published in the *Journal of Education for Library and Information Science* 42 (Summer 2001): 228–240.

52. Richard J. Cox, "The Masters of Archival Studies and American Education Standards: An Argument for the Continued Development of Graduate Archival Education in the United States," *Archivaria* 36 (Autumn 1993): 221–231.

53. See my "Accountability, Public Scholarship, and Library, Information, and Archival Science Educators," *Journal of Education for Library and Information Science* 41 (Spring 2000): 94–105 and my two books, *Closing an Era: Historical Perspectives on Modern Archives and Records Management* (Westport, Conn.: Greenwood Press, 2000) and *Managing Records as Evidence and Information* (Westport, Conn.: Quorum Books, 2001). See also Richard J. Cox and David Wallace, eds., *Archives and the Public Good: Accountability and Records in Modern Society* (Westport, Conn.: Greenwood Press, 2002).

54. I wrote about this in "Millennial Thoughts on the Education of Records Professionals," *Records and Information Management Report* 15 (April 1999): 1–16.

55. See H. Larry Eiring, "The Evolving Information World." *Information Management Journal* 36 (January/February 2002): 20–22, 24; Robert Meagher, "The IM Building Blocks." *Information Management Journal* 36 (January/February 2002): 26–32, 34; Sue Myburgh, "Strategic Information Management: Understanding a New Reality." *Information Management Journal* 36 (January/February 2002): 36–38, 42–43.

56. The *Handbook* can be obtained from http://www.certifiedarchivists.org/html/handbook.html.

57. John N. Berry, III, "Certification: Is It Worth the Price?" *Library Journal* February 15, 2001, p. 96.

58. Pemberton, "Records Management," pp. 6–8.

6

Archives, Records Management, and Distance Learning: Weighing the Options

INTRODUCTION

Distance education opportunities are growing in the records professions. There are various ways of considering this growth. We can consider it to be the result of the rapid expansion of the Internet, stimulating the development of asynchronous courses using Web sites combining full-text course materials, multimedia teaching resources, and self-paced evaluation products. Electronic mail, in addition to these materials, seems to promise to connect student and instructor for sustained training. We also can see these new opportunities as the result of a field hungry for continuing education that needs both advanced and basic training opportunities in order to enhance skills, improve knowledge, and keep pace with rapidly changing uses of technologies for records creation and maintenance. Both archivists and records managers have long relied on workshops, institutes, and conferences to sustain and strengthen their knowledge, and the emergence of more opportunities for such experiences via distance education only seems like an extension of what has been going on for some time in the records disciplines.

Distance education is not a neutral delivery mechanism for additional training. Nor is it universally welcomed as the answer to the education needs of any profession or other aspects of society. It has become extremely controversial, seen as threatening not only certain segments of the traditional providers of education but as possibly causing a serious blurring of the fundamental differences between education (building and sustaining knowledge) and training (supporting shorter term needs in developing and supporting skills). The purpose of this chapter is not to summarize all the opportunities for records professionals to indulge in distance learning (a Web search will turn up ample examples of what is presently available); rather in this essay I am trying to help archivists and records managers reflect on the *nature* and *implications* of distance education for them as individuals and collectively as a discipline. The increasing opportunities with their accompanying promises, require that records professionals carefully think about the positive and reactive implications of distance education. These opportunities also require organizations thinking of hiring an archivist or records manager to consider whether they want a graduate of a distance education program.

I am not opposed to distance education. I endorse the notion that distance learning, when designed and delivered *correctly* to the *right* audience, can be a powerful supplement to other educational approaches. However, I am seeing, as well, a rush to rely on distance education as a panacea for all or most challenges facing certain fields. At least several times a week I am contacted by individuals wishing to pursue studies in archival administration via distance learning venues. There is no question that there is a market for distance learning in the records fields, but economic reasons or even seeming to provide a service to the profession should not be the only reasons that are considered in designing and offering distance education programs (and too often this is precisely what happens). We also need to consider the full range of educational and training needs, where the records professions are moving and what their practitioners require, and whether distance education can meet some (and which) needs in education and training.

Administrators of records programs also might need to consider whether they can use distance education packages for additional training of their own staff. In some ways, this might constitute the best possibilities for distance education, since it can provide additional training in an environment where there are other professionals who can serve as resources for those taking such courses and where there is a records program with ample examples and potential cases for applying or enhancing what is being learned in the courses. It is important, however, for these administrators to be able to evaluate the positive and negative aspects represented by distance learning *before* they make use of such courses, and it is sometimes difficult to do this amidst all the hype generated about distance education.

MY OWN EXPERIENCE IN DISTANCE EDUCATION

I have had some experience with distance education. During the academic years 1997–98, I was involved with a modest distance education experiment in archival studies. This experiment occurred in an informal fashion, emanating from a few discussions with Margaret Hedstrom who, at the time, had recently joined the faculty of the University of Michigan School of Information. When we had these initial discussions, Margaret and I were the sole faculty members teaching in the archives and records specializations at our schools. With both schools, Michigan and my own school, Pittsburgh, interested in distance education and other collaborative ventures, our conversations led us to agreeing to exchange courses then lacking in each other's programs via distance education.

The experiment proceeded as follows. Margaret Hedstrom taught a course on electronic records management in the Spring 1997 term offered both at Michigan and Pittsburgh. I observed the electronic records management course, also serving as a liaison for the students; I participated in this way in order to prepare for my own distance education course and in order to observe how the students reacted to the experience. Margaret Hedstrom visited Pittsburgh twice during the term, once near the beginning of the course and again near the end of the course in order to meet individually with the students and with the groups working on projects; she taught two class sessions long distance to Michigan, giving those students a sense of what the Pittsburgh-based students were experiencing.

I visited Michigan twice, once at the beginning of that school's term (a week before our term formally begins) and then again after four weeks. During my second visit I taught two class sessions, met with students, and did an extra presentation for that school's SAA Student Chapter. Hedstrom did all the grading for the electronic records management course, and I did all the grading for the archival appraisal course; in order to keep matters as administratively simple as possible we each took responsibility for the grade sheets at our respective universities. Hedstrom and I kept each other informed via weekly telephone calls and regular use of e-mail; in addition, class discussion lists were set up for each course. Each school paid for all the expenses associated with the telecommunications connections, use of technicians, and other services; no money passed from one school to the other. Essentially the same process was followed during the 1997–98 academic year, although there was a change of personnel; David Wallace taught the electronic records management course and Elizabeth Yakel served as the course's liaison.

This was a fairly low-tech exploration of distance education possibilities, some of which was dictated by the technologies available at both schools. We relied on video or interactive television technology. I did use the electronic whiteboard and its capabilities in transmitting texts and images to the distant classroom. Our respective syllabi were available on our Web sites for consultation, but it appears that the students generally relied on the paper copies handed out in the classrooms. Hedstrom prepared a course packet, while I relied on readings placed on reserve at the two schools and a number of books required for purchase (in this I made no change from what I do in other courses).

We had both courses evaluated, using special survey instruments that the University of Pittsburgh Office of Measurement and Evaluation of Teaching developed for classes using interactive television. In general, what we found through this survey was that the quality of the educational experience is much better for the student in the classroom *with* the instructor. Such a conclusion has been borne out by other studies on distance learning, but it has been by no means a universal conclusion (or, at the least, one that distance education proponents want to accept).

The criticisms by students were generally directed at the obtrusiveness of the technology. Students at Pittsburgh, receiving the television transmission, made comments on the electronic records management course such as the "clumsiness in using microphones and waiting to be recognized to speak worked against the easy interchange of comments that makes graduate level education"; the "time delay due to transmission time was unsettling—as if the laugh track was not in sync"; "it was extremely difficult to either initiate or sustain useful dialog between the classrooms" and "it seems that whichever classroom had the instructor actually 'present' received more attention and participated to a much greater degree"; "interaction with members of the distance class and professor made students at the near end feel isolated" and "it was almost like viewing a class through a window rather than being an actual member of that class"; "the areas of protocol for asking questions or making comments from remote location [were] unclear"; "while much of the difficulty lies in the understanding of protocol and a lack of aggressiveness in students, it is still not an 'interactive' medium in an optimal sense, particularly in situations where team-based learning or active learning are promoted by the instructor"; and "I would absolutely never take another distance learning class. . . . Watching TV for 2 hours is definitely not stimulating."

Students at Michigan, with the instructor present, made the following kinds of statements: "The instruction was not as effective because it was at times difficult to hear and understand what people were saying at Pittsburgh"; "there is something critical about physical presence for building camaraderie and a sense of community and ownership of the course" and "I felt this community sense for my fellow UM students, but didn't really get to know the Pittsburgh students"; the "technology is both distracting and intimidating, and communication with professors and other students is more difficult"; and "at present, technology does not allow for free, unhampered communication." Similar comments were made about the archival appraisal class, with a focus on the problems or distractions of the technology.

The problems with or challenges of the technology may be the most serious issue regarding the use of distance education. These are certainly *not* unique concerns for our two universities. The recent study by Serena W. Stanford in the use of such technologies in library and information science uncovered virtually the same kinds of attitudes. As this study concluded, "student reaction was more positive at the originating site"; "students 'bonded' with their distant colleagues, or not, in approximately equal numbers"; "class discussions are not easy in distance mode"; and "students believe more face-to-face contact with the instructor would be helpful."[1] From my perspective, some of these conclusions are no more than common sense findings.

These are certainly real issues that need to be addressed, but I personally believe that they must be put into some perspective. At one point during the electronic records management course, Margaret Hedstrom contacted me about one student who was constantly complaining to her about *not* having the opportunity to participate in the course discussions, blaming the technology for these problems and arguing that she should not be penalized because of the technical glitches. Two problems were evident with this particular student's complaints. First, this student, who had been in two other regular courses taught by me, had not participated in these courses either. Second, I was present during all but two class sessions of this course and in a position to observe the students (I sat at the back of the room), and I noted little evidence of this student's efforts to participate.

Often the problem with evaluating distance education and other courses is that we conduct evaluations too close to the time of the courses, long before students are in a position to see the value of a course's content or an instructor's teaching approach in presenting the content. This kind of problem does relate to a greater challenge we face with distance education courses *and* other courses as well. Students who are taking the courses are usually not in a position to evaluate course *value* because they have not had any real practical experience and their knowledge of the field is quite limited. From *my* perspective, the student's opportunity to have Margaret Hedstrom, internationally recognized as one of the top authorities on electronic records management, as an instructor *far* outweighed the peculiarities of the classroom experience.

Nevertheless, there *are* obstacles to quality education in distance learning, but I believe these can be overcome or at least minimized by other strengths. There are no *more* difficulties in ensuring quality education via distance education than there are trying to teach a class of fifty to one hundred students or even striving to educate information professionals in a one-year curriculum (a time frame most faculty and a lot of students complain as being far too compressed or limited). What this does suggest, however, is that each course, whatever its delivery mechanism, needs to be carefully planned and evaluated in order to minimize the difficulties that may appear. The array of technologies involved in distance learning does enhance the potential number of problems that might result in teaching in this way.

There are many issues that the instructor of a distance education course needs to rethink. For example, in my case, my advanced courses (archival appraisal is one of these) tend to be run like reading seminars (brief introductions and intensive discussion of the assigned readings). As it turns out, this sort of course has an advantage over traditional lecture courses because it lends itself to more interaction and few lengthy discourses by the instructor. From the vantage of the distance education classroom, however, you can become distracted by having nearly as much equipment as used to run the *Enterprise* in the popular *Star Trek* television and movie series. The more experience in teaching in this manner, the easier it becomes. For most of us, we gain an opportunity to acquire some instruction about teaching for the *first* time, as you need to rethink *every* basic aspect of what you do in the classroom.

With distance education, there is, of course, much *more* that can go wrong. At the beginning of the electronic records management course, we had a number of difficulties with the technical compatibility of the two classrooms; as a consequence, both universities changed classrooms at least once early in that course. In another class session we had audio but no video, and the students got to look at a frozen image of Margaret Hedstrom while hearing her voice for two and a half hours (it was a surreal event and definitely distracting). When I taught my class on archival appraisal, I had one class session in which I wore a striped shirt that drove the Michigan students insane; every time I moved, the image of the stripes lingered. It was sometimes difficult to orchestrate running the class from behind the panel of computer and other screens; I finally worked with one of the technicians to mark the floor, similar to what stage directors and actors sometimes do, so that I did not wander too far away from the camera.

Such problems are more annoyances than major obstacles for creating an educational experience. There were a number of advantages to the exchange of distance education courses between Michigan and Pittsburgh. The quality of students and student work was substantially enhanced by the mixing of the two student bodies. Despite the students' perceptions that the technology was a barrier to discussion, I found that the discussion in both courses exceeded the quality of student discussion and interaction in other non-distance education courses in that academic year. The experience also provided a reality check of sorts for both schools' archives and records specializations. Through the offering of these two courses, we discovered the similarities in curriculum and educational objectives. While some of the Pittsburgh students believed that the Michigan students had had a more intensive introduction to archives and records *before* the electronic records management course, it turns out that both previous courses, as well as students' backgrounds and career objectives, were very similar. The class discussions and group projects also assisted the students gain a broader exposure to the range of archives and records challenges in modern society. During the electronic records management course, there were group projects that enabled students to understand that the modern records problems faced by universities were not unique to a single school. During the archival appraisal course, students were assigned a project evaluating an appraisal and acquisitions policy, and they discovered how alike issues were among certain kinds of institutions even in different regions.

Participating in the distance education experience was also an asset to both instructors' own knowledge. I sat through the electronic records management class in order to gain an update on some of these issues as well; I was especially interested in how Hedstrom would be using her recent experiences working as a consultant with a number of state government and national archives in this area. Margaret Hedstrom sat through part of the archival appraisal course in order to see what I was doing with this archival function; my teaching this course since 1989 has given our program one of its distinctions (although appraisal is recognized as one of the most important and difficult archival responsibilities, it is taught in only a few schools in North America). Distance education provides an educational opportunity for instructors as well.

Distance education is not free, of course, and all its possibilities and benefits must be weighed against the actual financial and other resource (mostly time) costs. While I do not have actual expenses for these courses, my understanding is that the costs of doing these courses then ran about $170 per connect hour (this included telecommunications costs and costs for the technicians). Each course cost, then, an *additional* $4500 or so over the costs of a typical course. In this particular experiment, no monies were exchanged between the two schools and, as a result, neither school lost or gained money from the courses based on student enrollment. As it turned out, the enrollment for the two courses from the two schools was nearly identical anyway, and whatever gains or losses would have been negligible; in fact, one could argue that the additional administrative costs of the two schools would have added costs for no real reason other than to serve bureaucratic processes. To these costs, of course, must be added the costs of visits by both myself and Margaret Hedstrom, probably increasing the necessary financial support by another $2000 or so.

There are other resource costs to be considered as well. It does take, for example, more time to prepare these courses. While this is difficult to estimate, my sense is that it took me about twenty percent *more* time to prepare each session. After doing my usual preparation, I found myself going back over the material in order to consider how it should be presented via interactive television. Experts tell you to make sure that you do not speak for longer than ten to fifteen minute segments and that you allow plenty of time for asking students at all classroom locations whether they have questions or comments to make. The more significant cost is the need to have a liaison in the classroom for the site receiving the course. A liaison needs to be present at all classes in order to troubleshoot for the students any of the additional possible problems that may result from the technologies, communicate with the instructor as necessary, ensure that reserve materials and other readings are available, help with whatever Web site is used for the course, and help provide some kind of lead for socialization of the students at the remote (receiving) classroom.

There may be other costs that will need to be absorbed, including guest lectures, instructional technology support, technical support for improved Web/Internet-based and CD-ROM-driven educational modules either as stand-alone, self-paced educational tools or as aids to the use of interactive television in the offering of regular courses. These are expensive undertakings, with a certain degree of risk involved in terms of recouping any of the financial investment. Some of these costs can be offset from other benefits that could accrue in distance education opportunities. These potential benefits include enticements for recruiting, developing more accessible opportunities for continuing education offered for a generation of better-educated archivists and records managers, and strengthening continuing education by moving far beyond basic issues and work that has characterized it to date. With each of these matters, we also have more things which can go wrong and become barriers to students learning.

The problem in all this is, of course, that we need more research about the effectiveness of education of archivists and records managers, both generally and specifically relating to distance education. More than a decade ago I described a research agenda concerning the education of archivists; very little research has been done to date concerning any of the areas I mentioned in that exploratory essay.[2] Records professionals might consider using distance education as a focal point for beginning to evaluate the educational needs of people already in this field and to evaluate the education of entry-level archivists and records managers. Newer Web-based courses also create the opportunity for gathering more data about what works and does not work, at least within the confines of the virtual classroom. This does not mean, of course, that records professionals do not have a need for longitudinal studies where they can assess former students three, five, or more years after entering the field or applying what they learned if they are already in the field, in order to determine the effectiveness of our teaching and the content of courses (at whatever level they are offered).

Seven years ago, after my brief foray into distance education, I posed some preliminary questions for my own school. Some of these questions (slightly revised to represent a more universal perspective) are:

- What are the incentives for faculty to be engaged in distance education ventures?
- How will distance education courses be counted as part of the normal teaching load for faculty?
- How will the addition of other faculty members in the archives and records management specialization and the changing curriculum for this specialization affect the potential for the use of distance education?
- Will the schools continue to develop an adequate technical infrastructure for distance education?
- How will the schools pay for distance education? Will it pay for itself?
- What is the maximum number of distance education courses the schools can support? How will it be determined who (student and faculty) participates in distance education?

Interestingly, even after my school embarked on a much more ambitious distance education venture, offering its MLIS degree in an alternative (although more limited) distance education mode in the past year, none of these questions had been fully addressed, and others had emerged as well. Enrollment and marketing issues seem to have caused us to throw caution aside, and to take risks (whether this is visionary or foolhardy remains to be seen).

DISTANCE LEARNING: THE DEBATE

Many of the pluses and minuses mentioned above take on a different and more profound meaning when we look at the more pervasive debate about distance education occurring in higher education and elsewhere. Despite the fact that some aspect of distance education long has been a fixture in higher and adult education, it continues to generate debate and controversy. As indicative that some of these debates stem from the rapidly changing nature of the technologies supporting this is the fact that there is now debate (and confusion) over what it is called. People who offer online courses mostly term it "e-learning" followed by online training, Web-based training, technology-based training, distance learning, and computer-based training. People who take online courses refer to it, in this order, computer-based training, Web-based training, online learning, distance learning, training, and e-learning.[3] Each of the terms has a particular meaning, and there can be considerable conflict between the perceptions and objectives assigned to them.

One of the more recent aspects of dissension about distance learning has developed because of the technological aspect that is integral to it. My favorite technology curmudgeon, Clifford Stoll, believes "Distance learning offers all the information, all the facts, all the boredom of an ordinary classroom, with none of the inspiration, none of the commitment, and none of the joy. It's ideal for the student who equates information with education. Perfect for the school that wants to hustle students through with minimal human interaction."[4] More pertinent to records professionals is the following Stoll reflection: "Distance learning appeals to those who need to maintain a professional license or wish to paper their walls with certificates. It's ideal for the school which wants to award diplomas with a minimum of student-teacher contact."[5] Some of his comments are particularly relevant to the state of affairs in the records professions and the views of its practitioners distance education, where graduate faculty, workshop instructors, and institute designers often find themselves facing students more interested in credentials than in knowledge (or, at least, it often seems this way).

The most serious criticism of distance education has come from historian David Noble, an expert on the history of technology in American life. This critic notes that distance education requires the "deliberate transformation of the educational process into commodity form, for the purpose of commercial transaction."[6] As part of his analysis, Noble points to the failure of correspondence education a century before, a merciless ploy for profits at the expense of real education. One of the connecting threads between the older correspondence model and the new distance education efforts of today, according to Noble, is that these courses are taught by "poorly paid and overworked low-status instructors, working on a per-course basis without benefits or job security and under coercion to assign their rights to their course materials to their employer as a condition of employment."[7] Most of Noble's criticisms are directed at what he sees as the decline of the modern university and the weakening of the professorate, subsumed by the corporate interests and part of a decades long takeover by business interests (often the same vendors of the network hardware and software). But much of the critique is relevant, since so much of what is going on in distance education is about money and not about the quality of education. Noble describes, for example, MIT's placement of all course materials on the Web for free access but quotes one of that school's professors as saying, the "syllabus and lecture notes are not an education, the education is what you do with the materials."[8] This often seems to be lost in distance learning programs.

Noble has been speaking at universities and on March 19, 2002, he spoke at mine, stressing the "corporatization" of universities, placing distance education in this transformation as merely another effort to make money by turning instruction into a commodity. My own notes on the lecture indicate that Noble compared distance education to being an "intellectual tapeworm, destroying the health of the host." Noble's views are not unique. Douglas Cremer likewise suggests that a "consumerist ideology makes of education just another product delivered by clicking a mouse, sitting at a terminal, and waiting for the package to arrive. . . . Higher education in the mode of distance learning opens the possibility of reducing the student, someone who should be actively engaged in the acquisition and critique of knowledge, to a consumer of intellectual property." Cremer is not arguing against distance education, seeing some opportunities for its bringing education to some who might not have the opportunity, but he wants it "rooted in a theory of truly collaborative learning between professor and student."[9] Otherwise, education becomes merely a commodity, and the student only a customer and something is lost along the way. If the essence of a profession is its knowledge, then the process of learning must be more than the sale of a product. Distance education venues seem to exaggerate such problems; all potentially lose something.

A good deal of the dissent about the role of distance education in the university has revolved about intellectual property issues related to the online materials, an issue that is probably not a concern for most records professionals considering distance education offerings, but which probably should get some attention as it could well affect who is teaching and, thus, have some impact on the quality of distance education. Some have argued that the concern of some academics about their ownership and control of online materials tends to transform teaching and other academic work into little more than a commodity, challenging the very core essence of academic freedom and the claims by the professoriate as having a special status in the university and in society.[10] If the student buys a course, he or she should expect to be taught by a recognized expert and the commodification threatens to undermine this.

Indeed, it is fairly easy to summarize the positive and negative aspects of distance education. One commentator on this educational approach suggested that the positive attributes were convenience, immediacy ("students receive speedier feedback on assignments"), contact ("more instructor/student contact and peer-to-peer contact"), learner control, technology ("students and teachers gain greater proficiency with the Internet and other tools for finding, using, and constructing information"), prestige ("online programs carry a cutting-edge cachet"), and new learning ("students and professors can construct new knowledge in ways they couldn't without new technology"). The same commentator views the negative aspects of distance education as being facelessness ("lack of verbal and facial cues, body language"), glitches ("technological breakdowns"), workload ("much more work to develop, produce, teach, and take an online course"), costs ("courses with audio, video, interactivity, etc., cost more to produce"), support (ranging from technical to the incentives for faculty to participate), and quality ("new methods required for accreditation and measuring 'outcomes'").[11] In other words, both purveyor and purchaser of these courses need to weigh the positive and negative aspects of distance learning.

DEBATING DISTANCE EDUCATION: A CASE STUDY

Over the past five years, my own school launched a distance education venture, called the Fast Track program, whereby students could complete all the requirements for the MLIS degree via distance with only limited onsite visits to the campus. At first, I was a strong supporter of the program, seeing in it possibilities for developing components of our archives and records management program that could be offered in this way. However, a number of factors soon led me to withdraw my support (not because of strong reservations about whether distance education can be useful but because of problems associated with its planning to ensure that it would be offered at a quality consistent with graduate education). Some of my reasons have to do with problems of communication and leadership, and those are not relevant to my discussion of distance education. A number of the reasons do relate to the kinds of problems identified by critics of distance education.

For example, the debate in my own school quickly divided into a discussion about quality versus quantity in terms of both education and enrollment. Those interested in enrollment numbers and tuition revenue, not unimportant concerns for sure, seemed pitted against others more interested in smaller classes, face-to-face teaching, and other matters traditionally associated with quality education. These differences were accentuated by other problems and questions about the need for an infrastructure to support the distance education initiative. Unfortunately, this is not a unique case either in higher education or in society generally. M. O. Thirunarayanan notes that we can divide the world of students into "three groups, namely the 'certification seekers,' the 'degree

seekers,' and the 'knowledge seekers.'" Then, he reveals what can become the Achilles heel of the distance education programs:

> The relationship between learning and degrees will become further
> blurred by the fact that the new breed of universities is too eager and
> willing to confer diplomas on their degree-seekers in the shortest pos-
> sible time frames. Since they are operating for profit, their survival de-
> pends on volume. The more clients that they can process in the shortest
> periods of time and in a most efficient manner, the more profits that
> they can make. Eventually, the bottom line becomes volume, not qual-
> ity. Conferring degrees in the shortest periods of time to thousands and
> thousands of degree-seekers is certainly more profitable than truly edu-
> cating smaller numbers of students. The economic imperative to serve
> "millions and millions" will outweigh the educational need to provide
> sustained learning experiences of high quality.[12]

Such concerns were raised very quickly in my own school, and while
there are intelligent and well-thought out opinions on both sides, there
seems to be little potential for resolving differences because of a rapid
commitment to a distance education program.

The advocates, promising evaluation of the program, quickly for-
got such promises (and even an additional two years has not seem any
evaluations delivered). While this is annoying, it may not be the most
critical issue. Avoiding the issue of an evaluation of distance education
is problematic, but even those institutions doing such evaluation is part
of what Cremer states when the "assessment of online education comes
more and more to resemble customer satisfaction surveys," something
that should be avoided and suggesting that many of the evaluators of
distance education efforts may not be very useful.[13] It is also at the heart
of David Noble's many complaints about distance education.

In the midst of this internal debate about distance education at our
school, I found myself again posing a set of fairly elaborate questions.
These questions (somewhat revised here again to reflect more universal
themes) were as follows:

- What are the reasons for expanding dramatically the cohort of students
  when the first cohort has not even finished year one of the program?
- What are the reasons for admitting students into a distance education
  program who live close to the campus?
- What data are available for now evaluating what has occurred with the
  distance education program and students?
- What is the impact of the distance education program on both faculty
  and onsite students?

- What are the cost figures for the present distance education program? Are we making or losing money?
- What are the realistic needs for an infrastructure for a ramping up of the distance education programs? How is the present infrastructure working? What IS the present infrastructure?
- What are the present repercussions with the University administration if we abandon the present distance education program by not admitting a second cohort but instead determine only to use the first cohort as a real test and evaluation?
- What are the present repercussions with the University administration if we restrict growth of the distance education program? Can we manage students in multiple cohorts with our present resources and infrastructure?
- What are the documents endorsing and supporting the present distance education program? What promises and claims have been made about the distance education program to the University administration?
- How many adjuncts will be involved in teaching in the distance education program? Who are they? How are they being selected? Is the faculty getting to review their vita before they are hired? How will we evaluate their teaching? Will students be satisfied with having adjuncts teach in the distance education program rather than regular faculty they might wish to have?
- How many students should be or will be in each distance education class? How many courses will be offered?
- How much additional time does it take for an individual faculty member to develop, mount, and teach a distance education course? Are they being compensated for this if it requires additional time? How does this impact their onsite teaching requirements?
- How do we advise distance education students? What are the differences in advising between onsite and distance education students?
- What is more important—revenue from enrollment, research grants, research and publication, onsite teaching, the masters or the doctoral program? What are our priorities? How does the apparent rapid expansion of the distance education program relate to our priorities?
- How do we define faculty governance, and has it worked or not worked in the administration of the distance education program?
- How do we define quality in teaching, and how is this related to onsite and distance education offerings? Do we care about teaching? Should we expand the distance education program to a much larger group of students, have adjuncts do all the teaching, and free up regular faculty to teach small seminars for doctoral students, advanced studies students, and a small cohort of onsite masters students?
- What is the impact, negative and positive, of the distance education program on the onsite programs?

All of these questions relate to the issue of evaluating distance education programs, especially their effectiveness in educational and training objectives. While some might seem peculiar to higher education, especially those connected to faculty governance and academic freedom, these questions nevertheless raise typical kinds of issues facing *all* distance education ventures, whether offered by universities, commercial vendors, or professional associations. And deep within these questions are additional questions and issues that prospective students need to think about as they contemplate signing up for onsite or distance education courses.

THE REAL OUTCOMES OF DISTANCE EDUCATION

There has been evaluation of distance education programs going on for some time. We can consider such evaluation in both library and information science education, the primary framework for supporting the education of records professionals in North America, and a smaller number of studies related directly to archives and records management distance education efforts. In studying the impact or implications of distance education, we discover that while some students feel uneasy with the mechanism, learning takes place and apparently does so in an effective manner. Examining the differences in learning outcomes in a single course at the University of Oklahoma School of Library and Information Studies, two library science professors discovered that "although the students expressed negative attitudes toward the delivery system, these attitudes do not appear to have interfered with their learning."[14] It appears that faculty and staff in library and information science (LIS) education, in general, see no difference in the educational programs of part-time or distance students from other full-time, traditional classroom students.[15] Another LIS educator argues, "Distance learning students benefit from cooperative learning activities in both the cognitive and affective domains."[16] Students feel that the quality of such courses is high, rate these courses on a high scale, and report that the courses provide the added benefit of feeling less isolated because of the carefully planned group exercises.[17]

In some studies of distance education offerings, student differences, mostly attitudinal ones, were noted. From San Jose State University we learn that there were no substantial differences between the perceptions of distance and other students in how they viewed the site setup, communication, or relationships between students and students and instructors. The significant differences come in the perceptions of instructors, technology, and learning, as well as the sense of community among students. Still, LIS educators generally will argue that this can be corrected by enhancing the quality of education in the distance mode (by providing training for those teaching in this way). Besides, most LIS faculty will argue that the more important consideration is the ability to serve a geographically dispersed clientele.[18] At the minimum, there is some suggestion that doing distance education transforms teaching into a public performance requiring new technical and managerial skills.[19] At the least, it is very probable that how students react to distance learning might rest on their own mental models of learning, even to the point that they will believe they have learned more in face to face classroom settings when it can be demonstrated that they learned more via an online course.[20] Another study surprisingly suggested that students participating in courses from a distance often feel more connected than resident students, because "Resident students have a more difficult time bonding with their peers and getting to know faculty. Distance students believe that they receive more personal attention and have greater interaction with faculty and other students than do resident students."[21] This study attributed this partly to learning styles: "As highly motivated, mature adults, most distance learners prefer a constructivist learning approach in which they construct their own internal representations of knowledge rather than accept an instructor's version."[22]

The public performance idea is an intriguing one, because it suggests the care with which instructors in distance education must choreograph their lectures and class sessions. One library science faculty considering the notion of audiographics—the "combination of voice-based and computer-based technology to permit simultaneous visual and audiotransmission to remote sites"[23]—suggests that "Ideally, the distance education experience should provide the distance learner with quality instruction that involves interaction and socialization with both the instructor and the other students in the course."[24] In other words, what can almost be taken for granted in a typical class must be carefully thought through when a course moves to the distance education mode. This forces even the most seasoned classroom veteran to rethink what he or she does, although how well this rethinking occurs may depend more on the kind of additional instructional technology expertise available to those embarking on distance education.

Considering the performance aspects of distance education is only part of the challenge posed by offering quality education remotely. Some experienced educators in the distance education mode relate that there are many challenges, including logistical ones, scheduling differences (between various universities and academic programs), disparate expectations by students taking such courses, arrangements for course credit, and faculty workloads.[25] These issues certainly appeared quickly in debates at my own school.

Others actually contend that students participating in distance education courses, especially those built around Web-based course materials, are being better prepared to work in modern organizations suggesting the "learning" organization—a "living, growing organization that can gain information and therefore grow."[26] Web-based distance education courses mimic these learning organizations, in that the classrooms become a "web of collaborative relationships rather than through a chain of commands."[27] This is a very provocative argument, although it ignores that there is much to learn *before* considering the nature of such organizations. Learning about the principles of organizational development, administration, culture, and for records professionals, the use of information and information technologies, probably needs to occur before an individual is enmeshed in a web of learning and information technologies. Moreover, thinking about distance education in this fashion can also blind a student to understanding how much organizational behavior and decision making is transacted through and influenced by much older communication techniques, such as face-to-face meetings and even gossip or informal and accidental encounters.

Studying the use of distance education courses in the health sciences librarianship area, a group ascertained that while using the technologies for such education suggests that "critical problems" about "updating and adapting practice to an ever-changing knowledge base and social milieu" are being addressed, in fact, they surmise, perhaps they are not, requiring more careful analysis of just what is happening. They conclude that distance education brings with it a degree of constant change, that some may or may not accept happily: "Students will change, student access to technology will change, student motivation will change, course content and resources will change, and instructor access to technology. In short, it is best to assume that everything will change and that these changes will not occur at the most convenient times nor will they be tidy and comprehensible at the times they do occur."[28] Of course, useful change is one thing, while change for change's sake is an altogether different matter.

EXPERIENCE OF DISTANCE EDUCATION IN THE RECORDS PROFESSIONS

While in comparison to some other disciplines, archivists and records managers have had limited experience with distance education approaches, there have been some efforts, some initial evaluation, and some lessons learned. But the degree of evaluation in the records professions is far more limited than what we see in closely related fields, suggesting that we need to be more mindful of reevaluating just what we are doing. The growth of distance education is rapid, and appears to be inevitable given the increasing opportunities to offer such courses and a growing potential market.

The Australians, contending with great distances between population centers, have been enthusiastic pioneers of distance education approaches. Some believe that distance education, because it forces students to become "familiar with computers and communication technology in the day-to-day pursuit of their studies," might also help students to become more aware of how offices are changing technologically and how electronic records challenges might be addressed.[29] There has been, however, little evidence that there have been enough of an effort on distance education in this realm for there to be much of a difference (but I recognize that there is some promise).

For distance education to be successful it must include carefully developed study plans, guides to the subjects, readers of articles and other literature, and workbooks for students to work through typical professional activities and problems. Undertaking something like this requires instructional designers and editors as well as subject experts writing the content, and such distance education draws on local tutors and others who can assist the students. In addition, the success of a distance education program must include "student access to lecturers via telephone and email and prompt response to student enquiries; support from local professionals who will provide opportunities for field trips and will accept students into their institutions on practicum placements; [and] a sound infrastructure to control the whole study process."[30] Potential students need to inquire about the strength of the infrastructure of the distance education course or program, and they should not assume that all programs are created equal in this regard.

A fairly detailed analysis of the students' experiences and educators' perspectives on a records management course offered via distance education at the Department of Information and Library Management at the University of Northumbria at Newcastle had some interesting conclusions about distance education, including that the "problems associated with the course were almost the mirror image of the benefits. The pluses that access to electronic communications bring were matched by the problems encountered when systems did not work."[31] Moreover, what made distance education successful for a student went far beyond anything specifically related to the mechanics of this kind of education, namely that "self-motivation, time and appropriate support from family and employer were commonly perceived as the major determinants of student success in the course."[32] Of more concern is, and this is my own interpretation of the study, that the instructors get a lot more involved with the use of the information technology than in some of the aspects of the course content. One begins to wonder whether what is really lost and gained from offering such courses over distance, except when it reaches groups that would otherwise have no access to any other form of instruction. However, if more and more is offered online, will we see a greater interest even by those living nearby a campus in only studying in this fashion? And, what will be the impact both on other classroom courses and in the nature of what is taught? And these are not just questions for faculty but for prospective students as well, who might wonder whether they are being given additional options or being shortchanged.

All of the above examples are efforts to evaluate specific continuing education efforts in the archives and records management disciplines. There are also some studies related to broader assessments of the range of interest in and needs about distance education. A major survey of members of the Society of Archivists and the Records Management Society in the United Kingdom was undertaken in the mid-1990s, concluding that availability to technologies that would support distance education is "substantial and growing."[33] However, only 9 percent of the respondents were "enthusiastic" about distance education although another 72 percent stated that distance education either "would suit their circumstances" or "would be prepared to try" it.[34] Those carrying out the survey concluded that attitudes about distance education were "somewhat ambivalent," but they then indicated that the next step in the project was planning a distance education program.[35] However, they also believed the survey suggested that both "students and employers are seeking much more flexibility in learning patterns,"[36] indicating a sensitivity to market circumstances that, according to the critics of distance education, may have little to do with matters of educational quality except in the most negative ways.

In North America the most ambitious effort has been the National Forum on Archival Continuing Education (NFACE), which has prepared some elaborate needs assessments for continuing education in the field, including providing a clearinghouse for emerging distance education offerings.[37] While the data does not seem to endorse, at least in any conclusive fashion, the utility of distance education (respondents seemed more committed to the use of traditional manual publications and other similar sources), this group is obviously exploring every distance education opportunity. At this point in time, other distance education efforts in archives are so flawed as not even being worth a mention.

David Gracy, a long-time educator of archivists and records managers, has tried to offer reasons why distance education in the field (primarily archives) has not developed more fully. Gracy notes that, "It may seem curious that in the United States, where we have so much distance, so many organizations and institutions producing records, and so great a quantity of historical record to preserve—that in light of these circumstances, we Americans have taken so little advantage of distance education for increasing the availability of courses in archival enterprise." Gracy offers three reasons:

> First, it has been thought that to satisfy the demands of the job market, we needed to produce no greater number of graduates in archives management than were being produced using traditional methods. Second, much education in records management has been offered in junior college, that is, at a technical level equivalent to the first two years of the baccalaureate degree. Because records management programs on the junior college level outnumber those on the graduate level, the number of records management education programs is sufficient to meet the need for records management specialists. Third, the impetus to offer courses using distance education technology came from the discovery by graduate schools of library and information science that a pool of potential students existed that the schools could expand to serve. As this pool consists of paraprofessionals unable to leave their jobs for school to obtain the master's degree which they need in order to attain professional status, the schools could turn the potential students into actual students only by taking the course work to them. These individuals did not demand courses in archival enterprise.[38]

These are interesting observations, and they may or may not be relevant, given that we have so little data concerning distance education or education of records professionals in general.

Gracy also believes that most North American educators will be involved in some dimension of distance education in the future, because the "number of regular students is projected to rise over the next several years"; "we are experiencing a growing demand for education by persons changing career fields in the middle of their working lives"; the "student population is growing more rapidly than is the number of faculty available to teach them"; and there are "calls by governing bodies that expenditures for more buildings and larger campuses be reduced."[39] The mistake of this assessment is that first the educators of archivists and records managers have responsibilities far more complex than merely delivering courses. And, as well, Gracy reduces the demand for education to little more than a market issue (a prevailing problem present in the way we often see advocating on behalf of distance education).

In 1999–2000 I chaired a task force on continuing education for the SAA that recommended a major shift in the Society's education program, primarily supporting a move from offering basic workshops to offering online courses (with a focus on more advanced and critically important topics and needs by advanced practitioners). While there is a market dimension to this approach, in some ways it repudiates the Society's previous marketing by which it tried to meet all the needs of all of its members. The new call urged the Society to be more strategic in how it defines the market. An example of the kind of discussion in this report is as follows:

> *Articulate a coherent continuing education framework of which all SAA courses and workshops are components.* Too often in the past the development of continuing education offerings has been at the instigation of willing members or in response to short-term opportunities. Several workshop presenters in the field of archival description, in an e-mail discussion prior to the meeting of this Task Force, expressed frustration at the varying levels of preparedness for their courses of the enrollees. They frequently face workshop participants who do not have the fundamental preparation in either archival theory or practice to successfully complete the workshop at the level at which it is being offered, or who sign up for a workshop because it is the only one being offered at a particular time and not because it meets their specific educational needs. Of course, this leads to workshops being taught to the lowest common denominator and, frequently and to the detriment of all enrollees, in the full range of material not being covered during the workshop. This situation, while perhaps in the short-term getting more bodies into seats at continuing education workshops, undermines the long-term success and health of the Society's continuing education program. The Education Officer should, in conjunction with CEPD [Committee on Education

and Professional Development], facilitate the development of a clear framework of courses and course progressions and, in conjunction with course and workshop developer(s), articulate minimum levels of professional practice and preparatory education for courses whose content is structured to challenge and educate mid-career archivists. As a part of a more robust and proactive clearinghouse function for archival continuing education offerings, . . . the Society's continuing education web site should assist potential enrollees who aren't adequately prepared for a particular SAA course or workshop in finding a continuing education offering elsewhere that is more appropriate for their level of experience, academic preparation, and professional need.[40]

This kind of assessment (and the above is merely an example) suggests the complexity of the factors affecting whether distance education should be developed, offered, or used in a particular sector of the records professions. Distance education is not merely a technology or technique; it has numerous implications for how we approach conveying and learning about the knowledge of archivists and records managers.

A CALL FOR STUDYING DISTANCE EDUCATION IN THE RECORDS PROFESSIONS

Records professionals need to evaluate, by systematic study, the effectiveness of distance education (not just study the market for distance education). While professional associations have issued guidelines covering the nature of continuing education, including distance education, these guidelines more often than not call for additional evaluation or provide in themselves the baseline for such assessments.[41] In fact, the Society of American Archivists statement on the challenges of copyright when applied to the use of archival materials in distance education courses suggests both barriers to developing such educational offerings and needs for all records professionals to wrestle through with the concerns posed by distance education as defined in the broadest possible manner.[42]

If one wants to consider the effectiveness of learning by distance education when compared with traditional classroom approaches, he or she could do so by examining written examinations, observations, interviewing, analyzing interactions with and between students, and using survey questionnaires to discover student attitudes.[43] The problem is, however, how to conduct analysis that goes well beyond just seeking immediate or near immediate feedback from students about how they like courses, both face-to-face and via distance.

One of the issues records professionals must address in the use of distance education in their disciplines is the matter of appropriateness for their fields. One individual trying to grapple with this in library and information science education sounds the cautionary note that distance education is successful when the "class tasks and activities are appropriate to the technology used; are consistent with the instructor's philosophy and style of teaching; provide maximum student interaction; are well organized and well presented; and when the technologies used are accessible and relevant to students."[44] One discerns in this a research agenda, and it is certainly one that could be carried out with archivists and records managers. Such concerns remind us that there is more to quality distance education than merely what we can do: "Improvements in technology, communication, and access to resources do not necessarily translate to better distance education."[45]

While we have considerably more information about what records professionals need in the realm of continuing education, we still lack suitable knowledge of what works. This paucity of evaluation weakens our ability to plan effective courses, workshops, and institutes, in whatever mode they are delivered. It also opens archivists and records managers up to the kinds of problems and controversies now raging about the mechanism of distance education. The archives and records management community has other more important challenges to deal with than such matters as these.

In the meanwhile, an individual thinking about taking a distance education course or an institution contemplating suggesting to its employees that they take a particular course offered via distance learning can consider some basic questions, such as:

- Does the course meet the learning objectives or styles of the individuals who might take it?
- Does the distance education approach meet the professional aims of the students, including the kind of credit offered for the course?
- Is the nature of the course content suitable for a distance education approach?
- Does the instructor possess qualifications both in the content of the course and in teaching via a distance learning mode?
- What kind of information technology is needed by the student to be able to take full advantage of the course?
- How well does the course fit into the practical needs of the student and their institutional host? Are the kinds of assignments required practical for the student?

Many of these questions and others need to be carefully asked by individuals who hope to learn something in such a course that will broaden their knowledge and enhance their skills. Organizations need to ask the same questions when interviewing a candidate who graduated from a distance education program.

A distance education course blending video lectures, interpersonal contact between students and instructor, well-designed curricular materials, suitable learning objectives, and reasonable practical exercises can be an excellent educational experience. It is essential, however, that careful evaluation be made of these opportunities before, during, and after the courses in order to ascertain whether the desired learning is achieved. What is also essential is that both the teachers of these courses and the students weigh all the options, positive and negative, that are represented by the mechanism of distance learning.

CONCLUSION

Advocates of distance education suggest that the approach liberates instructors to reach more potential students, more effectively spread their message, and make them better advocates for their professional mission or mandate. Distance education may be quite seductive for archivists and records managers since they are so intent on communicating the importance of their work. Yet, as I suggested in this chapter, there are many subtle implications, some quite negative, regarding the use of distance education delivery mechanisms. Distance education, well-designed and well-supported, can be very useful as an educational system, but it can also reduce education to selling credentials or generating revenue. Records professionals need to move into this arena slowly and carefully, ensuring that the use of distance education is the appropriate venue for their aim.

ENDNOTES

1. Serena W. Stanford, "Evaluating ATM Technology for Distance Education in Library and Information Science," *Journal of Education for Library and Information Science* 38 (Summer 1997): 180–190.
2. Richard J. Cox, *American Archival Analysis: The Recent Development of the Archival Profession in the United States* (Metuchen, N.J.: Scarecrow Press, 1990).

3. Dan Carnevale, "It's Education. It's Online. It's Someplace You Aren't. What Do You Call It?" *Chronicle of Higher Education*, December 8, 2000.

4. Clifford Stoll, *High-Tech Heretic: Reflections of a Computer Contrarian* (New York: Anchor Books, 1999), pp. 92–93.

5. Stoll, *High-Tech Heretic*, p. 94.

6. David F. Noble, *Digital Diploma Mills: The Automation of Higher Education* (New York: Monthly Review Press, 2002), p. 3.

7. Noble, *Digital Diploma Mills*, p. 22.

8. Noble, *Digital Diploma Mills*, p. 90.

9. Douglas J. Cremer, "Education as Commodity: The Ideology of Online Education and Distance Learning," *Journal of the Association of History and Computing* (2001), available at http://mcel.pacificu.edu/JAHC/JAHCIV2/ARTICLES/cremer/cremerindex.html.

10. Corynne McSherry, *Who Owns Academic Work: Battling for Control of Intellectual Property* (Cambridge: Harvard University Press, 2001).

11. Sara Aase, "Higher Learning Goes the Distance: Online Instruction is Radically Changing the Collegiate Experience–For Good and for Ill," *Pittsburgh ComputerUser* (October 2000): 13.

12. M. O. Thirunarayanan, "The Seekers," *Ubiquity* Issue 7 (April 3–9, 2001), available at http://www.acm.org/ubiquity/views/m_thirunarayanan_5.html.

13. Cremer, "Education as Commodity."

14. Kathleen J. M. Haynes and Connie Dillon, "Distance Education: Learning Outcomes, Interaction, and Attitudes," *Journal of Education for Library and Information Science* 33 (Winter 1992): 43.

15. Daniel L. Barron, "Perceptions of Faculty and Administrative Staff in ALA-Accredited Programs toward Part-Time and Distance Students in LIS Education," *Journal of Education for Library and Information Science* 34 (Summer 1993): 187–199.

16. Therese Bissen Bard, "Cooperative Activities in Interactive Distance Learning," *Journal of Education for Library and Information Science* 37 (Winter 1996): 2.

17. Bard, "Cooperative Activities in Interactive Distance Learning."

18. Stanford, "Evaluating ATM Technology for Distance Education."

19. Anita Coleman, "Public Performances and Private Acts," *Journal of Education for Library and Information Science* 37 (Fall 1996): 325–342.

20. Julie I. Tallman and Angela D. Benson. "Examining the Change in Personal Learning Models of Graduate Students Enrolled in an Online Library Media Course," *Journal of Education for Library and Information Science* 41 (Summer 2000): 207–223.

21. Ruth V. Small, "A Comparison of the Resident and Distance Learning Experience in Library and Information Science Graduate Education," *Journal of Education for Library and Information Science* 40 (Winter 1999): 37–38.

22. Small, "A Comparison of the Resident and Distance Learning Experience," p. 28.

23. Dietmar Wolfram, "Audiographics for Distance Education," *Journal of Education for Library and Information Science* 35 (Summer 1994): 180.

24. Wolfram, "Audiographics for Distance Education," p. 179.
25. Howard Besser and Maria Bonn, "Interactive Distance-Independent Education: Challenges to Traditional Academic Roles," *Journal of Education for Library and Information Science* 38 (Winter 1997): 35–42.
26. Eliza T. Dresang and Jane B. Robbins, "Preparing Students for Information Organizations in the Twenty-First Century: Web-Based Management and Practices of Field Experience," *Journal of Education for Library and Information Science* 40 (Fall 1999): 221–222.
27. Dresang and Robbins, "Preparing Students for Information Organizations in the Twenty-First Century," p. 222.
28. Mary Ellen C. Sievert, Diane Tobin Johnson, Teresa Hartman, and Timothy B. Patrick, "New Educational Strategies for Training Information Professionals: Building Awareness, Concepts, and Skills Through Learning Technologies," *Journal of Education for Library and Information Science* 38 (Fall 1997): 312–313.
29. Karen Anderson, "Distance Learning: A New Approach to Archival Education," *Archives and Manuscripts* 23 (May 1995): 53.
30. Karen Anderson, "Distance Education for Archival Education," *Janus* 1998, no. 2, p. 41.
31. Audrey McCartan, "Use of IT in a Postgraduate Distance Learning Course: Part 1: Students' Experiences," *Innovations in Education and Training International* 37, no. 3 (2000): 188. For another assessment of the program at the same school, see Julie McLeod, "Piloting A Postgraduate Distance Learning Course in Records Management for Practising Records Managers," *Records Management Journal* 5 (December 1995): 61–78.
32. McCartan, "Use of IT in a Postgraduate Distance Learning Course," p. 189.
33. Elizabeth Shepherd, "Continuing Vocational Education and Archives and Records Management: A Project Progress Report from University College London," *Records Management Journal* 7 (August 1997): 134.
34. Shepherd, "Continuing Vocational Education," p. 137.
35. Shepherd, "Continuing Vocational Education," pp. 142–143.
36. Shepherd, "Continuing Vocational Education," p. 144.
37. The Web site for this project is at http://www.coshrc.org/nface/index.html.
38. David B. Gracy II, "Defying Nature or Second Nature? Distance Education For Archival Enterprise in the United States," undated, available at http://www.gslis.utexas.edu/~issa/gracy.html.
39. David B. Gracy II, "Defying Nature or Second Nature?"
40. "Report of the SAA Task Force on Continuing Education," *Archival Outlook* (September/October 2000): 4–9.
41. Society of American Archivists. "Guidelines for the Development of Post-Appointment and Continuing Education and Training Programs (PACE)," available at http://www.archivists.org/prof-education/pace.asp.
42. Society of American Archivists. "Statement on Copyright Issues for Archives in Distance Education." Available at http://www.archivists.org/statements/distance_education.asp.

43. Haynes and Dillon, "Distance Education."
44. Deborah Barreau, "Distance Learning: Beyond Content," *Journal of Education for Library and Information Science* 41 (Spring 2000): 80.
45. Barreau, "Distance Learning: Beyond Content," pp. 80–81.

7

The Archivist in the Knowledge Age: What Have We Become?

INTRODUCTION

There are many ways records professionals can predict what will happen to their profession in the next decade or two, and there are many ways they can be wrong. However, it is important to speculate on the future because any profession must make decisions enabling it to meet its mission as effectively as possible. What has to be kept in mind, of course, is what professions represent. In the best analysis of the nature of professions, Andrew Abbott suggests, "professions are somewhat exclusive groups of individuals applying somewhat abstract knowledge to particular cases."[1] A profession, in order to maintain its status or identity as a profession, must focus on the application of that knowledge amidst the realities of constant organizational shifts.

There are at least two reasons why records professionals should be able to make helpful predictions. First, one area in which predictions have fallen short of expectations has been information technology and its applications. Archivists and records managers are deeply affected by this since records are products of technology. Records professionals must understand that the office creating the records is in a continual state of flux and that the origins of their functions and techniques stem largely from an earlier stage of the office's evolution.[2] Electronic information technology has been the crucial factor transforming the office, although other economic, cultural, and political dimensions mediate the ways in which the newer technologies are utilized. Second, professions with information as a fundamental aspect of their responsibility are in a stronger position to flourish because information management has become integral to the competition among professions and their continuing success or failure. Again, archivists and records managers, with their responsibility to identify and manage records possessing continuing value to their organizations and society should be able to compete well in the future.

Regardless of the importance of professionalism, I am not arguing that efforts to control entry into the records professions, strengthen credentials, or develop and use standards always should be the focus for the future. These are important, but the professions' focus should always be on the health of the mission to administer records for institutions and society. Archivists and records managers have strengthened themselves in the past half-century, but it is debatable whether the progress is as great as we should have expected. Records programs are under-funded and have a low societal profile, and the prospects for gaining the needed support do not appear to be much better than they were a generation or two ago; some might argue that the prospects have even lessened.

When archivists and records managers speculate on the future, they often tend to focus on internal professional issues.[3] We can suggest all sorts of things about records professionals—their educational backgrounds, the kinds of individuals attracted to the field, their credentials, the work they will do, and even where they will work—but these kinds of predictions only make sense *if* they are related to the current changing nature of the organizations and the society they work in.

Earlier speculative efforts have been important for understanding that such matters are important if records professionals are to be successful in their work and mission, but they do not help much within their work places if they only go a little further than internal professional debates and discussions. It is easy to either adopt a progressive viewpoint in which we see a healthy and vital records community, or a more fatalistic perspective in which we see the community gone from the array of professions in the twenty-first century.

We need to speculate on what society and its organizations might become and to consider the ramifications of these changes for the mission of archivists and records managers. The need to administer records will remain, but I am not altogether sure about whether archivists and records managers or their programs as we now know them will. We should first examine organizations (corporations, governments, cultural institutions), and then consider other, greater societal changes. This might help us to better understand what archivists should and should not be doing now and in the near future. Here I have attempted to do this by examining some popular concepts paraded about in business and organizational management—reengineering, reinventing, and knowledge management—that have captivated corporate leaders for more than the past decade.

REENGINEERING THE ORGANIZATION

Every few years a new management scheme comes along, takes center stage, produces some bestsellers, and fades into the background. However, some new concepts show promise for transforming the manner in which we administer institutions and programs; these are administration approaches records professionals must pay closer attention to, both for serving their organizational parents and managing their own records programs. Recent writings on "reengineering" and "reinventing" institutions, followed by more recent musings about knowledge management, represent three related management schools or trends that records professionals should carefully consider.

Reengineering strives to show why the management principles of the past century must be discarded or, at the least, radically transformed. The fundamental testament of this approach is Michael Hammer and James Champy, *Reengineering the Corporation: A Manifesto for Business Revolution*, originally published a decade ago. Their premise is that management has been built around "tasks" which, in turn, are built on the principle of the division of labor when it should be clustered around "coherent business processes."[4]

While the older, task-oriented managerial approach worked well for a long time, its own success bred its failures. Tasks expanded in number, production became more complicated, and managing the production process became harder and often impossible. And the managing of the process further removed the corporation from the customer, threatening service, quality, responsiveness and other aspects of producing for the customer. The premise of reengineering is a recognition that the corporation's business is to have a product. The limited lifespan of a product and its market makes the processes that enable the business to change and create products all the more important. As Hammer and Champy indicate, "good products don't make winners; winners make good products."[5]

For thinking about processes rather than tasks, Hammer and Champy provide reengineering as a means of starting over, as is evident in their definition of reengineering: "Reengineering . . . is the fundamental rethinking and radical redesign of business processes to achieve dramatic improvements in critical, contemporary measures of performance, such as cost, quality, service, and speed."[6] The authors focus on four key aspects of this definition: fundamental (why, how, what kinds of questions), radical (reinventing the business, not improving it), dramatic ("quantum leaps in performance"), and processes (the "collection of activities that takes one or more kinds of input and creates an output that is of value to the customer").[7]

What are the future implications of "reengineering" for records professionals? We must consider this question in two ways: the records professional working within the reengineered corporation and the records professional reengineering his or her own program. Working in the reengineered corporation creates some interesting challenges. Hammer and Champy contend that "Reengineering is about beginning again with a clean sheet of paper. It is about rejecting the conventional wisdom and received assumptions of the past."[8] This poses a question about a records professional, especially the archivist, arguing that his or her mission is to provide a corporate memory. The point here may be, of course, not whether this is a legitimate role, but whether it is the exclusive or most important purpose of the institutional archives.

Hammer and Champy also argue, with a full chapter on the topic, that information technology is not the *solution* to the problems of an organization, but a means by which problems can be resolved. The authors stress that the technology often provides the means to invent new ways of doing business. In other words, "the real power of technology is not that it can make the old processes work better, but that it enables organizations to break old rules and create new ways of working—that is, to reengineer."[9] Imagining the uses of information technology brings records professionals face-to-face with the matter of how to employ the technology itself for the functioning of their program.

There are other, more crucial, concerns for the records professional in the reengineered institution. A major emphasis of the reengineering advocates is on the issue of who will lead and carry out reengineering, challenging the organizational records professionals. Hammer and Champy write, "Leadership isn't just a matter of position, but of character as well. Ambition, restlessness, and intellectual curiosity are the hallmarks of the reengineering leader. A caretaker of the *status quo* will never be able to muster the passion and enthusiasm the effort requires."[10] The records community has leaders. However, archivists take their mission to conserve or preserve quite seriously, and records managers often function in a conservative fashion in order to protect their organization.

The records professionals seeking to reengineer their own programs also face other serious issues. Hammer and Champy state that "in order to meet the contemporary demands of quality, service, flexibility, and low cost, processes must be kept simple."[11] Simplifying processes includes combining several jobs into one, allowing workers to make decisions, ordering the steps in a process, ending standardization to have multiple versions of a process oriented to different markets, performing work where it makes the most sense, and reducing checks and controls.

How can records professionals simplify their processes? Archivists, for example, could bring together the continuum of appraisal, arrangement and description, preservation, and use into a more simplified version that enables the appraisal process to accomplish much of what constitutes arrangement and description and preservation so that records are ready for use more quickly and processing backlogs are eliminated. A thorough appraisal could result in a thorough description; or, archivists could adapt existing descriptions produced by the creators.

Hammer and Champy also believe that the reengineered organization moves from stressing management as a way for individual advancement to stressing working. Records professionals have often stressed administration as a means of personal advancement or have often found themselves in small operations where they have been forced to assume managerial responsibilities, whether they are qualified or interested. What records professionals need to do to reengineer their programs is to provide the means for their most capable workers to stay where they have been successful.

Reengineering also requires "insight, creativity, and judgment."[12] Many records professionals are suspicious of innovation or risk taking. Simplifying processes requires radical rethinking and more than just tinkering. Appraisal could be simplified from acquiring records for every conceivable use by every conceivable potential constituency to focus on organizational legal and evidence requirements. Arrangement and description could be done only for backlogged holdings when they are requested, thus eliminating the constant complaint about the immense resources needed for such work and the appeal to this responsibility as the archival priority in favor of a strategy that stresses meeting organizational and societal information and evidence needs. Records managers must strive to balance their emphasis on serving organizational needs to perceive bigger concerns such as compliance and the public good. There is an important principle here: records professionals must only do what will assist their parent agency to achieve its objectives. They must understand their organization's objectives in the first place, and then to tailor their work to meet these objectives.

Some features of the reengineered corporation parallel some current trends in the records community. One of those is education. Hammer and Champy stress education versus training that is compatible with the recent movement to develop graduate archival education programs that do not train but provide a basic knowledge: "Traditional companies typically stress employee *training*—teaching workers how to perform a particular job or how to handle one specific situation or another. In companies that have reengineered, the emphasis shifts from training to *education*—or to hiring the educated. Training increases skills and competence and teaches employees the 'how' of a job. Education increases their insight and understanding and teaches the 'why.'"[13] This reorientation will not be a problem for archivists, assuming support for the continued development of graduate archival education and continuing education programs, ensuring that these programs focus on education and knowledge rather than skills and attitudes.

REINVENTING THE ORGANIZATION

Reinventing—another management concept capturing a lot of attention—is closely related to reengineering. As described in the book by David Osborne and Ted Gaebler, *Reinventing Government: How the Entrepreneurial Spirit is Transforming the Public Sector*, the notion of reinventing is the management effort carried out by an entrepreneur who "uses resources in new ways to maximum productivity and effectiveness."[14] Osborne and Gaebler believe the last major effort at reinventing government occurred fifty years to a century ago, and this has created a problem *because* "the kind of governments that developed during the industrial era, with their sluggish, centralized bureaucracies, their preoccupation with rules and procedures, and their hierarchical chains of command, no longer work very well."[15] While Hammer and Champy stressed a perspective on processes, Osborne and Gaebler focus on results: In the old model, we attempted control and "we became so obsessed with dictating *how* things should be done—regulating the process, controlling the inputs—that we ignored the outcomes, the *results*."[16] They suggest, however, that the circumstances that led to the older models have disappeared or been greatly modified: "We live in an information society, in which people get access to information almost as fast as their leaders do. We live in a knowledge-based economy, in which educated workers bridle at commands and demand autonomy."[17] How fast can these organizations get access to information in their records programs? Will they tolerate needing to go through the archivist or records manager in order to get the access they need?

Osborne and Gaebler, examining examples of government success stories, developed a set of criteria for success (constituting the reinvention of government):

- promoting *"competition* between service providers"
- empowering of citizens by moving control from the bureaucracy to the community
- having performance measures stressing outcomes rather than inputs
- being motivated by their mission rather than by rules and regulations
- redefining their clients as customers
- preventing problems before they occur rather than offering services after a problem emerges
- focusing on earning, not just spending, money
- having an authority that is decentralized, stressing participatory management
- preferring market mechanisms rather than bureaucratic mechanisms
- possessing a "focus not simply on providing public services, but on *catalyzing* all sectors—public, private, and voluntary—into action to solve their community's problems."[18]

Records professionals who someday may labor in reinvented organizations face a number of interesting issues. Osborne and Gaebler contend that "in today's world, public institutions also need the flexibility to respond to complex and rapidly changing conditions. This is difficult if policy makers can use only one method—services produced by their own bureaucracy."[19] Archives, as well as records management programs, have often functioned as if they have a long time to respond to needs. Archivists often have slow processes for retrieving information from their holdings, and records managers often employ highly labor-intensive devices by which to schedule, store, and retrieve records. Records management programs have often been unresponsive to public needs, while archivists often defined their clients as only the public, losing sight of the services they should provide to the records creators.

The reinvented organization requires records professionals to rethink their roles, real and potential. Osborne and Gaebler note that "there are very few services traditionally provided by the public sector that are not today provided somewhere by the private sector—and vice versa."[20] This is not a new idea, but it probably has far more implications today than it did a few years ago. Rising dissatisfaction with the services of present organizations and a growing realization of the inadequacies of such organizations has created an environment where experimentation and new competition is probable, not just possible.

Archivists, in state government for example, want to be taken seriously as providing services for the ongoing, practical administration of such government, but there is plenty of competition for the kinds of information services that state archives provide, including state libraries, bibliographic utilities that all agencies can use, other commercial information services, and, especially, information technology and policy boards making decisions about the use of electronic information technology for recordkeeping purposes. Records management can be sourced out even now.

Records professionals need to reexamine such prospects and, rather than view them as a threat, they need to see them as an opportunity. Osborne and Gaebler contend, "when governments contract with private businesses, both conservatives and liberals often talk as if they are shifting a fundamental public responsibility to the private sector. This is nonsense: they are shifting the delivery of services, not the responsibility for services."[21]

State government archives (encompassing records management operations) need to reconsider their services, determining whether or not they must do them or whether they can be sourced out. State archives need to reinvent themselves as regulatory agencies, and they must cease thinking that they have to do everything. If they can gain the flexibility to use their funding in more creative fashions, they will probably be able to do far more with such funds in the past. Since their funding support is unlikely to increase in any appreciable manner, using some guiding principles, such as offered by reinventing an organization, may be the only real sensible alternative. And since governments are likely to adopt more competitive modes in the future, state records programs must reconsider how they can compete in meaningful ways.

Archivists and records managers working for reinvented organizations need to consider how they measure their success. Osborne and Gaebler think that "public entrepreneurs know that when institutions are funded according to inputs, they have little reason to strive for better performance. But when they are funded according to outcomes, they become obsessive about performance."[22] If this is true for any records operation, there is little description of such performance. It is inevitable that reinvented organizations will ultimately ask for their records programs to suggest appropriate measures, or they will be given measures to achieve. Archivists and records managers will have to come up with responses about how they have provided information crucial to solve certain problems, met real information needs, or achieved a full documentation of certain functions, trends, or special activities.

There will inevitably come a new level of accountability. It is viewed by some records professionals that accountability is precisely the business that archivists and records managers are meant to be performing, as suggested by the increasing array of writings about records for accountability purposes. As Osborne and Gaebler argue, "words like *accountability, performance,* and *results* have begun to ring through the halls of government. Luckily, we now have the technology needed to make such words mean something. We can generate, analyze, and communicate a thousand times more information than we could just a generation ago, for a fraction of the cost."[23] Records management for accountability, evidence, and corporate memory certainly fits with this. Archivists and their programs will be judged by their ability to support this, among other things ensuring that the information that their repositories contain can be made readily available. Archivists need to stress the integrity of the record, its appropriate management, and the ongoing need for records by the organization.

Records professionals who seek to reinvent their own programs can draw many suggestions from *Reinventing Government*. At one point its authors provide this description of the government worker: "Many employees in bureaucratic governments feel trapped. Tied down by rules and regulations, number by monotonous tasks, assigned jobs they know could be accomplished in half the time if they were only allowed to use their minds, they live lives of quiet desperation."[24] Archivists and records managers have often defined their jobs by only the most routine and time-consuming work—such as archival arrangement and description or records management inventorying—while they have often done less about the more important and intellectually stimulating of their functions, especially appraisal. Records professionals need to ask themselves if they are hiring bright individuals but assigning them virtually clerical duties or hiring individuals more interested in clerical responsibilities. Some of this attitude may be because archivists and records managers often reflect thinking more in tune with the older industrial-era office, stressing tasks and division of labor, out of which the earliest archives and records management programs emerged.

Osborne and Gaebler argue, "Most public organizations are driven not by their missions, but by their rules and their budgets. They have a rule for everything that could conceivably go wrong and a line item for every subcategory of spending in every unit of every department. The glue that holds public bureaucracies together, in other words, is like epoxy: it comes in two separate tubes. One holds rules, the other line items. Mix them together and you get cement."[25] Apart from the fact that there are many records programs in government reflecting this problem, there are also many records programs in other kinds of organizations also showing such characteristics. Many of these programs are waist-deep in concrete which they have mixed and poured themselves, and the professional staff of such programs need to rethink what they are doing, which means rethinking their mission. Osborne and Gaebler argue that in order to develop mission-ruled organizations we first "scrape off the dead weight of accumulated rules, regulations, and obsolete activities."[26]

Reevaluating an archives or records management mission has become a major activity of many such programs in the United States in the past decade or so. It may be, however, that archivists have tended to go about such work in the wrong fashion. Osborne and Gaebler state that "clarity of mission may be the single most important asset for a government organization."[27] But how clear can archival or records management missions be when it is obvious that archives and records management tend to be low-profile, often misunderstood functions? The authors note that "public organizations work best when they have *one* clear mission."[28] But records programs often possess an ungainly mix of cultural mission and service orientation, along with a confused sense of who they are serving.

Part of the problem derives from the fact that archivists and records managers have often seemed unable to change their mission, layering one old mission and traditional function or activity after another even as the larger organizational context of their operations has changed. Reinvented organizations are run by entrepreneurs and "entrepreneurs are people who fail many times";[29] archivists often either lack the entrepreneurial spirit or the opportunities to display it. Records managers, on the other hand, have tended to be extraordinarily entrepreneurial, but this has also made their mission difficult to comprehend because it always seems to be changing.

Osborne and Gaebler spend an entire chapter on their sense that government has lost sight of its customers. While we are a society that expects "products and services customized to our styles and tastes," it is nevertheless true that "traditional public institutions still offer one-size-fits-all services."[30] Archivists and records managers have been in a similar quandary. Although they don't fully understand their users needs, yet they continue to expend *great* efforts and resources on designing systems for access to their holdings.

How can this be? Is it, perhaps, that in their race to standardize archival arrangement and description, archivists, as one example, are in fact offering such one-size-fits-all services? The eventual outcomes might be disturbing. And, do I need to add, this government, in its failure, might take its records with it?

Perhaps the most important issues for records professionals presented in the *Reinventing Government* treatise are the ideas of "anticipatory" and "decentralized" government. Osborne and Gaebler argue for anticipatory government, doing two things: "they use an ounce of prevention, rather than a pound of cure; and they do everything possible to build foresight into their decision making."[31] Archivists spend too much time when they do appraisal thinking about future use, and I am sure this will strike some as contrary to the notion of anticipatory government. I don't think it is, at all.

When archivists speak of appraising for future use or when they discuss working for future users, it is often utilized as a rationale for their appraisal decisions. They do not understand enough about their present users to be able to build a foundation for predicting what will happen. In fact, both archivists and records managers tend to be notorious reactors to problems. Their institutions and their functions seem not to have changed very much over the past century, even in light of massive uses of electronic information technology.

The authors of *Reinventing Government* also discuss decentralization of programs as an essential aspect for future government agencies. The notion of decentralization probably sends shivers up the spines of archivists and records managers. Records professionals have spent most of their careers building programs that centralize recordkeeping functions. Osborne and Gaebler paint a different future for government and organizations on their canvas. They write that "fifty years ago centralized institutions were indispensable," especially as "there was plenty of time for information to flow up the chain of command and decisions to flow back down."[32] Now, because of better information systems, better-educated staff, and other factors, we see decisions being made at all levels and by many different types of employees. We also see new kinds of team work and different roles or the elimination of middle managers, allowing organizations to become more innovative and entrepreneurial and closer to the customer. If archivists or records managers don't participate in making their functions more decentralized then they may become obstacles—and obstacles in the reinvented organization are more apt to be eliminated than they are to be tolerated.

Has there been any response, for example, by the archival community in the United States to such ideas as reinventing and reengineering the organization? Not surprisingly, the one response has come from archivists involved in managing electronic recordkeeping systems. In a essay by David Bearman and Margaret Hedstrom, these authors take the concept of reinventing and examine it from the perspective of electronic archives management. They initially consider the reasons why current, conventional archival methods have failed in the management of such recordkeeping systems, and then they present what the reinvented archives must look like. It is worth summarizing their latter discussion. Some of their suggestions follow. Archival agencies

> monitor and provide oversight "while assigning responsibility to agencies for achieving adequately documented functions and programs"; "engage their communities in solving archival problems, then they can rely more on their communities to achieve mutually desired ends"; become more enterprising and "endorse strategies that turn the profit motive to public use, raise money by charging fees for some services, and spend money to save money in the long run through investments that pay a return"; develop "more relevant and responsive services that are oriented to the needs of customers"; and become "more effective and more productive" by decentralizing their operations.[33]

Whether or not one buys into such notions popularized by these best-selling books or adopts some other schemes, I believe they reflect one fundamental truth about corporations and government (the two most dominant institutions in modern society): they *are* changing, they *will* change, and they *will continue* changing for quite a while. This means that archivists and records managers must also adopt and adapt in order to play an effective role in such institutions.

A NEW WRINKLE: MANAGING KNOWLEDGE

Knowledge management gradually emerged in the 1990s, developing from earlier concepts such as information resources management and striving to make sense of the growing array of information technologies being used in organizations. The notion of knowledge management has generated both considerable interest and confusion, partly because it is "both a business practice and an emerging theoretical field of study."[34] What does the working records professional see from the vantage of his or her work responsibilities? What does an organization see? From the organizational vantage it is quite possible that the notion of any theoretical view is meaningless. The organization will look at, consider, and embrace or reject knowledge management because of how it fits the need for business practices. This does not mean that we can reject the theoretical perspective.

The working records professional must have a strategic perspective in order to make sense of a vast universe of records with an equally vast array of evidence, information, and knowledge for the organization. The key is, of course, not to lose sight of how the organization sees its own needs and how the records professional fits his or her mandate or sense of mission to the larger organizational mission and needs.

We have the persistent or traditional division between archivists and records managers, with the old view that one serves the scholar or researcher and the other serves the institution and its needs. This demonstrates a couple of things about the knowledge management debates. One is that the debates about knowledge management are nothing new at all. The other is that the prospects of bringing disparate groups together is very difficult, because of different perspectives, traditions, allegiances, and education. We have seen this before with information resources management and the concept of "islands" of information going back into the 1980s. Archivists and records managers, perhaps, will need to focus on how to build bridges rather than compete, while at the same time identifying and making their unique perspectives known.

In what follows, I am largely drawing on the knowledge management writings of Thomas Stewart, a business writer and editor, not because his books are the most comprehensive or even the best of the writings on knowledge management, but rather because they are the most accessible to the leaders of organizations. Stewart contends that there have been "three big ideas" concerning the management of organizations—Total Quality Management, reengineering, and intellectual capital. "Knowledge companies will, in short, have to think of themselves almost in biological terms, rather than in mechanical ones," he argues. "It is no wonder that we thought of organizations, too, as mechanical things, with pistons and valves, parts that wore out or broke down; no wonder we thought that corporations should be 'restructured' or 'rationalized' or 'streamlined' or 'reengineered'; no wonder we thought that duplication was the enemy of efficiency, redundancy the antonym of productivity."[35]

Stewart builds off of the idea of intellectual capital, and shows that there is more to organizational information than technology or records or, more crudely put, memos and directives. He believes "Intellectual capital is the sum of everything everybody in a company knows that gives it a competitive edge."[36] Intellectual capital is the essential ingredient in the mix, the "knowledge that transforms raw materials and makes them more valuable."[37] And this is not just the case for for-profit entities. There is competition in all organizations, even cultural ones such as museums and libraries—competing for resources, public attention, donations of objects, and in most any other activity that you can conceive of for virtually any kind of organization.

It is the source of intellectual capital that should get the attention of records professionals. Stewart contends that "One reason organizations don't manage knowledge is that it almost always comes wrapped in some tangible form—in the paper of a book, in the magnetic tape of an audiocassette, in the body of a speaker, in the stones of a historical monument."[38] "The stuff we're looking for, intellectual capital, takes two forms," Stewart believes. "First, there's *the semipermanent body of knowledge*, the expertise, that grows up around a task, a person, or an organization. . . . The second kind of knowledge assets are *tools that augment the body of knowledge*, either by bringing in facts, data, information— call them what you will—or by delivering expertise and augmentation to others who need them when they need them, that is, leveraging them."[39]

Archivists and records managers need to question just what is the expertise (and tools of this expertise) unique to them. Is it their knowledge of the record, why records are created, how records and record-keeping systems work, the manner in which business functions create records, or their great breadth of knowledge about how organizations work? These questions must be asked because otherwise organizations may simply bypass what they see as the least attractive aspect of knowledge—that which is wrapped up in mundane records clogging desks, file cabinets, and computer memory banks.

The focus on knowledge by commentators such as Stewart is very different from the more traditional ideas of records by archivists and records managers, books and reports by librarians, or even the contents of the growing World Wide Web by the innovative cybernauts. For Stewart, "Crucially, intellectual capital is not created from discrete wads of human, structural, and customer capital but from the *interplay* among them."[40] Later, Stewart pithily argues, "It has become standard to say that a company's intellectual capital is the sum of its human capital (talent), structural capital (intellectual property, methodologies, software, documents, and other knowledge artifacts), and customer capital (client relationships)."[41] How do records professionals fit into this interplay? Who are their customers and what are the talents they bring? Records professionals know the structural capital stuff, because this is what they have traditionally focused on.

The contrast between what archivists and records managers have often thought about their business and the new objectives of knowledge management is quite interesting. Archivist Jay Atherton writes, "Many archivists have considered . . . records management as merely an element of archives. For them, the ultimate purpose of records management is the permanent preservation of 'historically valuable' material in an archives. From this long-range point of view, the short time-span of administrative or operational use of records is a comparatively minor thing."[42] Of course, knowledge management changes this by demonstrating, I think, that we need to understand organizational missions and mandates.

Perhaps even more importantly, we need to realize that organizational managers are not probably going to see such nuances between archivists and records managers or even between librarians. What Atherton was describing in the 1980s was more of an internal squabble between siblings, at least when we step far enough back as those writing about knowledge management seem to be doing. Knowledge management is as much outwardly focused toward the customer as towards other units or agencies within an organization.

Knowledge generation and management becomes, then, a task of all business. Stewart argues, "Because knowledge has become the single most important factor of production, managing intellectual assets has become the single most important task of business."[43] Stewart expounds, "The knowledge economy stands on three pillars. The first: Knowledge has become what we buy, sell, and do. It is the most important factor of production. The second pillar is a mate, a corollary to the first: Knowledge assets—that is, intellectual capital—have become more important to companies than financial and physical assets. The third pillar is this: To prosper in this new economy and exploit these newly vital assets, we need new vocabularies, new management techniques, new technologies, and new strategies. On these three pillars rest all the new economy's laws and its profits."[44]

Such notions have caused some records professionals to seek ways of relating their mission, work, and practices to the seemingly more global fashion of knowledge management. Jan Duffy tries to identify the unique sources of knowledge brought to the table by records professionals, identifying their best practices and their knowledge about corporate memory. As she logically writes, "Corporate memory constitutes a historical record of an organization's significant events and decisions. It is the organization's corporate records *and* the accumulated knowledge, experience, expertise, history, stories, strategies, successes, and mythology of an organization as these exist in its employees. Much of this is likely to be maintained in the records or archives that form a history of an organization."[45]

While Duffy's work is derivative, it does at least provide a stronger connection between archives/records management and knowledge management. Sue Myburgh extends the argument substantially: "KM goes far beyond the technologies. For records managers as well as for other information professionals, it means new ways of looking at records as sources of potential knowledge. It also means educating other staff members. Knowledge management is the process of capturing a company's collective expertise whenever it resides—in databases, on paper, or in people's heads—and distributing it to wherever it can help produce the competitive advantage." Myburgh wants to get the new advocates of knowledge management to look at documents: "At the heart of knowledge management are rich, structured, highly functional documents." Still, she must see a substantial difference between knowledge and records managers (the latter certainly including archivists): "One major difference in the outlook of RMs is this: We have to look forward now, instead of back, if we wish to engage with and participate in KM. In the past, the major thrust of records managers and archivists was to preserve and conserve the records of an organization and its history—the corporate memory. . . . However, KM implies a learning organization, and that implies looking forward and being better able to deal with future crises or opportunities. . . . The corporate memory approach is dangerous if it looks only to the past."[46]

Archival educator Beth Yakel argues that archivists and records managers must be more aggressive in figuring out how they relate to a new regime like that represented by knowledge management: "Records professionals must be able to identify and acknowledge the competition in their organizations in order to influence the corporate information ecology. . . . After identifying the competition, records professionals must determine which services they are in the best position to provide in an exemplary manner and how to better target the clients most in need of those services."[47] Yakel urges that they assume leadership in forming partnerships, taking more of an auditing role in identifying records, and moving beyond professional standards "to embrace their parent organization's mission and to understand the key organizational functions that must be supported."[48]

Can knowledge really be managed? Thomas Stewart argues that it can be. "Knowledge and information take on their own reality, which can be detached from the physical movement of goods and services. From this divergence come at least two important implications. First, knowledge and the assets that it creates and distributes can be managed, just as physical and financial assets can be. . . . Second, if knowledge is the greatest source of wealth, then individuals, companies, and nations should invest in the assets that produce and process knowledge."[49] In arguing this position, Stewart identifies the limitations of information technology and approaches such as expert systems as often missing the most critical matters of importance to an organization.

Technology often does not deal with knowledge: "Information technology better suits information than knowledge. It even tries to change knowledge into information-like objects."[50] The preoccupation with information is often just that, a fixation with lots of stuff. Other commentators have focused on the location of knowledge, and it is not in the hardware or software: "Expert systems were created to 'capture' the knowledge of experts. The 'capture' approach continued with an emphasis on 'capturing knowledge' in databases, manuals, books and reports, and then sharing it in a hard form. The emphasis was placed on managing so-called 'knowledge assets' that were tangible, and could be structured and codified, such as patents, trademarks and documents." They continue, "However, it is important at this point to re-emphasize the key attribute of knowledge: that it exists in people's heads. Once explicit knowledge has been committed to paper (or any other medium), it becomes information." "If KM is to really be KM, and not just IRM with a new label, then all KM projects will have to recognize that some knowledge cannot be articulated."[51] We need to study about this from the vantage of records professionals. How is the stuff in records used? How could it be used? How is it used in comparison with other forms of information and knowledge? And, if archivists and records managers do not take advantage of the idea of the knowledge management culture, what are the long-term prospects for these disciplines and the uses of their records?

Like the earlier books on reengineering and reinventing, the more popular treatises on knowledge management emphasize some poignant advice about the nature of professionals. For Stewart, "Professionals are measured not by the tasks they perform but by the results they achieve."[52] What are the results for records professionals? Archivists and records managers have been task-oriented, and this poses some serious issues about how they will be perceived in the knowledge management environment. A new emphasis on knowledge means a new stress on education and qualifications. Stewart thinks that "Far from being alienated from the tools of his trade and the fruit of his labor, the knowledge worker carries them between his ears."[53] Where does this come from? For the archivist and the records manager, does this mean formal education, experience, networks of colleagues, independent study, or some combination of these?

Indeed, Stewart and other proponents of concepts such as knowledge management fit individual professionals into a broader community. "Swiping secrets is odious to both law and etiquette, and that's a legally enforceable document. It is also hornswoggle. First, you swap proprietary information all the time; in fact, the company probably wouldn't prosper unless you did. Second, the real genesis and true ownership of ideas and know-how aren't corporate. Nor personal, for that matter. They belong to something that is coming to be known as a 'community of practice.'"[54] Just how have archivists and records managers fit into a community of practice? Who else is in that community? The split between archivists and records managers has been severe. Archivists are often looking outward, while records managers are looking inward. Of course, it is precisely this notion of belonging to a community of practice that often makes managing professionals like archivists and records managers so difficult. Modern organizations have made this even more complex.

When people view their own work, their livelihood, how do they define it? Thomas Stewart contends, "A paradox lies at the heart of the Information Age organization: At the same time that employers have weakened the ties of job security and loyalty, they more than ever depend on human capital; for their part, knowledge workers, because they bring to their work not only their bodies but their minds—even their souls—are far more loyal to their work (though not to their employer) than those tire-makers whose first love was for the hobbies that waited for them at home."[55]

Is this true of records professionals? Both archivists and records managers have tended to define themselves as part of their employing organizations. Even certification programs for individual practitioners have tended to identify themselves with employers because the examining processes are practice-oriented. One must wonder whether an organization bought into the knowledge management paradigm will buy into this approach. Stewart, admittedly in a for-profit business context, provides some direct advice for modern workers. "Instead of security, seek resilience. Chart your contribution, not your position. Careers will be defined less by companies . . . and more by professions . . . ; they will be shaped less by hierarchies and more by markets."[56]

This is not a new view. The architectural historian and critic, Witold Rybczynski, provides a historical benchmark: "Since there were no architects' guilds or associations in the sixteenth century, there was no period of formal training or apprenticeship. In that sense, to be an architect did not mean to be a professional; it meant, rather, to hold a position."[57] Some professions seem to have achieved truly disciplinary independence long before others.

What is amazing about this is that records professionals such as archivists and records managers ought to be in unique positions to capitalize on how these organizations work. Stewart connects quite strongly the issue of access to information with the ability to understand the nature of these new communities. "Embedded in the e-mail of a company is a rich picture of its employees, customers, and suppliers. Just as circulating correspondence showed me who did what and knew what, e-mail reveals communities of practices and pockets of expertise."[58] Others have been more cynical. One observer notes, "Now if Knowledge Management is largely the management and support of expertise, then, unlike data and information management, it is primarily the management of individuals with specific abilities, rather than the management of repositories of data and information."[59]

One of the greatest challenges with relating the responsibilities of records professionals to knowledge management is that, just like the former fads of reengineering and reinventing, paperwork is seen as the great (mythical?) nemesis. Stewart falls into this easy stereotyping of the problems in organizations today when he writes, "Unleashing the human capital already resident in the organization requires minimizing mindless tasks, meaningless paperwork, unproductive infighting."[60] Yet, Stewart seems inconsistent with such concerns. At one point, he muses, "We produce an extraordinary amount of the stuff [knowledge]—annual worldwide production of new information is somewhere between 700 and 2,400 terabytes, each terabyte being the equivalent of a million ordinary books. Sure, a lot of it is garbage, but there's no reason to think the ratio of wheat to chaff is any worse (or any better, for that matter) than it ever was. Much of this production is never sold: For example, only a fifth of the information produced on paper can be found in books, newspapers, and periodicals; the rest is office documents."[61] Do we need to eliminate all this paperwork, or do we need to try to mine it in new and innovative ways? Clearly, making paperwork part of the old evil empire of inefficient organizations seems counterproductive and counterintuitive to what we need to be doing in modern organizations.

Stewart and other knowledge management proponents are struggling with what to make of their organizations' paperwork piles. "What do your customers expect you to know? What intellectual materials—facts, bodies of knowledge, technologies, and so on—do you call upon? Are they found in documents or brainpans?"[62] Stewart can't let go of the idea that documents are dead knowledge. "Preserving institutional memory requires 'documentation.' The word is in quotes because, as we shall see, more is involved than documents. Documentation is an aftermath, however, of doing knowledge projects."[63] The problem may be, however, that what Stewart is reacting to are not just stereotypes but what archivists and records managers seem to portray by their practices and approaches.

Other commentators on knowledge management have been a little more kind to the connection of knowledge management to traditional records and recordkeeping systems. We have the idea of the knowledge artifact, as one example. "In a knowledge management program it is the knowledge artifact, or the thing, that is managed, not knowledge itself, and the knowledge representation must reflect the action of knowledge acquisition." "Eventually, these knowledge artifacts would comprise a collection of materials that could be codified and placed in a repository for access by everyone in the organization."[64] Others have expressed concern that knowledge managers not go overboard with how they approach existing information and knowledge sources.

Commenting on the great progress in storing more information on computers, David Blair worries, "When information is put on a computer it is usually removed from the informal social networks of the employees who use and produce it. Removing information from these pragmatic contexts is OK for relatively context-free data, and low-context information, but it can be harmful to remove the more context-dependent information that experts often use in the execution of their expertise." Blair uses documents as his example: "When documents exist only as paper, they tend to be physically managed by individuals who understand them and have some use for them." Blair also understands some of the fundamentals of traditional records management: "Finally, because the storage of paper documents has an explicit cost, the gatekeepers will be selective about what they keep, and will often weed out and discard documents that are no longer useful. This makes it more likely that social information networks will provide access to information that is useful for the purposes of the organization." Blair doesn't see only "messy offices populated by desks and tables piled with stacks of papers. As humorous as this image is, there is a hidden efficiency in it."[65]

There is, then, a persistent problem with how knowledge management advocates see records. Bruce Dearstyne has been particularly concerned about this: "Records are an important embodiment of, and source for, knowledge derived from past practices. They document a company's strategies, products, services, customer information, and the achievements of its employees. Records are bound to be an important source of knowledge. However, KM literature seldom mentions records or, for that matter, the corporate library." Dearstyne notes that knowledge managers often see "records in a slighting, misleading manner, portraying them as paper-based documents that slow decision making and that need to be converted to digital format to make them more available and useful."[66] Dearstyne argues that records managers need to learn about knowledge management and better promote the connection of archives and records management to it. Conversely, one would hope that knowledge managers could learn more about archives and records management, especially the importance of standard, transactional records as knowledge carriers.

One of the more critical values expounded in the knowledge management panoply of ideas and practices is the moving forward to a more central role: serving the customer. Stewart lays out the focus quite clearly: "It is a principle of managing intellectual capital that *when information is power, power flows downstream toward the customer.*"[67] Sometimes substituting for customers is the notion of an emphasis on outcomes, as Bouthillier and Shearer argue, with "The ultimate goal of IM is to ensure that information is stored and retrievable, while the ultimate purpose of KM is tied more closely to organization outcomes."[68] Earlier arguments about the records management-archives continuum suggest this, so thinking about customers ought not to be a stretch for either archivists or records managers (although they will conceive of these outcomes in somewhat different ways).

Atherton shifts around the old life cycle model to unite archivists and records managers into one phase of scheduling records and then a final phase of the "maintenance and use of the information—whether it be maintained in the creating office, an inactive storage area, or an archives." "The function that ties the process together is that of service—to the creators of the records and all other users, whoever they may be and for whatever reason they may wish to consult the documentation. Records are created to serve an administrative purpose, usually to document a transaction or decision. Their value is directly related to their availability to those requiring them. . . . Much of the use made of records in any corporate archives usually comes from the agency officers or employees, searching for precedent or background on current policies and administrative procedures. Here the archives acts simply as the continuation of a process that started at the moment of creation, ensuring the preservation and availability of records of enduring value. If you like, acting as the memory of the creating agency."[69] Atherton is even more harsh with the archivist, who sometimes conceives of the clientele in much more restrictive fashion, stating a "major concern of the continuum as a whole must be administrative efficiency. Records are not created to serve the interests of some future archivist or historian, or even to document for posterity some significant decision or operation. They are created and managed to serve immediate operational needs. . . . While an archivist obviously is obliged to acquire the right material and ensure its preservation, that archives had better be prepared to serve its immediate clients and serve them well if it wishes to prosper."[70]

Thinking about knowledge management also includes some issues about changing behaviors. Archivists and records managers sometimes act as if they always have to be hovering around their records. Stewart argues that for a knowledge management environment to be created and sustained, people have to be working with each other—that is, interacting with each other in substantive ways. He states that "One of the most consistent, important, and ignored pieces of research about knowledge sharing is this: *It won't happen if people are not near each other.*"[71]

There is an opportunity implicit in such notions. Another knowledge management expert thinks that an organization with a knowledge culture "offers opportunities to create knowledge and one that encourages learning and the sharing of what is known. Encouragement can come in the form of establishing small group meeting rooms, conducting on-site seminars, rewarding those who pursue learning and who will teach others what they know, offering informal 'water cooler'-type meeting places throughout the workplace, etc. Creating a knowledge culture ensures the continual creation and sharing of knowledge through the environment of trust and dialogue."[72] Archivists and records managers will need to be mobile and facile in order to pursue their agendas, especially if they want records to be factored into the equation or organizational administration.

What has worried some of the proponents for and critics of knowledge management is whether knowledge management is simply another management fad. Thomas Stewart takes this on directly: "Fads aren't necessarily bad. Sometimes—often—faddists fail; in so doing they perform a service for the rest of us, showing where not to tread, showing us the boundaries of the possible. Sometimes, against all odds—or at least against conventional wisdom , they succeed—performing a greater service, showing us possibilities we never imagined, the penicillin in the mold."[73]

One of knowledge management's staunchest critics, Tom Wilson, after criticizing the various approaches to knowledge management and claiming that even some of the founders of knowledge management have questions about it, writes: "Of course, academic researchers and teachers do not need to be 'stuck with' anything that fails to stand up to rigorous analysis. . . . The inescapable conclusion of this analysis of the 'knowledge management' idea is that it is, in large part, a management fad, promulgated mainly by certain consultancy companies, and the probability is that it will fade away like previous fads. It rests on two foundations: the management of information—where a large part of the fad exists (and where the 'search and replace marketing' phenomenon is found) and the effective management of work practices. However, these latter practices are predicated upon a Utopian idea of organizational culture in which the benefits of information exchange are shared by all, where individuals are given autonomy in the development of their expertise, and where 'communities' within the organization can determine how that expertise will be used."[74] Wilson ignores how information science could be scrutinized in much the same fashion, and fails to see how responses to such fads sometime speak volumes about the real needs of modern organizations. McInerney sees this potential, assessing that "Knowledge management is another big idea that may not always retain its current cache, but it is bound to continue to influence the way we think about organizational processes and assets."[75] Records managers and archivists will have to ask themselves some serious questions about whether newer developments such as represented by knowledge management are in fact filling voids left by the failures of archives and records management programs.

CONCLUSION

The popular trends in organizational administration—reinventing, reengineering, knowledge management—all are arguing that they are accurate reflections of a new organization, one going beyond paper documents to entrepreneurial uses of knowledge that might or might not be found within these documents. Archivists and records managers need to pay attention to what is happening within their own organizations, both at the most mundane level of daily activity and in the value systems that ideas like reengineering or managing knowledge might suggest.

Records professionals will have plenty of opportunities. As organizations and society make the transition from traditional paper-oriented recordkeeping systems to electronic systems, there will be heightened concern about the continuing management of such records, their access and privacy, the notion of a record, and other such basic concerns that have long been the province and interest of archivists and records managers. For the past two decades, we have seen books raising concern about computer use, ethics, and misuse, but we can now see a flow of interest to more basic issues about the management of electronic records, including a shift from a stress on information to a stress on the record.

The knowledge possessed by records professionals should be more highly valued than ever before, even if the records they administer might seem to be ignored. Assuming that records professionals will be able to refocus their attention on the needs of their organizations, they should be able to cease worrying about their status in the information professions. Those needs will have a lot more to do with matters of accountability and evidence than ever before, and archivists and records managers will need to develop the means by which they can respond to their organizations' constantly shifting needs and concerns.

Is there a linchpin in these characteristics? What will be the most important element for archivists and records managers to have in place in this new century? In my estimation it is education, or, what records professionals know. Much of what archivists and records managers will face in the years ahead will require new strategies, ideas, methods, and a healthy dose of imagination and risk-taking. Educated archivists and records managers are the key to this. They need to be well versed in archival theory and methodology, with some orientation to practice.

A decade ago I thought this meant the promulgation of stronger professional guidelines for separate masters degrees, but this change has not occurred. What will have to suffice is to recruit bright, capable individuals into the best graduate programs available, and build within them a knowledge of archives and records management systems that takes into account the perspectives reflected by Osborne and Gaebler, Hammer and Champy, and Stewart as a means of rethinking how the records professionals' mission can be kept current in our ever-changing world.

ENDNOTES

1. Andrew Abbott, *The System of Professions* (Chicago: University of Chicago Press, 1988), p. 318.
2. Vincent E. Giuliano, "The Mechanization of Office Work," *Scientific American* 247 (September 1982): 149–164.
3. Frank G. Burke, "The Future Course of Archival Theory in the United States," *American Archivist* 44 (Winter 1981): 40–46 and Richard M. Kesner, "Automated Information Management: Is There A Role for the Archivist in the Office of the Future?" *Archivaria* 19 (Winter 1984/85): 162–172 are examples of such writing.

4. Michael Hammer and James Champy, *Reengineering the Corporation: A Manifesto for Business Revolution* (New York: HarperBusiness, 1994), p. 2.
5. Hammer and Champy, *Reengineering the Corporation*, p. 25.
6. Hammer and Champy, *Reengineering the Corporation*, p. 32.
7. Hammer and Champy, *Reengineering the Corporation*, pp. 33–35.
8. Hammer and Champy, *Reengineering the Corporation*, p. 49.
9. Hammer and Champy, *Reengineering the Corporation*, p. 90.
10. Hammer and Champy, *Reengineering the Corporation*, p. 105.
11. Hammer and Champy, *Reengineering the Corporation*, p. 51.
12. Hammer and Champy, *Reengineering the Corporation*, p. 64.
13. Hammer and Champy, *Reengineering the Corporation*, p. 71.
14. David Osborne and Ted Gaebler, *Reinventing Government: How the Entrepreneurial Spirit is Transforming the Public Sector* (New York: Plume Books, 1992), p. xix.
15. Osborne and Gaebler, *Reinventing Government*, pp. 11–12.
16. Osborne and Gaebler, *Reinventing Government*, p. 14.
17. Osborne and Gaebler, *Reinventing Government*, p. 15.
18. Osborne and Gaebler, *Reinventing Government*, pp. 19-20.
19. Osborne and Gaebler, *Reinventing Government*, p. 34.
20. Osborne and Gaebler, *Reinventing Government*, p. 43.
21. Osborne and Gaebler, *Reinventing Government*, p. 47.
22. Osborne and Gaebler, *Reinventing Government*, p. 139.
23. Osborne and Gaebler, *Reinventing Government*, p. 141.
24. Osborne and Gaebler, *Reinventing Government*, p. 38.
25. Osborne and Gaebler, *Reinventing Government*, p. 110.
26. Osborne and Gaebler, *Reinventing Government*, p. 114.
27. Osborne and Gaebler, *Reinventing Government*, p. 130.
28. Osborne and Gaebler, *Reinventing Government*, p. 131.
29. Osborne and Gaebler, *Reinventing Government*, p. 135.
30. Osborne and Gaebler, *Reinventing Government*, p. 168.
31. Osborne and Gaebler, *Reinventing Government*, p. 222.
32. Osborne and Gaebler, *Reinventing Government*, p. 250.
33. David Bearman and Margaret Hedstrom, "Reinventing Archives for Electronic Records: Alternative Service Delivery Options," in *Electronic Records Management Program Strategies,* ed. Margaret Hedstrom (Pittsburgh: Archives and Museum Informatics, 1993), pp. 82–98.
34. Claire McInerney, "Knowledge Management and the Dynamic Nature of Knowledge," *Journal of the American Society for Information Science and Technology* 53 (October 2002): 1009.
35. Thomas A. Stewart, *The Wealth of Knowledge: Intellectual Capital and the Twenty-First Century Organization* (New York: Currency, 2001), p. 335.
36. Thomas A. Stewart,. *Intellectual Capital: The New Wealth of Organizations* (New York: Currency Books, 1999), p. xix.
37. Stewart, *The Wealth of Knowledge*, p. 12.
38. Stewart, *Intellectual Capital*, p. 56.
39. Stewart, *Intellectual Capital*, p. 71.
40. Stewart, *Intellectual Capital*, p. 78.

41. Stewart, *The Wealth of Knowledge*, p. 13.
42. Jay Atherton, "From Life Cycle to Continuum: Some Thoughts on the Records Management-Archives Relationship," *Archivaria* 21 (Winter 1985–86): 44.
43. Stewart, *Intellectual Capital*, p. xxiii.
44. Stewart, *The Wealth of Knowledge*, p. 5.
45. Jan Duffy, *Harvesting Experience: Reaping the Benefits of Knowledge* (Prairie Village, KS: ARMA International, 1999), p. 12.
46. Susan Myburgh, "Knowledge Management and Records Management: Is There a Difference?," *Records & Information Management Report* 14 (September 1998): 13.
47. Elizabeth Yakel, "Knowledge Management: The Archivist's and Records Manager's Perspective," *Information Management Journal* 34 (July 2000): 26.
48. Yakel, "Knowledge Management," 27.
49. Stewart, *Intellectual Capital*, p. 31.
50. Stewart, *The Wealth of Knowledge*, p. 123.
51. Paul M. Hildreth and Chris Kimble, "The Duality of Knowledge," *Information Research* 8 (October 2002), available at http://informationr.net/ir/8-1/paper142.html.
52. Stewart, *Intellectual Capital*, p. 48,
53. Stewart, *Intellectual Capital*, p. 51.
54. Stewart, *Intellectual Capital*, p. 95.
55. Stewart, *Intellectual Capital*, p. 101.
56. Stewart, *Intellectual Capital*, p. 201.
57. Witold Rybczynski, *The Perfect House: A Journey with the Renaissance Master Andrea Palladio* (New York: Scribner, 2002), p. 9.
58. Stewart, *The Wealth of Knowledge*, p. 128.
59. David G. Blair, "Knowledge Management: Hype, Hope, or Help?" *Journal of the American Society for Information Science and Technology* 53 (October 2002): 1022.
60. Stewart, *Intellectual Capital*, p. 87.
61. Stewart, *The Wealth of Knowledge*, p. 8.
62. Stewart, *The Wealth of Knowledge*, p. 129.
63. Stewart, *The Wealth of Knowledge*, p. 170.
64. McInerney, "Knowledge Management and the Dynamic Nature of Knowledge," p. 1011.
65. Blair, "Knowledge Management: Hype, Hope, or Help?" p. 1022.
66. Bruce W. Dearstyne, "Knowledge Management: Concepts, Strategies, and Prospects," *Records & Information Management Report* 15 (September 1999): 12.
67. Stewart, *Intellectual Capital*, p. 149.
68. Frances Bouthillier and Kathleen Shearer, "Understanding Knowledge Management and Information Management: The Need for an Empirical Perspective," *Information Research* 8 (October 2002), available at http://informationr.net/ir/8-1/paper141.html.
69. Atherton, "From Life Cycle to Continuum," p. 48.

70. Atherton, "From Life Cycle to Continuum," p. 49.

71. Stewart, *The Wealth of Knowledge*, p. 204.

72. McInerney, "Knowledge Management and the Dynamic Nature of Knowledge," p. 1011.

73. Stewart, *The Wealth of Knowledge*, p. 110.

74. T. D. Wilson, "The Nonsense of 'Knowledge Management,'" *Information Research* 8 (October 2002), available at http://informationr.net/ir/8-1/paper144.html.

75. McInerney, "Knowledge Management and the Dynamic Nature of Knowledge," p. 1016.

8

Records, Documents, and Stuff in the Digital Era

INTRODUCTION

Let's start with the obvious. We have access to more information (and records, however defined) today than at any other time. One historian states, rather casually, "Per person, we consume about 20,000 times as much reading material as our medieval ancestors."[1] Some translate such statistics into a characteristic of our modern era as *The* Information Age, and others suggest that somehow we are better off for all this information than we were before. Given the general propensity to believe in a Western notion of progress—where with our faith in technocratic and scientific solutions we believe that the more information we have the better off we are and the better we will continually get—it is obvious why so many grab onto the idea that we are living in a grand and glorious era in which we can muster all of human knowledge to solve virtually any problem or challenge confronting society and its institutions. Winifred Gallagher, in her book about her search for the divine, believes that "For most of history, there were no hard lines between the intellectual, emotional, and spiritual."[2] The promises of our present technocratic age seem to be erasing the lines once again, except that technology has become god and information the divine message. Even records professionals, often contending with seemingly mundane matters, sometimes fall prey to seeking technological solutions to problems that are more moral, ethical, economic, or cultural.

As a faculty member in a school of information sciences, observers might expect that I could muster a much more precise explanation for what this present age (the Digital Era with greater and easier access to information) means and offers or at least some scientific or formulaic definition of information. For sure, the twentieth century was one in which we saw varying explanations for information, such as the formulations offered via the documentalists, information theorists, cybernauts, information scientists, and so forth.[3] What I am discussing and arguing about here concerns my own work, my professional calling, and my livelihood. There are fallacies with this approach.

Margaret Atwood, poet and novelist, notes, "Even if we are writers ourselves, it is very hard for us to watch ourselves in mid-write, as it were: our attention must be focused then on what we are doing, not on ourselves."[4] I am trying to do both, ruminating about my work in mid-work in a manner intended to provide some self-reflection about the notion of information in the Information Age. As it turns out, trying to assess the nature of information in an age we have termed as being demarcated by information itself might be an impossible task, if not an improbable one. Perhaps, trying to mull over information through the teaching one does in a school of information studies in the so-called Information Age might be an even more ludicrous assignment. Of course, it is an assignment I have given myself.

There are other reasons why this has become a difficult task. Bill Stumpf, renowned designer, draws on the Dutch historian Johan Huizinga to remind us how "not to forget how much we have sanitized natural experiences. We are warm in winter, cool in summer, we light up the night and darken the day. Our technology has allowed us to separate the visceral reactions from the experience producing these reactions."[5] We are like the frogs slowly and unconsciously heated in a pot of water in our high school biology classes. Words are everywhere, books pour from the publishers, Web sites proliferate at an immense rate, the television news programs and talk shows run twenty-four hours a day, and e-mail piles up on our desktops. In such a time, how we gain, read, and think about information is crucial. The issue is not how much information we have, but how we use it and how it helps us function in the real world. And for this, we have immense quantities of articles, books, software, and advice trying to guide us.

And, now, let me add a few thousand more words to the cacophony of opinions, assuring you that this is what academics do best. Lewis Lapham, editor of *Harper's*, senses that "we assign to education the powers that other societies award to religion, the word itself invested with so many meanings that it can be confused with Aladdin's lamp, made to serve as synonym for the way out and ticket home, offered as an answer to every mother's prayer."[6] I don't think I am offering the way home or a ticket out, but rather I am describing what my own road map seems to indicate about traveling in the present Information Age. Ironically, education has been one of the weaker aspects of the records community, with archivists having only in the past couple of decades established small (by university standards) graduate programs and with records managers still reliant more on continuing education and post-appointment forms of training. One must wonder whether the underpinning of the records community is as substantial as it should be, or, at least, sufficiently defined so as to withstand the constantly changing winds that characterize the digital era.

PARADOXES OF THE DIGITAL ERA

Let me provide my perspective on the great and reigning paradoxes of our age of information wealth. My professional affiliation is that of the archivist—the professional responsible for selecting, preserving, and making available the portion of the documentary heritage that has continuing (some would say enduring) value to society, its citizens, and its organizations. If you carefully study the writings of both the theorists and practitioners (those who write) in my field, you will find a curious trait. Every commentator on the nature of records and recordkeeping laments the quantity of records created, and many of these commentators suggest a range of guiding theories and methods by which to manage the documentary universe. It is also not difficult to find critics of the "too many records" syndrome, whether they are lambasting government waste and inefficient bureaucracy or simply observing how much paper piles up in offices and homes.

Likewise, we can find many critics, pundits, and others who write about the wonders and challenges of our modern Information Age. While it is relatively easy to break these observers into camps of either complainants about too much information or predictors or proponents of the saving virtues of readily accessible information, more than ever before and cheaper than ever before, all groups readily acknowledge that we are immersed in information in unprecedented fashion. At the least, we recognize that the new information technologies of the past decade have transformed American governance and society, with extremely mixed results, both increasing access to more information about our government, institutions, and society while simultaneously making some aspects of our lives much more difficult than ever before.

Haynes Johnson's discussion of these technologies and the O. J. Simpson trial, the Clinton political scandals, and corporate influences on society provides some interesting insights into the contradictions of the vast potential of the information technologies with how those technologies are used.[7] At the same time, we must recognize that our immersion in these modern technologies tends to have us assign them greater revolutionary significance than we should. Deborah Spar recently argued, "Cyberspace is indeed a brave new world, but it's not the only new world. There have been other moments in time that undoubtedly felt very much like the present era, other moments when technology raced faster than governments and called forth whole new markets and social structures. Other entrepreneurs sensed that, they, too, were standing on the edge of history, bending authority to their will and reaping fabulous profits along the way."[8] Todd Gitlin, more caustically, notes that the "centrality of media is disguised, in part, by the prevalence of the assured, hard-edged phrase *information society*, or, even more grandly, *information age*. Such terms are instant propaganda for a way of life that is also a way of progress. . . . *Information society* glows with a positive aura. The very term *information* points to a gift—specific and ever replenished, shining forth in the bright light of utility. Ignorance is not bliss . . . information is."[9] How many times have records professionals been duped into thinking that their primary responsibility is information rather than records and their evidence, sometimes through appeals and promises about enhanced status, greater visibility, and better compensation (all of which can be serious problems).

There is obviously a ready connection between these groups and an obvious reason why archivists, and their colleagues such as records managers, have an important role in the Information or Digital Age. A large portion of what holds information is represented by records, and a substantial amount of these records remain of traditional types—letters, receipts, checks, licenses, diaries, to name only some—and these appear now in both analog and digital forms. We are also seeing new kinds of records, such as Web sites, reports with audio-visual and constantly updated statistics, and other complex records with infinite possibilities and problems. However, what really holds the attention of Information Age pundits and the critics of bureaucratic documentation may be that their concerns are eternal.

A half-century ago, the scholar Jacques Barzun observed that "every age has carried with it great loads of information . . . deemed indispensable at the time."[10] When we look at the abundance of modern records and the flood of contemporary information, we are simply too close to our sense of the documents to comprehend that others looking out over the documentary universe in 2000 or 1950 or 1850 or 1750, or at anytime before, might have had the same sense of euphoria or melancholy about what they observed. A photograph of an old industrial building with the sign 'information' over its door given to me by a student, shows a building from an early industrial site." Even a hundred years ago, information was important enough to be featured in a separate building at the entrance of an industrial complex. People needed information even then to navigate among the various buildings, to find a particular individual, or to deliver a product or package. If the site was still an active one, we might expect it to have an information kiosk with a Web directory and GIS-guided maps and directories; and, someday, too, these might sit vacant, a relic of an earlier age and different hopes and sensibilities. We might wonder, as well, what kinds of records were stored and used in that building and where those records have gone.

Despite the great widening notion of information objects, artifacts, or documents, we also see immense paradoxes in our Information or Digital Age. In the midst of high-tech, flashy new concepts of documents that talk, read, and sing to us and blink and wink to sell, convince, and amuse us, we have seen a new sensitivity to the importance of very traditional records, many still kept as paper forms and housed in file cabinets and records center storage cartons. The story of the use of government archives and banking records (along with the opening of vast quantities of formerly classified records in both government and non-government entities like museums and libraries) in the Holocaust assets case has elevated the public's understanding of the importance of even the most routine of the most bureaucratic seeming records.

Stuart Eizenstat's powerful book about this provides a window into what we see happening. He comments in a number of places about the opening of the records and data banks of eleven federal agencies, noting how such cooperation is unusual: "The project demonstrated the awesome resources the U.S. executive branch can muster when it receives presidential backing. I was amazed at the powerful story that was emerging by drawing from the data banks of these different federal agencies."[11] Eizenstat relates that about a million records were declassified, the "largest single declassification in U.S. history."[12] At other points in the book, Eizenstat contrasts the cooperation and openness of the American federal government with the reluctance of many corporations and institutions and other national governments to open records or even to admit that they had records. Still, he relates that one of the project's successes was in ultimately seeing twenty-eight historical commissions established around the world to open other archives, a stellar achievement in the importance of open government and attesting to the significance of records. Eizenstat believes that the "most lasting legacy of the effort [he] led was simply the emergence of the truth. . . . Historical facts can be suppressed, but eventually they bubble to the surface. What started as a tiny trickle from long-buried U.S. archives became a torrent of information that helps provide a final accounting for World War II."[13]

And we can see such comments, about numerous other cases, reflecting on the essential importance of records to society, especially in holding governments, corporations, public officials, the media, and other entities and groups accountable to society.[14] We only have to consider the case of the Enron/Arthur Andersen scandals and the dramatic stories of the shredding of Enron's records. The normally hurried efforts to destroy bureaucratic choking paper and other records were cast in another light, where "Enron failed because its leadership was morally, ethically, and financially corrupt."[15]

In Enron's case, we find false financial books cooked up to hide questionable activities; adoption of accounting procedures intended to favor certain kinds of risky speculative behavior and to inflate the sense of financial profits intended to produce raises and bonuses; the buying off of the auditors to look the other way; reports fabricated in ways to make them difficult to understand and allowing a range of interpretations; and a host of other strange and wonderful activities with multiple implications for what corporate records managers and archivists will face in their future work. The information buried in formerly mundane records suddenly looked much more important and critical than as a mere by-product of large corporations and excessive government regulations. Where are the records professionals in such organizations, with their professional codes of ethics, in this age of the celebrated whistleblower?

An essential paradox of our present age is, however, that we see the vocal advocates of the power of information and the technologies supporting the use of information often depicting traditional records as either bureaucratic obstacles needing to be reengineered or reinvented out of the way, or as objects that are far too limited in their analog, cumbersome state. The Information Age pundits conjure up pictures of inefficiency, ineptitude, waste, and other such obvious barriers—all serious matters—with the promise that new hardware and software will solve these problems or that these challenges will be resolved by the creation of new kinds of documents. The chief problem with such promises is, however, that concerns such as accountability are usually not part of the equation.

The activities of the Third Reich or Enron, admittedly far apart in the degree of evil represented, were not factored in; governments and businesses would simply use the best information technologies in rational and orderly manners. How many times have you talked with a vendor promising you the world, until you asked some very specific questions about long-term maintenance, how the system enables you to keep the organization or yourself compliant with external regulations and best practices, or other such concerns? There is substantial evidence that both the long dreamed of idea of the paperless office is only that, a dream, and that the promise that the computer will bring greater efficiency is also still only a promise.[16]

The paradoxes go much deeper and are much more blatant. The advent of the Internet has been heralded with promises of greater access to information, more open organizations, easier methods of working in organizations with professionals working from home or anywhere, and stronger democratic societies in which citizens have more information and greater opportunities for influencing their elected and appointed officials.[17] The reality has been somewhat different. It can be a mistake to believe that the modern information technologies are no more intrusive than those of earlier eras, or that there may not be something distinctive about this particular information age. There have been invasions on privacy and the quality of life.

There are, for example, immense differences in the modern workplace related to or caused by information technologies. A recent study on the corporate workplace notes that the "overwork, stress, and insecurity of today's workplaces has been exacerbated, not relieved, by the proliferation of high-tech equipment—laptop computers, cell phones, electronic desk calendars, beepers, portable fax machines, Palm Pilots, and more—that help people try to keep up with growing workloads while also making it impossible for them to fully escape their jobs and rules. New technologies, meanwhile, facilitate intrusive efforts by employers to monitor everything from their staffers' comings and goings to computerized keystrokes and mouse taps, e-mails sent and received, and personal productivity on a weekly, daily, or even hour-by-hour basis."[18]

It gets worse. After a decade of opening up government records, we have seen a severe closing down of records, post-September 11, 2001, in the name of national security (even though many of the activities to shut down access to records seems to be only peripherally related to security matters). At the beginning of this year the *New York Times* ran a long, chilling front page news story by Adam Clymer about how the current Bush administration is clamping down on the access to its records. Clymer provided an accounting of all of the various steps taken by this administration and reasons why such actions are underway and the picture was not an attractive one: "Some of the Bush policies, like closing previously public court proceedings, were prompted by the Sept. 11 terrorist attacks and are part of the administration's drive for greater domestic security. Others, like Vice President Dick Cheney's battle to keep records of his energy task force secret, reflect an administration that arrived in Washington determined to strengthen the authority of the executive branch, senior administration officials say."[19]

Another recent report confirms such problems. Jack Nelson's study on government secrecy describes how the Bush administration has set an "all-time record" for classifying records, coupled with such sponsored legislation as the Patriot Act, the Homeland Security Information Act, and the Homeland Security Act. Nelson describes the history of such secrecy, dating back to the First World War, but he focuses primarily on the very recent past because of the greater intensity of government efforts to be more secret and to stop-up leaks. The most interesting description of activities relates to an unofficial government body named the "Dialogue," a group of media executives and government officials brought together to try and discuss the nature of information leaks and their role in a democratic state. "Dialogue" has been meeting for the past year, and it seems to have made some positive steps in convincing government officials that harsher actions taken against individuals who may leak information is counter to how a democratic society works and, in fact, the efforts to cease leaks may be impossible and cause damage to the work of the administration and government agencies.[20]

MORE PARADOXES: RECORDS AND DOCUMENTS

One of the more interesting paradoxes, for me at least, has been the nearly simultaneous narrowing of the notion of record and the broadening of the concept of document in this age of the ubiquitous computer and growing faith in technology. If nothing else, these contrasts point to the wild frontier that is cyberspace.

Archivists and other records professionals have worked with electronic information technologies for more than three decades, and while there is still a great deal of consternation about just how successful the preservation and maintenance of electronic records systems has been, there are obvious discernible features of the processes involved in confronting such challenges. In the 1960s, most archivists either ignored what were then called machine-readable records (since these were mostly large-scale statistical databases) or more adamantly declared the early electronic records to be non-records and, therefore, not their responsibility. Within a decade, as the personal computer took over, such attitudes changed and archivists and records managers knew that they needed to expand their horizons and that they needed to be in the game. Debates followed about the nature of archival theory and knowledge, calls for practical case studies and the subsequent appearance of how-to manuals, expressions of the need for research and stronger partnerships with both the creators of records and the creators of the hard- and software, and some research into the challenges and nature of electronic records management.[21]

Most of the research, all with a heavy bit of theorizing as well, has led to efforts to more precisely define records.[22] In the major research project I was involved with, we concluded that records were the products of business transactions, that each record must possess a structure, content, and context in order to be a complete record, and that each record was the result of a warrant (deriving from legal, fiscal, or acceptable best practices).[23] Another research project, drawing on the older science of diplomatics, came up with a much more restricted notion of record: "When a record is said to be trustworthy, it means that it is both an accurate statement of facts and a genuine manifestation of those facts. Record trustworthiness thus has two qualitative dimensions: *reliability* and *authenticity*. Reliability means that the record is capable of standing for the facts to which it attests, while authenticity means that the record is what it claims to be."[24]

One of the primary investigators in this latter project defines an electronic record, presenting its components (medium, content, physical form, intellectual form, action, persons, archival bond, and context), and arguing that "electronic records possess essentially the same components as traditional records," but "with electronic records, these components are not inextricably joined to one another as they are in traditional records" but are "stored and managed separately as metadata . . .", all of these needing to be used to "embed procedural rules for creating, handling, and maintaining such records in an agency-wide records system, and to integrate documentary procedures with business processes."[25] In such projects, we can readily see that in order to manage records as precise objects they need to be defined as precisely as possible to enable their requirements to be engineered into the software.

While such interesting projects in the archival and records management corner of the information professions have been going on, other information professionals have been expanding the notion of the information document. David Levy and John Seely Brown and Paul Duguid in their recent books provide the best glimpse of the broader sense of a document. David Levy argues that documents are "bits of the material world—clay, stone, animal skin, plant fiber, sand—that we've imbued with the ability to speak."[26] These things are fixed, they can be repeated, and they are essential to the social order.

Out of such writings comes a very broad concept of a document that is fitting to the expansive landscape that is cyberspace and beyond. Documents are cultural artifacts, the adhesiveness for community, imbued with symbolic value and power, representative of other activities, full of content, responsible for performing a task, and both fluid and fixed (depending on their medium). As Levy very poetically muses, a document is a "surrogate, a little sorcerer's apprentice, to whom a piece of work has been delegated."[27]

Brown, Duguid, and Levy are all trying to rein in, to some degree, what is the main building block of the Information Age. Still, it is relatively easy to surmise that the archivist's or records manager's notion of a record is, at best, a subset of the concept of document as it is now being more popularly used. This is certainly not a problem. Indeed, if we tried to diagram the universe of information along with the various information professions, we would readily discern that there are many other disciplinary groups (librarians, museum curators, information scientists, knowledge managers) in addition to archivists and records managers who have carved out a niche of that universe. Each of these groups has developed different means to define or assess an aspect of information, and it is when we think more broadly that we begin to see another fuzzy and challenging aspect of what we are dealing with in our particular information era.

INFORMATION EVERYWHERE

An amusing aspect of being a professor in a school of information sciences and being part of what we call the information professions is to be on the front line of what remains continuing and confusing discussions about what *information* is and how the various information disciplines array themselves. I have followed listserv discussions whereby information scientists viciously attack the concept of *knowledge* as used by knowledge managers even though there are hundreds of definitions of information, a phenomenon that I suspect students of social interaction, if not ethics and religion, would be best at explaining. Many of my library and information science colleagues wonder why I am buzzing around and discussing concepts like evidence as manifested by records and which are important for purposes such as accountability, corporate memory, and social memory. At best what holds us together (and sometimes this is very tenuous) is that we (the disparate faculty members) are convinced of the importance of information to improve the performance and quality of society, the life of its citizens, and its institutions. While we have many different perspectives about how information is defined or we focus on different elements of information, we all share a commitment that information is critical to life as well as a commonsense notion that information needs to be managed, preserved, accessible, protected, reliable, and processed in forms that are practical.

One of the values of the Levy and Brown-Duguid models of documents is that they both open up the possibility of cutting across the diverse disciplinary orientations to information and provide a common notion (even if it is somewhat imagined) that can unite all who are working in the somewhat amorphous information-knowledge management realms. For teaching purposes, it actually breaks open the more rigid quantitative or qualitative measures of information that are often assumed by library and information scientists, broadening the students' world to see that information is not something that is confined to a record, a book, an archives, or a library, but that it is something we are all immersed in.

I have used the information document notion as a unifying theme in my version of one of the core courses (Understanding Information) for our Masters in Library and Information Science degree, where students are intended to gain knowledge about the responsibilities of the information professionals, comprehend the complexities of information in modern society, and understand how the various notions of information affect or should affect the work of any information professional. Course objectives include defining the nature of information, providing historic background on the nature of information systems, orienting students to concepts of information systems, integrating views of the physical and virtual library and other information providers, orienting students to technology issues related to information systems, making students aware of professional issues, making students aware of human factors influencing information systems, providing an orientation to information services, and providing an awareness of social, economic, political, and other issues affecting information systems. Students learn about some obvious information documents (obvious to people planning to work in a library or archives) such as books, records, newspapers, photographs, and maps, but they are also asked to explore other information documents such as movies, artifacts, monuments, landscape, and buildings. The last information document we consider is the Web page, a place that most of the younger students seem to see as both the beginning and end of the essence of information or documents.

These are all things we read, or to adopt some of the language of experts like Levy, these are all things that speak to us. We tend to assign document-like characteristics to many artifacts or objects. Geologist Robert Thorson's book on New England's stone walls commences, "Abandoned stone walls are the signatures of rural New England." These "stone walls have an important story to tell." Thorson adds, "A stone pulled from an authentic New England wall speaks, all at once, of ancient seas, glacial mud, and the tip of a scythe being broken during spring mowing a century ago."[28] We can "read" all sorts of things. Alberto Manguel's discourse on reading pictures notes "I would say that if looking at pictures is equivalent to reading, then it is a vastly creative form of reading, a reading in which we must not only put words into sounds into sense but images into sense into stories." In other words, reading pictures can be complex and confusing. Pictures provide stories, riddles, witnesses, nightmares, reflections, philosophies, memories, theatrical performances, and the like, sometimes all at once or sometimes bits at a time as experienced by different individuals at different times and in different cultures.[29]

Reading these documents is a complicated and challenging process, for sure, but every aspect of the effort involves some aspect of what can be termed "information." The Irish historian R. F. Foster describes a visit to a country estate where he was doing research; he encountered a late-nineteenth century story about the reluctance to cut down an old tree because it was "unlucky." When some workers finally agreed to remove the tree, they discovered it was "densely peppered with lead." Foster continues: "The tree stood for more than bad luck. In the 1798 Rising, particularly bloody [in the area of the estate], local rebels had been tied to the tree and shot. The memory persisted, and the taboo: the actual association was suppressed, whether for reasons of tactfulness or trauma. Or both."[30] There was, then, something to the tree's story that allowed its deciphering, in this case, the unraveling of memory and legend back to a particular incident.

Brown and Duguid, in their interesting analysis, worry that the "myth of information . . . is overpowering richer explanations," whereby we have a "tunnel vision" or "infocentric" explanation to everything primarily associated (such as computers and the Web) with the Information Age.[31] Kicking open a broader array of information documents helps students, and me, to comprehend that every age, every socioeconomic group, every culture is part of an information culture. For sure, the high-powered computer networks, massive digitization projects, the pervasive daily dumping of e-mail messages are all part of something that seems unique to our times, but it is certain that most people in other eras believed themselves to be immersed in information in very similar ways.

Michael Pollan describes reading books in this way: "Rather than a means to an end, the deep piles of words on the page comprised for me a kind of soothing environment, a plush cushion into which sometimes I would remember almost nothing the moment I lifted myself out of the newspaper or magazine or paperback in which I'd been immersed. . . . Mostly I just let the print wash over me, as if it were indeed warm water, destined to swirl down the drain of my forgetfulness."[32] In the same way, we are surrounded by objects that can be read (sometimes literally, sometimes figuratively). We must, for example, learn that museum exhibitions are "fundamentally theatrical, for they are how museums perform the knowledge they create."[33] We learn to read the weather: "Weather writes, erases and rewrites itself upon the sky with the endless fluidity of language; and it is with language that we have sought throughout history to apprehend it. Since the sky has always been more read than measured, it has always been the province of words."[34]

Monuments or memorials, with or without texts, are the "most traditional kind of memory object or technology,"[35] and as a result they have to be learned to be read and re-read. Landscapes are covered in texts, but they can also be read as texts even if no words are evident. Surveying Antebellum New York, David Henkin notes, "writing and print appeared on buildings, sidewalks, sandwich-board advertisements, the pages of personal diaries, classroom walls, Staffordshire pottery, needlepoint samples, election tickets, and two-dollar bills, to name just a few locations and contexts."[36] Looking over our contemporary cityscape, Dolores Hayden sees that "urban landscapes are storehouses for these social memories, because natural features such as hills or harbors, as well as streets, buildings, and patterns of settlement, frame the lives of many people and often outlast many lifetimes."[37]

We could continue this exercise of considering just how far-reaching the scope of information documents is, and how this provides perhaps a richer context for considering the salient features of the Information Age. Suffice it to say that my students now grasp that understanding information, and hence the nature of the current era, is more complicated than they thought before considering the broader array of documents. In addition to the information documents I presented, students considered diaries, nutritional labels on food products, poetry, tattoos, pictograms, oral tradition and storytelling, music recording liner notes, personal names, advertisements, cookbooks, county courthouses, the family snapshot photograph, zines, and comic books (in their own research projects) as other document forms.

Their papers added to a rich discussion, enabling us to see that the world, for generations and across cultures, has been distinguished by information eras. Robert Darnton reminds us that France in the mid-eighteenth century was also an information society—"we imagine the Old Regime as a simple, tranquil, media-free world-we-have-lost, a society with no telephones, no television, no e-mail, Internet, and all the rest. In fact, however, it was not a simple world at all. It was merely different. It had a dense communication network made up of media and genres that have been forgotten"[38]—and we can demonstrate how nearly every era has been one in which information plays a crucial defining role.

SAVING EVERYTHING: RETHINKING SOME BASIC TENETS OF EDUCATING RECORDS AND INFORMATION MANAGEMENT PROFESSIONALS

One result of seeing all this information and believing that information technology is the defining metaphor for our present Information or Digital Age is to come to believe that we must also be able to save everything. It may be that we need to expand our notions of information away from the purely scientific or theoretical to a much more practical, working definition or concept. Just as scholars are working the treasures of eBay because they find materials they do not believe are held in most archival or library repositories, information scholars and professionals probably need to expand how they research, write, and teach about information. One commentator writes, "Academic sleuths once relied almost exclusively on the archives of major research libraries to track down facts and colorful details. Now, historians, literary critics, and museum archivists across the country incorporate a regular search of eBay into their research routine." This assessment continues, "Overall, the availability on eBay of historical objects and ephemera from Americans' attics has given scholars access to information that traditionally has been ignored by major research institutions."[39]

All this makes sense. It is, however, quite something else to think that we can save everything found on eBay because of its potential information value. Archivists, records managers, and other information professionals are waking up to such challenges. One archivist from South Africa notes, "Even if archivists in a particular country were to preserve every record generated throughout the land, they would still have only a sliver of a window into that country's experience."[40] We can probably say this about the task of saving all print and digital information as well; it is only a miniscule part of all human experience and for sure only a minor portion of all documents that can be read in some fashion.

A few years ago most of us would have laughed at even the possibility that anybody would posit the notion that everything with some information content or value must be preserved. We would have thought it hilarious that someone might have decided that not only should everything be saved but that it must be saved in its original format. Then along came novelist and literary essayist Nicholson Baker and his *Double Fold* bombshell. The media took to his rambling, saber-rattling, conspiratorial diatribe like a duck to water. Laudatory review after laudatory review appeared, and in short order the word got out that librarians and archivists were destroyers, that they were violating a sacred covenant with the public, and that preservation administrators and conservators alike were willing accomplices in the destruction of our documentary heritage.[41] We were all vandals in the stacks, as the *New York Times Book Review* dramatically portrayed on the cover of its issue reviewing the controversial Baker book.

The purpose of understanding information and the documents that constitute and convey information is to comprehend that the universe of documentation is so large that not everything can or should be saved. As an educator of archivists and records managers, members of professional groups who cleave quite closely to the notion of highly selective appraisal approaches and results, I work to help their future colleagues perceive that even every record with archival value might not be able to be saved. The understanding of the archivist and the records manager derives from his or her knowledge about records and recordkeeping systems. Likewise, the reason that we teach a course like "understanding information" is to assist students to grasp that information and the information documents are multitudinous, complex, fragile, ubiquitous, redundant, and constantly expanding in size, scope, variety, and nature. By understanding the kinds of information documents that society builds on, we can begin to understand the kinds of decisions that must be made about how to manage the information and its supporting technologies.

The challenge for a library and information science educator is, of course, that these schools are often easily caught up in the hype of the information age. We (the faculty) can become believers of the importance of information as the crux of what makes society function. We can become technocrats, immersing people into the nature of tools as if these tools and the requisite skills to use them are the only critical matters. Over the years, library and information science programs pushed out rare books and history of printing courses in order to accommodate more courses on information technology, partly to grab onto the revenue gravy train of funding agencies and partly out of belief that the printed book was dying and digital information was to replace everything.

Now, schools are finding that they need to introduce new courses because the book persists and, just as importantly, because the e-book demands its historical context if we are to understand what it represents. In order to value the true worth of the present era and the growth and wonders of the World Wide Web, we must be able to place it as well into its historical context. Otherwise, we become prey to every new fad, gimmick, buzzword, and trite trend that run in newspaper and television advertisements promising a kind of digital salvation. Our schools often do not educate the next generation of information professionals; they seem merely to turn out unquestioning people who lack the big picture and the skills to be problem solvers, critical analysts, and wise leaders.

While it is critical for us to understand that we acquire information from multitudinous sources, we also must recognize that certain of these sources assume different levels of importance because of what they document. The memory of the destruction of the Congo and its people by King Leopold II of Belgium in the late-nineteenth and early-twentieth centuries was nearly eradicated because of the deliberate destruction of the state archives by Leopold and his officials. Oral tradition and other eyewitness accounts did not compensate for the loss of the records, or, at least, did not keep memory of these events alive and vital.[42] What Leopold did was a deliberate act of wanton destruction, a kind of informational genocide as well as the more traumatic real kind. If we persist in believing all the promises and hype of the Information Age, we will inadvertently destroy the critical information documents and documentary heritage of our own generation.

Yes, these are exciting, complex, and trying times, and information professionals (including archivists and records managers) have a very important role to play in their society and culture—if we can get our collective minds and disciplines wrapped about the primary questions and issues. One university professor, commenting on the purpose of higher education, argued for a "more holistic approach to learning, a disciplinary training for people who teach in college that takes into account the fact that we are educators of whole human beings, a form of higher education that would take responsibility to the emergence of an integrated person."[43] This is especially difficult in a school of information sciences, where tools and numbers and rhetoric can easily get in the way of teaching the full dimensions of information use and nature in our lives, places of work, and society.

We need to not just manipulate and massage information, but to *understand* it. Information, no matter how good it is or how much, is meaningless without understanding. Otherwise, we are just playing with lots of stuff, and the people and organizations relying on records and documents for evidence, accountability, and memory will be lost in cyberspace. Novelist and science fiction writer Bruce Sterling writes about technology in our Information Age, arguing that "Technology never leaps smoothly from height to height of achievement; that's just technohype, it's for the rubes. In the real world, technology ducks, dodges, and limps."[44] For Sterling (and for me), both the present and the future are messy and complex, and the roles that information plays in all this just as messy and complex. As an information professional and the educator of information professionals, I have to convey to my students and colleagues, both in the academy and in the field, that these complexities are what makes our tasks both so important and so interesting. The sheer bulk of information tests and taunts us, and I love it. And when I discover that another individual fifty or a hundred or more years ago also struggled with the same challenges, I am reassured that the records, documents, and stuff of our present digital era are worth even more attention and care, connecting us both to the past and the future while serving the needs of the present.

In a fascinating history of the compass, Amir Aczel gives us a glimpse into the complexities of understanding information. Aczel writes, "Ancient mariners were astute observers—their trade was not only a science, it was an art." A mariner "would use all the tools available to him—astronomical observations, soundings, estimation of the directions of winds and currents, and even the directions followed by migrating animals—to guide his ship as close as possible to its destination. Once the coastline was sighted, he would use his knowledge of the terrain to correct the vessel's heading accordingly and guide it into port."[45] Likewise, we need to use all of our faculties to bear on understanding information and the nature of our present era. Are we really very different from those of a century, five centuries, or a thousand years ago in our reliance on both information and the technologies that support its creation and use? Yes, the technologies are different, and they pose new possibilities as well as problems, but how we best use information may still be as much a factor of cultural, economic, political, and other dimensions as anything else, necessitating us to be "astute observers" as well. Many worry that we are being numbed by all of the information out there, but I hope my students, at least, take away with them a greater appreciation of information and its present age. I hope the tool my colleagues and I give them is the counterpart of the compass for the Information Age.

CONCLUSION

Archivists and records managers often walk away from discussions such as this wondering about their relevance for basic, applied work in the trenches that are real organizations. Without a firm grounding in thinking about the nature of records and information, the concept of the Information or Digital Age, the relationship between the confusing array of various information professions, and basic values of and objectives for archives and records management, it will be hard to be clear and precise without our own organizations. Here are some practical points that I think emerge from such reflections:

- We cannot take for granted that the importance of records is understood.
- We cannot take for granted that all the attention devoted to information encompasses records.
- Information Age hype often brings no clear focus on the experts (professionals) responsible for managing the information and most certainly the records.
- Professional differences and schisms between archivists and records or knowledge managers and others are not comprehended outside the narrow circles of these professional guilds.
- It is easier to pontificate about the wonders and powers of information technologies than it is to harness these technologies into meaningful administrative processes for creating, administering, maintaining, and accessing information (including the evidence contained in records).
- The same technologies promising organizations and societies renewed freedom from the perils of managing information and records also generate new and sometimes more complex challenges.
- Human nature is such that we need to maintain a focus on the seemingly simpler aims of managing records for accountability, evidence, and corporate or social memory.
- Having a lot of records and information is not the same as understanding what these records and information tell us.

These, and other concerns, if neglected or botched, certainly will undermine the effectiveness of the work of any archivist or records manager within an organization.

ENDNOTES

1. John Man, *Alphabeta: How 26 Letters Shaped the Western World* (New York: John Wiley & Sons, 2000), p. 14.
2. Winifred Gallagher, *Working on God* (New York: Random House, 1999), p. 55.

3. Ronald E. Day, *The Modern Invention of Information: Discourse, History, and Power* (Carbondale, Ill.: Southern Illinois University Press, 2001).

4   Margaret Atwood, *Negotiating with the Dead: A Writer on Writing* (Cambridge: Cambridge University Press, 2002), p. 55.

5. Bill Stumpf, *The Ice Palace That Melted Away: How Good Design Enhances Our Lives* (Minneapolis: University of Minnesota Press, 1998), p. 9.

6. Lewis H. Lapham, "Study Hall," *Harper's* 303 (September 2001): 9.

7. Haynes Johnson, *The Best of Times: The Boom and Bust Years of America Before and After Everything Changed* (New York: Harcourt, 2002).

8. Deborah Spar, *Ruling the Waves: Cycles of Discovery, Chaos, and Wealth from the Compass to the Internet* (New York: Harcourt, 2001), p. 3.

9. Todd Gitlin, *Media Unlimited: How the Torrent of Images and Sounds Overwhelms Our Lives* (New York: Metropolitan Books, 2001), p. 5.

10. Jacques Barzun, *The House of Intellect* (New York: Perennial Classics, 2002; originally published 1959), p. 12.

11. Stuart E. Eizenstat, *Imperfect Justice: Looted Assets, Slave Labor, and the Unfinished Business of World War II* (New York: Public Affairs, 2003), p. 99.

12. Eizenstat, *Imperfect Justice*, p. 100.

13. Eizenstat, *Imperfect Justice*, p. 346.

14. Richard J. Cox and David A. Wallace, eds., *Archives and the Public Good: Accountability and Records in Modern Society* (Westport, Conn.: Quorum Books, 2002).

15. Robert Bryce, *Pipe Dreams: Greed, Ego, and the Death of Enron* (New York: Public Affairs, 2002), p. 12.

16. Thomas K. Landauer, *The Trouble with Computers: Usefulness, Usability, and Productivity* (Cambridge: MIT Press, 1995); and Abigail J. Sellen and Richard H. R. Harper, *The Myth of the Paperless Office* (Cambridge: MIT, 2001).

17. Howard Rheingold, *Smart Mobs: The Next Social Revolution* (New York: Perseus Books, 2002); *The Virtual Community: Homesteading on the Electronic Frontier* (New York: HarperPerennial, 1993); and *Virtual Reality* (New York: Touchstone Book, 1991).

18. Jill Andresky Fraser, *White-Collar Sweatshop: The Deterioration of Work and Its Rewards in Corporate America* (New York: W. W. Norton, 2001), p. 10.

19. Adam Clymer, "Government Openness at Issue as Bush Holds On to Records," *New York Times*, January 3, 2003.

20. Jack Nelson, *U.S. Government Secrecy and the Current Crackdown on Leaks*, Working Paper Series #2003-1 (Cambridge: The Joan Shorenstein Center on the Press, Politics and Public Policy, Harvard University, 2002).

21. For my views about such matters see my *The First Generation of Electronic Records Archivists in the United States: A Study in Professionalization* (New York: Haworth Press, 1994).

22. See, for example, David Bearman, *Electronic Evidence: Strategies for Managing Records in Contemporary Organizations* (Pittsburgh: Archives and Museum Informatics, 1994); *The Concept of Record: Report from the Second Stockholm Conference on Archival Science and the Concept of Record 30–31 May 1996* (Skrifter utgivna av Riksarkivat 4, 1998); Richard J. Cox, *Managing Records as Evidence and Information* (Westport, Conn.: Quorum Books,

2001); Luciana Duranti, Terry Eastwood, and Heather MacNeil, *Preservation of the Integrity of the Electronic Record* (Dorddrecht: Kluwer Academic, 2003); Trevor Livelton, *Archival Theory, Records, and the Public* (Lanham, Md.: The Society of American Archivists and Scarecrow Press, 1996); Sue McKemmish and Frank Upward, eds., *Archival Documents: Providing Accountability Through Recordkeeping* (Melbourne: Ancora Press, 1993); Heather MacNeil, *Trusting Records: Legal, Historical, and Diplomatic Perspectives* (Dorddrecht: Kluwer Academic, 2000); and Elizabeth Shepherd and Geoffrey Yeo, *Managing Records: A Handbook of Principles and Practice* (London: Facet, 2003).

23. For my summary views of this, see my *Managing Records as Evidence and Information*.

24. MacNeil, *Trusting Records*, p. xi.

25. MacNeil, *Trusting Records*, pp. 96, 98.

26. David M. Levy, *Scrolling Forward: Making Sense of Documents in the Digital Age* (New York: Arcade Publishing, 2001), p. 23; and John Seely Brown and Paul Duguid, *The Social Life of Information* (Boston: Harvard Business School Press, 2000).

27. Levy, *Scrolling Forward*, p. 38.

28. Robert M. Thorson, *Stone by Stone: The Magnificent History in New England's Stone Walls* (New York: Walker, 2002), pp. 1, 9, 229.

29. Alberto Manguel, *Reading Pictures: What We Think About When We Look at Art* (New York: Random House, 2002; originally published 2000), p. 149.

30. R. F. Foster, *The Irish Story: Telling Tales and Making It Up in Ireland* (London: Penguin Books, 2001), p. 211.

31. Brown and Duguid, *The Social Life of Information*, pp. 1, 16, 32.

32. Michael Pollan, *A Place of My Own: The Education of an Amateur Builder* (New York: Random House, 1997), p. 54.

33. Barbara Kirshenblatt-Gimblett, *Destination Culture: Tourism, Museums, and Heritage* (Berkeley: University of California Press, 1998), p. 3.

34. Richard Hamblyn, *The Invention of Clouds: How An Amateur Meterologist Forged the Language of the Skies* (New York: Picador USA/Farrar, Straus and Giroux, 2001), p. 11.

35. Marita Sturken, *Tangled Memories: The Vietnam War, the Aids Experience, and the Politics of Remembering* (Berkeley: University of California Press, 1997), p. 10.

36. David M. Henkin, *City Reading: Written Words and Public Spaces in Antebellum New York* (New York: Columbia University Press, 1998), p. 6.

37. Dolores Hayden, *The Power of Place: Urban Landscapes as Public History* (Cambridge: MIT Press, 1995), p. 9.

38. Robert Darnton, "An Early Information Society: News and the Media in Eighteenth-Century Paris," *American Historical Review* 105 (February 2000), available at http://www.Indiana.edu/~ahr/darnton/.

39. Noel C. Paul, "Scholars Scour eBay," *Christian Science Monitor*, January 14, 2003, available at http://www.csmonitor.com/2003/0114/p11s02-lecs.htm, accessed January 16, 2003.

40. Verne Harris, "The Archival Sliver: A Perspective on the Construction of

Social Memory in Archives and the Transition from Apartheid to Democracy," in *Refiguring the Archive*, ed. Carolyn Hamilton, Verne Harris, Jane Taylor, Michele Pickover, Graeme Reid, and Razia Saleh (Dordrecht: Kluwer Academic, 2002), p. 135.

41. Nicholson Baker, *Double Fold: Libraries and the Assault on Paper* (New York: Random House, 2001); and my response; *Vandals in the Stacks? A Response to Nicholson Baker's Assault on Libraries* (Westport, Conn.: Greenwood Press, 2002).

42. Adam Hochschild, *King Leopold's Ghost: A Story of Greed, Terror and Heroism in Colonial Africa* (Boston: Houghton Mifflin, 1998).

43. Jane Tompkins, *A Life in School: What the Teacher Learned* (Cambridge, MA: Perseus Books, 1996), p. 218.

44. Bruce Sterling, *Tomorrow Now: Envisioning the Next Fifty Years* (New York: Random House, 2002), p. 26.

45. Amir D. Aczel, *The Riddle of the Compass: The Invention That Changed the World* (San Diego: Harcourt, 2001), p. 27.

9

Forming the Records
Professional's Knowledge

INTRODUCTION

We have many versions of when, how, and why the modern archival profession started, traversing from a science of records in the Renaissance; the organization of the first archival associations a century ago; the establishment of the various national archives and their efforts in codifying both practice and the knowledge supporting the practice; influences of the dominant archival theorists and the publication of their writings; and the sociologically determined attributes of professions as a foundation for analysis. Explanations for the start of the archival profession are endless, and consensus elusive.[1]

No matter how we consider the origins of archival professionalism, archival knowledge is critical to our understanding of and appreciation for the work of the archivist. Can anyone be called an archivist who has not mastered the rudiments of archival theory, methodology, and practice encompassing an understanding of records and recordkeeping systems? But, how do we get at the notion of archival knowledge? How we answer that question depends on how we conceive of the archivist's responsibilities in society, where the archivist acquires knowledge, and whether the archivist is part of the vast and ever-changing panoply of information disciplines or a first cousin to the historical scholar (matters that have largely shaped the contour of debate about archival knowledge, identity, and practice for the past half century).

Knowledge is a tricky business, as the recently emerged field of knowledge management suggests. David Snowden, Director of IBM's Institute for Knowledge, writes of knowledge as both a "thing" and a "flow." Building on the work of earlier knowledge management theorists, Snowden identifies four domains of knowledge, one of which is professional and codified in a profession's literature (the others are bureaucratic, informal, and uncharted) and focuses on the challenge of knowledge flow between such domains.[2] Sociologists hold similar views, and Eliot Freidson sees "formal knowledge" as "specialized knowledge that is developed and sustained in institutions of higher education, organized into disciplines, and subject to a process of rationalization. . . .

So delineated, formal knowledge may be found empirically by examining the literature produced by its creators and custodians—the professions' teachers and researchers who are usually located in universities."[3] Freidson reminds us, however, that professionals include "practitioners, administrators, and teacher-researchers,"[4] all with different attitudes about such knowledge and its uses. While the published textbooks are critical, there are always differing views about what they represent, and professional knowledge is constantly in flux as debate about the knowledge continues. Such knowledge is not merely fixed by such publications, but it "lives only through its agents, who themselves employ ideas and techniques selectively as their tasks and perspectives dictate."[5] While this chapter tries to provide an understanding of the formation of archival knowledge through professional literature, such perspectives remind us of the limitations of doing this.

It is important that archivists and other records professionals understand the extent to which they can lay claim to a particular knowledge; the ability to meet their professional objectives may depend on this. While sometimes the debate about aspects of knowledge can be acrimonious, or, in the view of some, superfluous to the nuts and bolts of practice, both the theory and practice *and* the debate about knowledge are essential to working as a professional. As Preben Mortensen recently observed, "archives and archival theory must be understood in their practical context, and that theory and practice cannot be separated."[6] Nevertheless, there seems to be a growing gap between some aspects of archival theory and its application in the real world, perhaps because of growing disparities between professional objectives and the content of the more conceptual components of the professional literature. Brien Brothman, for example, argues that the writings of Jacques Derrida may have been ignored by some archivists because they reject all philosophical orientations, accept a matter-of-fact professionalism built about management science and organizational theory, and find Derrida's works too difficult to understand practically.[7] On the other extreme, Victoria Lemieux argues, "the current body of archival literature fails to meet the needs of working level archivists on several scores. It is particularly weak in terms of suggesting how to operationalize theories and methodologies."[8]

Today, the archival literature captures, even if imperfectly, best practice, research deliberately seeking to add to the knowledge, and the reification of professional knowledge through debate about the literature. Prior to the formation of national archives, archival professional associations, and graduate archival education programs, archival literature was dispersed in content, appearance, and purpose. In North America, until the critical formation of national archives and professional associations, there were no *major* texts, aiming to be comprehensive, published on the nature of archives administration.[9] From the nineteenth century antiquarian-oriented historical societies and the fledgling libraries and museums until after archivists adopted more rigorous elements of disciplines (professional associations, journals, and university-based education) by the eve of the Second World War, practice and experience were the distinguishing marks for archival knowledge. Even today, for many archivists working in the field with minimal educational preparation and only the Internet as a connector to the mainstream activities of a larger archival community, practice and experience remain their chief claim to being an archivist (although the emerging sophistication of an archival knowledge as reflected by the published literature has made this claim more tenuous). Records managers have witnessed similar patterns, just lagging behind what has happened with their archival progenitors.

What follows is an assessment of the formation of archival knowledge in North America, based on the nature of its professional literature. It has some limitations, such as excluding the archival literature published outside of the United States and Canada, while recognizing that some foreign publications (such as the UNESCO RAMP studies and Australia's *Keeping Archives* textbook)[10] have had substantial impact on both theory and practice, especially in the past couple of decades as the field became more legitimately international. Other than a few basic manuals, before 1940 we see only articles and reports on archival topics scattered in a variety of historical and library science journals, internal newsletters, and various government organs. Annual meetings, the proliferation of discipline-specific journals, special conferences, the maturation of the professional associations, and the growth in numbers of practitioners all eventually led to the development of a healthier and more sophisticated knowledge supported by both textbooks and scholarly monographs. By the late 1960s, archivists assumed that their professional literature was eternally expanding, although it was not yet the rich archival knowledge we see at present. These patterns should be familiar to records managers, who have had similar publication patterns and forms.

CHARACTERIZATIONS OF THE PROFESSIONAL KNOWLEDGE

Following the establishment of the National Archives and the Society of American Archivists, professional literature grew slowly (as it did later for records managers after they established their separate professional organization). The primary catalyst for a more robust literature was the *American Archivist*, starting in 1938, although initially it was more a record of professional conferences. Slim volumes on basic preservation and other archival topics appeared—mostly in the form of the U.S. National Archives *Bulletins* on topics that the institution's staff was preoccupied with resolving—but the profession eagerly swept them up and many remain well known and consulted even today.[11] Professional literature was becoming an important source for codifying and sharing experiences about practice, first in the self-reflective volumes on the history of archival and historical manuscripts repositories; later, as records managers would stress stories about the formation of their programs. Individual archivists, sometimes sanctioned by their employing institutions, studied how archival matters were dealt with in other times and places as a means of grappling with current challenges. Concerns about the safety of records due to World War II and the need for management solutions to deal with the unprecedented growth of government and business records led to new kinds of publications that would ultimately be typical of the spin-off field of records management.

Books on building and storage specifications, filing and classification systems, and recommendations for reprographic miniaturization all were noted by archivists, and such works, with their very practical and narrowly focused topics, greatly outnumbered works on archival theory and practice. Books considering particular kinds of documents, the use of archival records in various kinds of research, and autograph collecting—many from outside the profession, but with illuminating insights into the nature of the archival universe—enriched the compact literature of the time.

Someone entering the archival profession fifty years ago, at about the time records managers were organizing into their own discipline, would find an extremely mixed group of publications about archival work. By reading the *American Archivist* and the publications of the National Archives, someone could gain a *sense* of archival work. A new archivist would then have to scour the historical and library and information science literatures to find additional guidance about records and recordkeeping systems. The profession was building repositories and programs, but the knowledge supporting archival work always seemed to be catching up; in many cases, practice was outrunning systematically defined knowledge in the field's published literature. Some archivists looked abroad for writings about archival theory, and the Hilary Jenkinson tome (published in 1922 and revised in 1937) and the 1940 English translation of the Dutch manual had some influence,[12] but the influence was extremely limited for many decades until the emergence of graduate archival education, the establishment of international communication networks, and the rebirth of interest in diplomatics. Records managers had to read through the archival literature since they had none of their own.

The fifties featured the publication of the first truly North American basic archives manual, T. R. Schellenberg's *Modern Archives*, a work that continues to resonate in the modern archival profession.[13] No research, practice manual, or theorizing about archival work starts without reference to Schellenberg's first book. Even when his publications are not directly referred to, the language often mimics or echoes Schellenberg's (and this is true in the records management literature as well). He systematized practice at the National Archives, adding his own useful insights and perspectives on archival work, drawing from or commenting on the archival literature in other countries and traditions.

In this manner, Schellenberg best embodies the symbiotic connection between professional knowledge and literature. Schellenberg's publication reflects the beginning of a time of more self-conscious archival theory, as the field matured with subsequent generations of practitioners and as its journal, *American Archivist*, grew in size and scope, capturing writings where archivists set forth principles and collected and analyzed data about practice.

The substance of the professional literature in this era showed, however, modest change from what preceded it. T. R. Schellenberg, in reviewing a volume of conference proceedings on archives in Australia in 1959, commented that "controversial questions and observations are not avoided, as they often are in the discussion of similar problems in the United States. . . . "[14] The major difference was the publication of some monographs, conference proceedings, and *festschrifts*. Nearly all of these publications and what can best be called "reports" (publications issued by or commissioned by archival and other organizational entities) focused on the historical development of the profession (mostly institutional biographies). One encouraging sign was the issuance of research reports on technical functions such as preservation and conservation, but the emergence of records management as a function and unique discipline generated most of the books covering basic policies and procedures, reprographics, filing, punch cards, retention scheduling and disposition, and vital records management and security. As corporations and governments contended with growing quantities of records, and as these entities often had more staff and fiscal resources for resolving these challenges, publications of practice, forms, and processes appeared with increasing frequency.

The decades of the sixties and the seventies were turbulent in the North American archival community. Among the changes came a dramatic growth in the number of archival programs (especially university archives). Moreover there was an overall expansion and diversification of the field, including the influx of individuals from graduate history programs (especially with a social history background, which led to the creation of many creative collecting programs and a subsequent impact on archival theory and practice). This was also a time with a fledgling interest by library and information science education programs in the education of archivists (aided by the increased numbers of university archivists who could teach as adjuncts in these programs).

This was the era when the challenges of forming a substantial archival knowledge were made more complicated by a disciplinary fragmentation among what we can only call the records professions—with records management solidifying itself as a separate field and the fragmentation becoming more complex as archivists became more engaged in both information science and new historical research paradigms. The schisms bifurcated the nature of conceptualizing and administering records and their systems, thus weakening archival knowledge. These problems continue to the present. For example, an essay published in a records management journal tends to be read by only a small portion of archivists, and an essay appearing in an archival journal will be dismissed by a records administrator.

All of these changes were reflected in the publications of this era. There were a growing number of basic textbooks published for both archivists (including Schellenberg's second book)[15] and records managers (including the first edition of one of the pioneering textbooks on this topic by William Benedon).[16] New specialized manuals on preservation management and conservation also appeared for the first time, reflecting a growing interest in developing and applying basic principles on caring for archival and library materials learned from the continuing research. The number of books, manuals, and reports on records management indicated an increasing preoccupation with the efficient and economic control of records—and the widening schism between the missions of records managers and archivists. Basic guides to paperwork, filing systems, micrographics, fire protection, and security proliferated across institutions.

There was a greater tilt towards a more expansive archival knowledge with an increasing number of monographs, edited works, and important conference proceedings. A cluster of monographs by H.G. Jones, Walter Muir Whitehill, and Ernst Posner represent one of the most important eras in evaluating the nature and health of historical manuscript and government archives repositories, all calling for change and new leadership.[17] Like these studies, most of the monographs and other similar publications focused on historical or biographical topics, examining pioneer archivists and records professionals, institutional biographies, the history of archives and historical manuscripts repositories in a particular state, and the use of archives as historical sources. Even the monographs published outside of the archival community focused on similar themes of research in archives and the historical nature of records and recordkeeping.

While basic records management continued to be the prevalent interest, there was a promising improvement in archival knowledge as reflected in the primary publications of the field, with a higher degree of scholarship emerging that was noticed by other disciplines concerned about archives and historical manuscripts (although the lack of any bibliometric studies concerning archival literature prevents me from arguing this with any conviction). The heavy historical flavor of the topics and methodologies reflected the connection of the archival profession to the historical discipline and to a cultural mission, aspects that would change (with debate and considerable angst) in future decades. The literature was beginning to reflect a complexity in professional knowledge not seen before. Most records managers, however, did not appreciate the focus on the historical orientation of the literature.

About thirty years ago, the intense publishing of basic manuals for guiding practice began, continuing until the present. At first glance, little distinguishes this period in the formation of archival knowledge from the previous decade, with only a few basic comprehensive manuals being published. However, this was the decade that the SAA entered the basic manual publishing business with a vengeance. In 1977, SAA launched its Basic Manual Series covering every essential function of archival work, with each manual focused on a specific function.[18] For whatever reason, perhaps due to the rapid spurt in growth of the North American archival community or due to the recognition of the need to establish cogent descriptions of professional best practice (the publication of basic comprehensive bibliographies suggest this), this was a time of immense industry in publishing basic manuals on every archival topic from elemental functions, to repository type, to records and media forms. While a small number of these manuals were published outside by standards setting bodies, most were the productions of professional associations and archival institutions.

Added to these publishing ventures was the normal array of conference proceedings and special journal issues. What weakened, especially in comparison to the outpouring of basic manuals, was the publishing of monographs on archival topics. The decade continued to stress the historians' use of sources with some minor growth of interest in such topics as secrecy, access, privacy, research about technical issues related to preservation, and some records forms such as maps and film. There were a few outstanding monographs published with great interest to the archival field, such as Cutright's study of the history of the Lewis and Clark journals and McCoy's serious study of the history of the National Archives[19] (along with the earlier work by H. G. Jones the only serious study of this institution).[20] However, these were exceptions and they reflected the strong connection of history to archives at the exclusion of other aspects of archival development, practice, and theory. This was a time of solidifying best practice, at its must rudimental level.

The seeds of a revolution in archival knowledge were sowed in the 1980s and have blossomed in the past decade. A rich monographic literature developed in the past two decades, with growing evidence of the emergence of a core group of archival scholars and increasing interest in archives by scholars from other fields. There are, perhaps, many reasons for these substantial changes, including: the establishment and growth of graduate archival education; the challenges of electronic records management; the emergence of descriptive standards; greater questioning about basic functions such as archival appraisal; an intense self-evaluation by the profession mostly manifested by a vast array of planning documents; recognition of the importance of public programs and public policy; the apparent internationalization of the archival profession; and controversial cases about the creation, maintenance, and use of records. But why these elements should merge in the past two decades rather than in an earlier era is still uncertain. Could it be the difference in graduate archival education, the most notable difference from earlier eras?

The recent decades have continued to rely on basic manuals and with this we see the persistence of some tension between theory and practice, between specific application and a broader scholarship. The SAA continued to publish a growing variety of specialized manuals, and in the early to mid-1990s, it replaced its older Basic Manual Series with the Archival Fundamentals (and the Society is now revising and replacing the Fundamentals with the first volume appearing in 2004). Other publishers—including other professional associations and professional, university, and trade publishers—also entered the market, causing an avalanche of specialized and general manuals. In the 1990s, the North American profession published more general basic manuals and nearly doubled the quantity of specialized basic manuals. Added to these basic manuals was a wide array of bibliographies and other basic reference tools reflecting the profession's efforts to keep pace with its expanding literature and more demanding responsibilities (although the means of controlling the literature has not kept pace, and there is still no comprehensive bibliographic utility or clearinghouse covering the expanding literature). Such manuals often have served useful roles in supporting professional practice and in delineating professional knowledge. In Terry Cook's important essay about the generations of electronic records archivists, he reflects on such roles with the 1984 publications of the Margaret Hedstrom and Harold Naugler electronic records management manuals. These publications, Cook says, "indicate clearly to any sensitive reader the debt which the archival profession owes to the first-generation pioneers who, starting with almost nothing, produced within the confines of the prevalent data structures and computer technologies of the period, a lasting legacy of theory and practice. . . . Both monographs are . . . transitional, summing up the best of what went before and anticipating the new generation. . . . "[21]

Even as the profession gobbled up every new basic publication related to archival work, this was the era when doubts about the utility of such publications were sounded. Michael Lutzker, reviewing the 1984 *A Modern Archives Reader*, wrote, "The profession is undergoing rapid change, and even some of the traditional archival functions will have to be considered as continually evolving. As admirable a compendium as this volume is, one would hope to see timely revisions as outstanding articles appear in the professional literature."[22] Despite fears that these manuals and basic readers were inelastic, they often stayed in print.

Other troublesome issues about such publications materialized in these years. Barbara Craig, assessing William J. Maher's 1992 manual on college and university archives, wrote, "As a teacher of archives, I finished the book with a nagging sense of *ennui*. As much as I like the book, and I shall use it often, I was, in the end, somewhat unsettled by its larger implications. Should archivists overcome the barriers of ignorance or should we encourage isolation by addressing manuals to specific settings? The dictates of a 'unique' environment appear overwhelming and may undercut a consensus on a universal theory and common practice."[23] Terry Eastwood, more critical of basic publications when considering SAA's Archival Fundamentals Series, laments the gaps and omissions in topics covered, the target audiences, theoretical or conceptual confusions, and other problems, especially the authors failure to "delve beneath the surface of the subject to work out its [archival science] principled foundation. Instead, they veer off into description of practice, perhaps with some justification of the way it is done."[24] The archival community seems to have a nearly insatiable appetite for these manuals, creating an uneasy tension between professional need and desirability (that, in my opinion, perhaps can only be addressed effectively within the classroom, a place that still not everyone entering the profession has the opportunity to reside in for a time).

This was also a period of considerable scrutiny about the nature, mission, and future of the North American archival profession. From the early 1980s until well into the next decade, numerous national, regional, and institutional plans were formulated, released, debated, refined, or shelved and forgotten (as is often the case with self-study and planning).[25] In Canada a national archival plan was completed; in the United States individual states created plans and conferences led to efforts to articulate a national mission and priorities as well as to create institutional self-study documents.[26] Many of these planning efforts were also advocacy efforts, intended to gain broad public and policymaker support for archives and historical records programs and the archival mission—trying to understand the societal perceptions of archives and archivists.

Increasing threats to the preservation of archives, especially those posed by new technologies, added to controversies, crises, and critiques challenging the modern archival community's efforts to sustain useful practices and procedures—suggesting another source for the creation and text of new archival knowledge. Not surprisingly, archivists turned to new audiences, developing and offering teaching packets for schools, as well trying to manage the growing professional literature of their own field. Like other professionals, archivists struggled to manage their own knowledge while in the midst of a new kind of information age. All of these efforts reflected that archival knowledge was both shifting and stabilizing, implying an unprecedented breadth and depth within the literature.

The emphasis on local, regional, and national planning, while remarkable, was not the most notable change in the formation or presentation of archival knowledge. Research and other monographs began to appear regularly in the early 1980s, and have gained momentum since then. In 1980 the first research study on any aspect of archival appraisal was published, quickly followed by studies on the U.S. National Archives, the Historical Records Survey, and descriptive practices.[27] At the end of the 1980s David Bearman's groundbreaking *Archival Methods* was published, questioning nearly every cherished assumption held by archivists,[28] a precursor to new literature on the archival profession. Research reports appeared on electronic records and appraisal and documentation issues,[29] including the first major monographs on electronic records and other matters followed by important volumes on similar themes throughout the 1990s.[30] The first systematic study of archival appraisal methodology was conducted and published in 1991,[31] followed by other significant writings on archival appraisal such as Helen Samuels's analysis of documenting colleges and universities.[32] The first critical analysis of the ethical dimensions of access to personal information in archival records appeared in Heather MacNeil's *Without Consent* in 1992.[33] The profession's first book-length study of users at a single repository appeared in 1994, authored by Paul Conway.[34] One of the most unusual publications in the history of North American archival work was the memoir of former U.S. Archivist Robert Warner describing his efforts to lead the U.S. National Archives to independence.[35] This was also a time when important writings on archival theory, especially on the nature of the record, began to appear, perhaps best delineating this era from earlier ones as a time of new archival reflection and discourse.[36]

The newness of the monographic publishing also created some critical assessments of such research. For example, while Ann Pederson praised Richard Berner's 1983 *Archival Theory and Practice in the United States: A Historical Analysis* as "our profession's first comprehensive, effective work," she also lamented some of its failings. Pederson argued that the book's "narrative does not sustain the standard of objectivity required of high-quality historical work beyond its first three chapters. . . . Thereafter, the book becomes more and more openly prescriptive, with Berner justifying and promoting his own concept of a comprehensive finding aid system that will offer researchers a single point of access to all holdings."[37] These were the growing pains of a richer archival knowledge. Pederson's characterizations of the Berner book probably captures well much of the monographic publishing of this recent era, and in such assessments we recognize the work of both busy practitioners and the early efforts of a transitional group of archivists developing graduate archival education programs. From this point on, it was unlikely that the only litmus test for a new archival publication would be its practicality in the repository.

Archivists and records managers were more likely to read outside of their fields to learn about the historical, political, cultural, and economic nature of the modern Information Age, with many studies providing extended discussions about records and recordkeeping systems. One explanation for this may have been the immense changes in graduate archival education, with the emergence of both full-time academics supporting these programs and a stronger curriculum in both library and information science schools and history departments—even though the establishment and continuing development of regular, full-time academics focused on archival studies may not yet have had the desired results in archival research and theory.

There has been a corresponding growth in the number of doctoral students focused on archival studies and number of doctoral dissertations on archival topics in the past half-century. In general, it was a time when *new* ideas were generating because of *new* issues caused by *new* technologies, as evident in the writings of the iconoclastic David Bearman or the visionary Hugh Taylor. This was the era of Taylor's most creative forays into the nature of archival knowledge. Gordon Dodds, reviewing the 1992 *festschrift* in Taylor's honor, reflected on the variety of "Taylorisms" served up to us—"information ecology," "paper archaelogy," "sea changes," "dust to ashes," "cloistered archivists," "transformation of the archivist," "media of the record," "totemic universe," "the conjuring text," "Clio in the raw,"—and suggested that a volume of Taylor's own writings would not only capture his nimble mind and imagination, but reveal a formative period in new archival knowledge.[38]

Some of this interdisciplinarity suggested that the old dichotomy between history and information science was at an end, such as Terry Cook's assertion, "It is long past time for archivists to set aside the false dichotomies of historians *versus* information specialists. . . . It is now time to realize the wisdom both can offer to archival work, and to take strands from each and weave them into a rich texture archivists can call their own" (a stronger archival knowledge).[39] Yet, within the creative cross-fertilization of archival studies with other disciplines resides both great promise of intellectual riches and substantial dangers about a loss of core knowledge.

The past twenty years have also been marked by an outpouring of new volumes of collected essays from conferences or freshly assembled on a theme, covering every aspect of archival work. A prominent effort in this publishing genre was Tom Nesmith's work in assembling a reader on the contributions of Canadian archivists to archival theory and practice.[40] Another important volume was the collection of essays on appraising American business records, edited by James O'Toole, generating from a conference at the Minnesota Historical Society.[41] The education of archivists was the focus of a number of important conferences, with resulting published proceedings reflecting the increasing emphasis on the new energy devoted to this aspect of the profession. Archival appraisal attracted new scrutiny as archivists searched for ways to evaluate the success of this function, as well as for new approaches. Arrangement and description, buoyed by an immense new interest in descriptive standards and authority control and access to archival records, also was a conference topic.[42] Every aspect of archival work or archival record was featured in one or more conference proceedings or collected essays. Special journal issues and other volumes of collected essays ruminated on the relationship of archivists to other professions, especially historians and public historians (mirroring the tensions and growing distance between historians and archivists), librarians, and rare books and special collections curators.[43] Closely related groups, such as rare books and special collections librarians, have also been carefully analyzed.

As electronic information systems grew more sophisticated, issues like intellectual property and other public policy matters attracted greater attention and concern, as did oral history, other documentary forms, and the history of individual and institutional collecting.[44] *Festschrifts* in honor of senior members of the field also appeared, most notably the essays edited by Barbara Craig in honor of Hugh Taylor, a volume frequently cited for its substantial essays on a number of archival topics.[45] Archivists, along with closely allied colleagues, love to hold conferences to set new agendas, resolve issues, articulate new objectives, and answer persistent archival questions—suggesting the dynamic nature of a knowledge unlikely to be captured in a one-volume primer. Even conference proceedings and edited thematic volumes that were uneven or weak often featured one or two stellar essays captivating the attention of the profession and adding to its knowledge.

Monographic publishing on topics related to archives and records are published in noticeably larger numbers than ever before. Some focus on persistent matters like privacy and access, public policy, the development of office and information technology, all with direct relevance for archivists and records managers.[46] Pioneers of archival and historical manuscripts collecting and private and public historical societies also received a fresh look, with some of the best analyses to date.[47] However, there has been intense interest in the nature of particular kinds of records, such as photographs, maps, oral tradition, census documentation, government reports, letter writing, and diaries, adding considerably to our knowledge of these document genres.[48] A new generation of writing about autograph collecting, and collecting in general, emerged, although this avocation still has not received its scholarly due.[49] More notable was the growing interest by journalists, freelance writers, and scholars in archives. Janet Malcolm's riveting book on access to the Sigmund Freud papers at the Library of Congress still remains a useful case study in archival access and ethics.[50] A number of journalists provided intense scrutiny on the murder, forgery, and other controversies regarding the Mormon Church and early records related to its history[51]—in fact, forgery of historical manuscripts and archives continues to attract increased attention by both scholars and the public.

Historians analyzed how societies and organizations function by the creation and use of information and record systems, with an influential study of business communication systems in 1850–1920 and another on the struggles of a seventeenth-century Dutch notary to make a transition to the newly dominant English culture (with haunting lessons about the problems of cultural shifts for records keepers).[52] Public controversies and social issues featured records, such as the tobacco litigation case and a scathing indictment of the management of U.S. Internal Revenue Service records.[53] All of these volumes are just as relevant to the records manager as to the archivist.

The schism between archivists and records managers continued to be evident as records professionals contended with the continuously emerging challenges posed by digital media. Archival programs, especially in government, continued to publish basic records management manuals. Meanwhile, the publications program of the Association of Records Managers and Administrators, along with other professional records and information resources management associations, published a wider array of texts on records and information resources management, reflecting a widening gulf in perspectives between archivists and records managers. Basic records management textbooks, published by a variety of commercial textbook publishers, appeared with relentless frequency, most providing little information about archives as an integral element of records management.[54] National studies and specialized manuals intended to assist various kinds of institutions implement records management programs became common.

By the mid-1980s archivists certainly understood that records management functions were crucial in an organization administering its records, and they also understood that records management texts provided useful information about the mechanics of records and recordkeeping systems. Unfortunately, the evidence does not suggest that records managers had the same appreciation for the archival perspective. Among archivists, skepticism about the role of records management surged, perhaps because many archivists held to a cultural role and were critical of any emphasis on records and evidence.[55]

In these publications, we see a fracturing of the archival community. At the advent of the 1980s, archivists wrestled with whether they were or should be distinct from librarians and historians, prompting a heated debate in North America in the mid-1980s and again in the early 1990s (with little resolution and with modest contributions to the concept of an archival knowledge).[56] Reports on the nature and purpose of documentary editing also accentuated differences between documentary editors and archivists.[57] There were increasing signs of deepening schisms between archivists and records managers and even archivists and preservation administrators (the latter developing a highly specialized technical literature). And, then, there were emerging archival specializations (like moving image archives) leading to new professional associations. Most of the writings about the splintering of various disciplines from archivists concentrated on the relationship between archivists and historians with complaints about stereotyping by historians and desires for demonstrating stronger links between the fields. However, the schismatic nature of the archival discipline has been far more complicated than generally acknowledged. Despite the debates there were some who persisted in holding to a static view of theory or who viewed these debates as merely wasting archival resources.

While the archival profession seems to have splintered in a thousand directions, a scholarly context for understanding the nature of archives and archivists has emerged with great promise for influencing nearly every aspect of the archivist's knowledge. The emergence of scholarly interest in public or collective memory, mixed with new cultural and literary studies and postmodernist textual criticism, has considerably enriched the historical and contemporary understanding of archives—from the news media serving as an archival record, photography functioning as a mechanism for cultural memory, and Americans interacting with the past, including archival records, as a means for forming collective memory.[58] The relevance of public memory studies should be obvious, since, as Barbara Craig comments, "All archives originate in the conscious act of memorializing some thing by the giving, receiving, and keeping of documentary records."[59] Nearly all the recent studies on public memory comment to some degree on the nature or role of archives, although in many respects such studies from the outside both enrich and detract from a broader understanding of archives.[60] With their increasing intensity of focus on records, one might assume that records managers would be more conversant with this emerging scholarship, but that appears not to be the case.

There are other troublesome; even if seen as promising to some aspects of the broadening of archival knowledge, as represented in both the profession's own literature and that on its borders. Not too many years ago the notion of convergence of various information professions was a spicy topic, although some in the archives field shunned the idea. Rather than convergence, we have seen a centrifugal force at work, creating more spin offs and subfields than commitment to a core knowledge. Peter Wosh, for example, argues that while we should "nurture diversity," the archival community is far too fragmented.[61]

Still, we need to pay attention to a wider variety of disciplinary scholarship, such as James O'Toole contends with historical literacy studies: "What does writing do and not do? How does written communication circulate in modern organizations or personal life? What are its formal and informal means? What is the interplay of forces that are expressly literate and those that are non-literate, such as voice-mail, person-to-person transactions, and (perhaps) e-mail?"[62] It is critical to do this if we are to develop a more coherent sense of how theory and practice relate to each other. Tom Nesmith, reflecting on Trevor Livelton's 1996 *Archival Theory, Records, and the Public*, wonders if we don't require a broader notion of theory encompassing a "wider study of various understandings of the broader world," one that would "reorient some archival theorizing . . . from a focus on what the classic archival texts say an archives, a record, or a public record is in 'nature,' to a study of how human perception, communication, and behavior shape the archives, records, and public records we actually locate and create as archivists and records creators." As Nesmith suggests, "to explore the wide terrain of human perception, communication, and behavior in relation to archives would also require us to consult the leading works of theory in these areas."[63] At the least, it requires archivists to read more than ever before.

VISUALIZING THE CREATION OF ARCHIVAL KNOWLEDGE

What do the publication patterns mean for the state of North American archival knowledge? The reliance on basic manuals suggests that archival knowledge is easily summarized or, perhaps, that most archivists look for convenient summations describing practice essentials. This is, however, challenged by the publication trends of specialized manuals, a phenomenon indicating that there is, indeed, more substantial changes occurring in the field in both practice and knowledge. Another indication that archival knowledge is transforming is the recent burst of scholarly monographs on archival topics (from a diversity of fields), providing a more complex meaning of archives, the nature of recordkeeping systems, and the role of records in society.

Some of this recent scholarship challenges some long-held basic precepts of archival knowledge and practice, or suggests how archival knowledge will be reevaluated in future years. This scholarship also is being buttressed by an unprecedented growth in doctoral dissertations on archival topics, a trend indicating that a new research foundation is being built with great promise for expanding archival knowledge. Providing greater insights into records and their administration, these studies also will benefit the work of records managers.

From our vantage point, North American archivists seem preoccupied with basic manuals. Such publications, as an indicator of best practices and consensus of how practices and theories mesh, are quite valuable to all those interested in understanding archives and archivists. If we only consider the publication of basic manuals, those trying to cover all functions and activities in a single volume, we might not be very impressed by the professional community's demand for such volumes. Figure One reveals that the publication rate of such volumes has been steady over the past half century, never totaling more than five in any of these decades (although for a field as small as archives a new basic manual every two years suggests over saturation of the market).

The questions that emerge about the publication rate of such general texts are, however, quite troubling. Is archival knowledge changing so rapidly that we must have *new* manuals every few years? How does the content of these general texts differ from one to the other? Are these manuals being pitched to different levels of experience and education in the practitioners' ranks or aimed at archives and archivists in different types of settings? Do they adequately reflect the changing aspects of archival knowledge, whatever these may be? Do these archival manuals demonstrate that they are being prepared and published as efforts to keep up with changing records and recordkeeping technologies? Although such questions will be debated for a long time, there are elements of basic archival practice and theory that seem quite fluid (such as the shift in archival description from standardizing repository finding aids to standardizing national and international inventories), requiring manuals to be regularly revised or replaced.

Over the past thirty years, however, the proliferation of basic manuals on specialized topics suggests that the parameters of archival knowledge are expanding. These manuals range from a focus on specific archival functions (such as appraisal or reference), to specific types of records forms (photographs, maps, and architectural drawings), and issues (such as legal concerns and intellectual property). Figure Two reveals a remarkable growth of such publishing, 177 volumes in thirty years—a rate of more than five a year. The primary question is whether

Figure One
Publication of General Basic Archives Manuals,
1950–1999

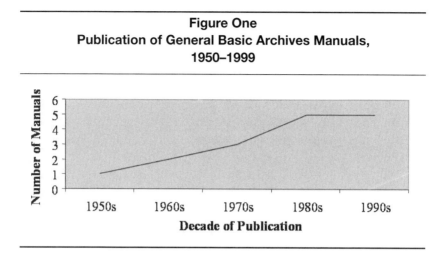

the knowledge portrayed in all these volumes is being incorporated into the more general texts or captured in other ways by the archival community. Nearly twenty years ago Helen Samuels and her colleagues, authoring the pioneering manual on appraising the records of science and technology, felt compelled to write a follow-up essay demonstrating how their approach to these records could be applied to other record types.[64] This problem continues to this day, suggesting that the scattering of publications across records and repository types, archival issues and functions, is not being assimilated into a coherent archival knowledge. Indeed, while general manuals may provide a kind of foundational unity about the fundamentals of archival practice and knowledge (and these manuals need to be examined more closely to help archivists discern what the unifying features are), the specialized manuals may suggest a continuing fracturing of the archival community into sub-specializations (think of the increasing complexity of specialized listservs).

The reliance on basic manuals may be an attribute of any modern information profession, so we must be cautious in how we characterize the North American archival community. While it is easy to suggest that the publication of such manuals means that there is a heavy orientation to basic skills rather than a sophisticated knowledge, we need to place the archives field into a broader context of the information, library, and historical disciplines. Other components of the professions related to archival work continue to publish a lot of basic (both general and specialized) manuals. In history, numerous basic works in historiography

Figure Two
Publication of General and Specialized Archives Manuals,
1970–1999

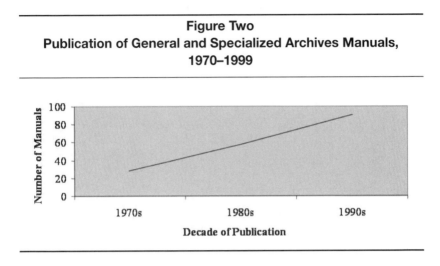

and historical method are regularly published and many of the best basic remain in print for a considerable time; the difference is that the historical discipline also produces countless scholarly monographs on all aspects of historical research, themes, and controversies. Perhaps a better comparison is what occurs within the records management discipline, a professional group that splintered from the mainstream archival field nearly half a century ago. Figure Three demonstrates that the records management community is even more focused on basic textbooks, reflecting perhaps its lower educational standards and more practice-oriented field. The records management field also supports a wide array of specialized manuals, just like the archives field, but there is little evidence of scholarly research monographs.[65]

A recent survey conducted by ARMA of its *Information Management Journal* concluded that records managers desire articles on how-to/best practices, technology, news, and other such matters: "The survey also found that topics readers would most like to see covered or emphasized more in future issues of the *Journal* include electronic records management, more RIM how-tos, and more content geared toward beginning RIM practitioners."[66] This came after a short-lived effort by ARMA to support this journal being more scholarly in content.

A mark distinguishing the archival discipline from the records management field is the recent burst of scholarly monographic publishing, indicating a new interest in the broadening of knowledge that supports basic archival practice. Figure Four shows a strong spike in publishing

Figure Three
Publication of General Archives and Records
Management Manuels, 1950–1999

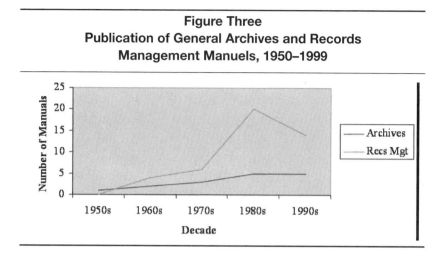

such research in the past decade, with evidence that this trend is continuing. In 1980, shortly before such publishing began, Maynard Brichford said that "archivists' avoidance of empirical research is somewhere between the pathological and the scandalous," and that the field needed a "scientific research methodology."[67] One response was the proliferation of research agendas,[68] but the more important change has been monographic publication.

Most of these publications eschew the idea that their content must have any practical intent, aimed to contribute more depth to a particular aspect of archival knowledge or to reform and continue strengthening of the profession and its mission. The lack of a practical aim sometimes irritates reviewers of these publications, but more often than not, the reformation aspect upsets commentators even more. Unfortunately, at times, it appears that the field still has not developed an adequate sense of how to engage in scholarly debate that advances its own knowledge, perhaps because the archival discipline has only recently become accustomed to having monographs rather than primers available to it about its mission and work.

If we add the increasing number of doctoral dissertations to the number of monographs, we see an even stronger transformation in the scholarly foundations of archival knowledge. More dissertations on archival topics at North American schools or on North American topics have been completed in the past decade than in the entire rest of the century (see Figure Five). The impact of this research on archival knowl-

Figure Four
Publication of Scholarly Monographs on Archival Topics,
1950–1999

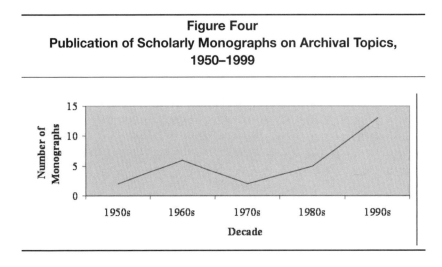

edge still seems suspect at this point with only one in three dissertations leading to article publication and about one in ten leading to a monograph. However, this, along with the spurt of monographic publishing, suggests that we are witnessing a new era of archival knowledge. When we consider the growing number of publications on the "archive" by a variety of scholars outside the archival community, we can surmise that we might be witnessing a true revolution.

The idea that an archives is a reasonably static place has been all but destroyed by scholars in the past few decades, as just one recent book, *Refiguring the Archive*, suggests. In this volume's introduction, three of the editors write, "For the archive is . . . always already being refigured: the technologies of creation, preservation and use, for instance, are changing all the time; physically the archive is being added to and subtracted from, and is in dynamic relation with its physical environment; organizational dynamics are ever shifting; and the archive is porous to societal processes and discoveries."[69] The instability of archival knowledge, in that it is growing and changing rapidly, is part of a revolution that seems to hold considerable promise (as well as some dangers) for the archival field and its relevance in modern society.

It may seem ironic to suggest that such a characteristic of archival knowledge, its instability, is also a strength of the discipline. Ever-changing recordkeeping systems and their technologies, along with constantly appearing new threats to society, its citizens and its organizations, require that archivists and records managers continuously update their

Figure Five
Completion of Doctorial Dissertations on Archival Topics,
1950–1999

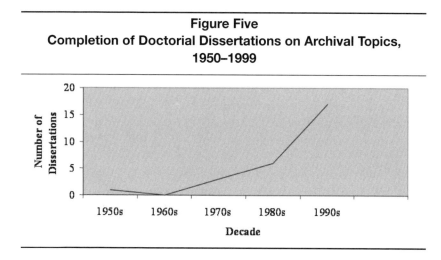

knowledge of records systems. One of the critical new contributors to the dissemination of archival knowledge is the Internet. Archivists were quick to take advantage of listservs and Web sites, although the full potential of these electronic means of transmitting knowledge has not been tapped. Most listservs don't discuss research, theory, or the archival literature, but operate fairly exclusively at the level of rudimentary practice. The longest messages and the most extensive discussions often focus on the most mundane matters, such as labels that won't adhere to boxes. The disseminating of policies, reports, case studies and conference proceedings is just beginning, and the promise of this for enhancing archival knowledge seems unlimited. The development of e-journals with a focus on archives and the publication of fully digital publications is the most underdeveloped aspect of archival work, but I expect this will change in the next decade. The influence and potential of the World Wide Web as a publishing venue may be the most critical aspect of the real revolution to occur in the continuing formation in archival knowledge, but its role will only be critical if the archival community has matured to sustain a high-quality professional and research literature.

CONCLUSION

At the outset of this chapter, I enumerated some limitations in my analysis of the archival literature. In this concluding section, it is important to consider additional limitations since they suggest how much more there is to understanding the general state of archival knowledge. The primary limitation may be that my comments suggest that somehow the *form* of a publication (whether it is a basic manual or a scholarly monograph) indicates the quality of knowledge that the publication communicates. Obviously, there are excellent basic primers and deficient scholarly monographs, so it is not my intent to make an absolute connection between the publication form and the quality of a publication's content.

My aim is to demonstrate that in the increasing diversity of research and publication there has been a substantial change for the better in archival knowledge, with the promise of more improvement to come. One of the most obvious, and perhaps notable, features of the literature is that every aspect of the archival field and its knowledge is becoming too complex to characterize in a single essay. Even when experts write about the literature of a part of the field, with all its weaknesses and strengths, they still find a considerable array of books, conference proceedings, technical reports, and journals that must be evaluated.

Another limitation of this analysis may be giving an impression that as time passes, archival knowledge increases and improves. Another analysis could certainly suggest that while we can see some substantial improvement in the professional literature, closer examination of particular aspects might suggest otherwise. Hopefully, an example will suffice to demonstrate my point. Prior to the advent of the U.S. National Archives, Schellenberg's theoretical musings, and records management techniques, the idea of archival appraisal was limited. From the 1940s until well into the 1970s, the evidential/informational model of archival value governed appraising. In the 1980s, appraisal became more complicated as neo-Jenkinsonism took root in parts of North America, other concepts (such as "total archives," "documentation strategies," "functional analysis," and "macro-appraisal") were introduced, and the task of appraising became more challenging.

Even though now we are beginning to see some specific case studies of appraisal methodologies and more theorizing about the nature and aims of archival appraisal, there are still many weaknesses in our knowledge of archival appraisal. There is little evidence that individuals outside of the archival community understand or appreciate the notion of appraisal. There is also very little known about the notion of success (saving the right records) and failure (destroying or saving the wrong records) in archival appraisal activities. Indeed, the idea of failure as a means of elevating professional or any knowledge seems something mostly avoided by archivists, manuscript curators, and records managers—an avoidance bound to have a negative influence on a continual maturation of archival knowledge.

My point is, however, that we need to keep examining, testing, and poking at our own assumptions about what constitutes the knowledge that distinguishes someone as an archivist, since archivists never take anything for granted about what is known or not known about archives and the archival discipline. We also need to make sure that archival knowledge is continually tested in the crucible of organizations creating records and recordkeeping systems and in the reference room where researchers ultimately strive to use archival records.

Another important limitation is the visibility of archival knowledge to other fields. Archivists have not contributed greatly to public scholarship, in going outside of their own disciplinary boundaries to discuss records, archives, and manuscripts. The business of public scholarship is a difficult one, requiring contacts, support, and resources (especially time) that most archivists do not possess. Writing outside of the archivists' own discipline is problematic. Given their knowledge about the nature of source material and its uses, often displayed in critical essays within their own journals, it is surprising, despite the barriers, how little such writing and publishing archivists have done (especially given the rampant opportunities of breaking news stories in which records and archives prominently figure). Such opportunities are not confined to public venues, but they also reside in new forms and approaches of scholarship. In surveying the possibilities of postmodern scholarship for archives, Tom Nesmith very neatly describes the potential:

> The postmodern outlook suggests an important new intellectual place for archives in the formation of knowledge, culture, and societies. It helps us to see that contrary to the conventional idea that archivists simply receive and house vast new quantities of records, which merely reflect society, they actually co-create and shape the knowledge in records and thus help form society's memory. This implies that studying the archiving process itself (and not just using archives in the familiar way to study other things) is a vital aspect of the pursuit of human understanding. The study of archives is no longer just the seemingly esoteric interest of a few archivists who believe it makes them more effective on the job, or provides an underpinning for professional culture, valuable as these internal pursuits may be.[70]

We must also recognize that in this expansion of the sense of archives and archiving that there is a danger of losing sight of the very unique aspects of what makes some things archives. Despite the promises of postmodernist scholarship (and I concur that the promises are immense), there is also the danger that the boundaries of archives become considerably blurred (prompting debate about the nature of records in the postmodernist milieu). In his impressive survey of archival ideas over the past century, Terry Cook indicates, "archival theory now takes its inspiration from analysis of recordkeeping processes rather than from the arrangement and description of recorded products in archives."[71] Will the infusion of a postmodernist scholarly bent allow archivists to maintain such a focus? Tom Nesmith believes it will, since the "central archival concerns now and in the future are not primarily technical or procedural. . . . The study of archives is very much a study of human beings (including archivists) and why and how they act when recording, keeping records, and placing, using, and perceiving them in archives."[72] And in a sense, whether more prone to a postmodernist inclination or not, such a recognition suggests that a real maturation has occurred with archival knowledge.

Undoubtedly, some will worry that many frontline archivists—the practitioners—will not be tied into this newer form of archival knowledge. However, fixating on this issue only churns up the older issue of the relationship of theory and practice, a relationship that, while continuing to be vexing, is also the wrong issue to focus on. Stephen Jay Gould, in his last book before his death, helped us to see that such a dichotomy that exists in all professions in their views toward theory and practice is deeply ingrained in the human psyche: "I strongly suspect that our propensity for dichotomy lies deeply within our basic mental architecture as an evolved property of the human brain. . . . "[73] In other words, our wrestling with what is clearly something never to be resolved is only useful to us if we are engaged in building—from *both* practice and research revolving about theoretical concepts—an archival knowledge that communicates to archivists, guides them, and engages other disciplines and the public in appreciating what archives are and why they are important. Gould pokes fun at the dream of unifying science and the humanities, when he says he wants the "sciences and humanities to become the greatest of pals, to recognize a deep kinship and necessary connection in pursuit of human decency and achievement, but to keep their ineluctably different aims and logics separate as they ply their joint projects and learn from each other."[74] Perhaps, in the same way, archivists should be a little self-mocking, and hope that archival practitioners and theorists keep their aims and logics separate while they learn from each other. An already strong archival knowledge has only more to gain. And records managers need to join in.

ENDNOTES

1. For some suggestive writings about this, see Luciana Duranti, "The Odyssey of Records Managers," *Records Management Quarterly* 23 (July 1989): 3–6, 8–11 and (October 1989): 3–6, 8–11; Luke J. Gilliland-Swetland, "The Provenance of a Profession: The Permanence of the Public Archives and Historical Manuscripts Tradition in American Archival History," *American Archivist* 54 (Summer 1991): 160–175; William F. Birdsall, "The American Archivist's Search for Professional Identity, 1909–1936," Ph.D. dissertation, University of Wisconsin, Madison, 1973; Terry Cook, "What is Past is Prologue: A History of Archival Ideas Since 1898, and the Future Paradigm Shift," *Archivaria* 43 (Spring 1997): 17–63; and Peter J. Wosh, "Creating a Semiprofessional Profession: Archivists View Themselves," *Provenance* 10 (Fall 1982): 1–13.

2. David Snowden, "Complex Acts of Knowing: Paradox and Descriptive Self-Awareness," *Journal of Knowledge Management* 6, no. 2 (2002): 100–111.

3. Eliot Freidson, *Professional Powers: A Study of the Institutionalization of Formal Knowledge* (Chicago: University of Chicago Press, 1986), 225–226.

4. Freidson, *Professional Powers*, 211.

5. Freidson, *Professional Powers*, 217.

6. Preben Mortensen, "The Place of Theory in Archival Practice," *Archivaria* 47 (Spring 1999): 22.

7. Brien Brothman, "Declining Derrida: Integrity, Tensegrity, and the Preservation of Archivy from Deconstruction," *Archivaria* 48 (Fall 1999): 64–88.

8. Victoria Lemieux, "An Archival Practitioner's Views on Archival Literature: Where We Have Been and Where We Are Going," *Archivaria* 40 (Fall 1999): 200.

9. There were some early preliminary efforts to reflect the work of some archival and historical manuscripts repositories, such as the Library of Congress's 1913 publication of an archival cataloguing manual based completely on internal practices and the stillborn effort to write and publish a major archives textbook based on more conceptual notions and sponsored by the Public Archives Commission; see, Robert D. Reynolds, Jr., "The Incunabula of Archival Theory and Practice in the United States: J. C. Fitzpatrick's *Notes on the Care, Cataloguing, Calendaring and Arranging of Manuscripts* and the Public Archives Commission's Uncompleted 'Primer of Archival Economy,'" *American Archivist* 54 (Fall 1991): 466–482.

10. Michael Cook, "UNESCO's RAMP Programme: A Pause to Reflect," *Archivaria* 31 (Winter 1990–91): 163–170 and my "RAMP Studies and Related UNESCO Publications: An International Source for Archival Administration," *American Archivist* 53 (Summer 1990): 488–495 evaluate the RAMP publications. Julia Marks Young's review of the Ann Pedersen edited 1987 volume *Keeping Archives* states that this volume "stands without parallel as the best comprehensive guide to archival management now available"; review in *American Archivist* 52 (Spring 1989): 250–251.

11. See Donald R. McCoy, *The National Archives: America's Ministry of Documents 1934–1968* (Chapel Hill: University of North Carolina Press, 1978), chapters 6 and 7.

12. Hilary Jenkinson, *A Manual of Archive Administration* (London: Percy Lund, Humphries and Co., Ltd., 1966; reprint of 1937 ed.); S. Muller, J. A. Feith, and R. Fruin. *Manual for the Arrangement and Description of Archives* (New York: H. W. Wilson, 1968; orginally published 1940). The latter volume has recently been reprinted by the Society of American Archivists.

13. T. R. Schellenberg, *Modern Archives: Principles and Techniques* (Chicago: University of Chicago Press, 1956).

14. Review in the *American Archivist* 22 (January 1959): 339.

15. Lucile Kane, *A Guide to the Care and Administration of Manuscripts* (Madison, Wisc.: American Association for State and Local History, 1960); and T. R. Schellenberg, *The Management of Archives* (New York: Columbia University Press, 1965). Many government programs were also publishing basic manuals as well, such as H. G. Jones and A. M. Patterson, ed., *The County Records Manual* (Raleigh, N.C.: North Carolina State Department of Archives and History, 1960).

16. William Benedon, *Records Management* (Englewood Cliffs, NJ: Prentice–Hall, 1969).

17. H. G. Jones, *The Records of a Nation: Their Management, Preservation, and Use* (New York: Atheneum, 1969). Walter Muir Whitehill, *Independent Historical Societies: An Enquiry Into Their Research and Publication Functions and Their Financial Future* (Boston: Boston Athenaeum, 1962); and Ernst Posner, *American State Archives* (Chicago: University of Chicago Press, 1964). See also Clement M. Silvestro and Richmond D. Williams, *A Look at Ourselves: A Report on the Survey of the State and Local Historical Societies in the United States* (Madison: American Association for State and Local History, 1962).

18. The first volumes were on appraisal and accessioning, surveys, arrangement and description, reference and access, and security. More information about the series can be found at the SAA's Web site (www.archivists.org).

19. Paul Russell Cutright, *A History of the Lewis and Clark Journals* (Norman: University of Oklahoma Press, 1976) and McCoy, *The National Archives*.

20. Jones, *The Records of a Nation*.

21. Terry Cook, "Easy to Byte, Harder to Chew: The Second Generation of Electronic Records Archives," *Archivaria* 33 (Winter 1991–92): 205.

22. Review in *American Archivist* 49 (Spring 1986): 194.

23. Barbara L. Craig, "Archival Sallies: Words and Deeds from the Ivory Tower," *Archivaria* 36 (Autumn 1993): 240.

24. Terry Eastwood, "From Practice to Theory: Fundamentals US Style," *Archivaria* 39 (Spring 1995): 149.

25. In addition to the numerous planning documents published, a fairly considerable body of commentary emerged during this period trying to make sense of what the planning efforts meant and how they were being used or should be used. See, for example, Nicholas C. Burckel, "National Historical Publications and Records Commission State Assessment Reports in Historical Perspective," *Archival Issues* 14, no. 2 (1989): 71–78; Larry J. Hackman, "State Government and Statewide Archival Affairs: New York as a Case Study," *American Archivist* 55 (Fall 1992): 578–599; F. Gerald Ham, "NHPRC's Records Program and the Development of Statewide Archival Planning American Archivist," 43 (Winter 1980): 33–42; Ham, "Planning for the Archival Profession," *American Archivist* 48 (Winter 1985): 26–30; Stephen G. McShane, "Planning as Prologue: The Planning Process and the Archival Profession," *Archival Issues* 15, no. 2 (1990): 108–116; and for a set of essays about the role of the NHPRC in this and other aspects of the archival profession, see the *American Archivist* 63 (Spring/Summer 2000): 16–96.

26. Key publications include *Canadian Archives: Report to the Social Sciences and Humanities Research Council of Canada by the Consultive Group on Canadian Archives* (Ottawa: Social Sciences and Humanities Research Council of Canada, 1980); Task Force on Institutional Evaluation, Society of American Archivists, *Evaluation of Archival Institutions: Services, Principles, and Guide to Self-study* (Chicago: Society of American Archivists, 1982); Lisa B. Weber, ed., *Documenting America: Assessing the Condition of Historical Records in the States: Consultant Reports Presented at the Conference of the National Historical Publications and Records Commission, Assessment and Reporting Grantees, Atlanta, Georgia, June 24–25, 1983* (Atlanta, Ga.: NASARA in cooperation with NHPRC, 1984); *Planning for the Archival Profession: A Report of the SAA Task Force on Goals and Priorities* (Chicago: Society of American Archivists, 1986); and Committee on the Records of Government, *Report* (Washington, D.C.: The Committee, March 1985).

27. Michael Stephen Hindus, Theodore M. Hammett, and Barbara M. Hobson, *The Files of the Massachusetts Superior Court, 1859–1959: An Analysis and A Plan for Action; A Report of the Massachusetts Judicial Records Committee of the Supreme Judicial Court, 1979* (Boston: G. K. Hall, 1980); Victor Gondos, Jr., *J. Franklin Jameson and the Birth of the National Archives 1906–1926* (Philadelphia: University of Pennsylvania Press, 1981); Burl Noggle, *Working with History: The Historical Records Survey in Louisiana and the Nation, 1936–1941* (Baton Rouge: Louisiana State University Press, 1981); and Richard C. Berner, *Archival Theory and Practice in the United States: A Historical Analysis* (Seattle: University of Washington Press, 1983).

28. David Bearman, *Archival Methods* (Pittsburgh: Archives and Museum Informatics, 1989).

29. Some highlights include Clark A. Elliott, ed., *Understanding Progress as*

Process: Documentation of the History of Post-War Science and Technology in the United States (Chicago: Society of American Archivists for the Joint Committee on Archives of Science and Technology, 1983); Bruce H. Bruemmer and Sheldon Hochheiser, *The High-Technology Company: A Historical Research and Archival Guide* (Minneapolis: Charles Babbage Institute, Center for the History of Information Processing, 1989); and Avra Michelson, ed., *Expert Systems Technology and its Implication for Archives* ([Washington, DC]: National Archives and Records Administration, 1991).

30. Charles M. Dollar, *Archival Theory and Information Technologies: The Impact of Information Technologies on Archival Principles and Methods* (Macerata, Italy: University of Macerata, 1992); David Bearman, *Electronic Evidence: Strategies for Managing Records in Contemporary Organizations* (Pittsburgh: Archives and Museum Informatics, 1994); and Richard J. Cox, *The First Generation of Electronic Records Archivists in the United States: A Study in Professionalization* (New York: Haworth, 1994).

31. Frank Boles, *Archival Appraisal* (New York: Neal-Schuman, 1991).

32. Helen Willa Samuels, *Varsity Letters: Documenting Modern Colleges and Universities* (Metuchen, NJ: Society of American Archivists and Scarecrow Press, 1992).

33. Heather MacNeil, *Without Consent: The Ethics of Disclosing Personal Information in Public Archives* (Metuchen, NJ: Society of American Archivists and the Scarecrow Press, 1992).

34. Paul Conway, *Partners in Research: Improving Access to the Nation's Archive: User Studies at the National Archives and Records Administration* (Pittsburgh: Archives and Museum Information, 1994).

35. Robert M. Warner, *Diary of a Dream: A History of the National Archives Independence Movement, 1980–1985* (Metuchen, NJ: Scarecrow, 1995).

36. Trevor Livelton, *Archival Theory, Records, and the Public* (Lanham, Md.: The Society of American Archivists and Scarecrow Press, 1996); and Luciana Duranti, *Diplomatics: New Uses for an Old Science* (Metuchen, NJ: Society of American Archivists, Association of Canadian Archivists, and Scarecrow Press, 1998).

37. Ann Pederson, "Analysis or Prescription? Richard Berner on Archival Theory and Practice," *Midwestern Archivist* 9, no. 1 (1984): 35, 41.

38. Gordon Dodds, "Archival Excursions," *Archivaria* 35 (Spring 1993): 274. Appropriately, we have now Terry Cook and Gordon Dodds, eds., *Imagining Archives: Essays and Reflections by Hugh Taylor* (Lanham, Md.: Society of American Archivists, Association of Canadian Archivists, in association with Scarecrow Press, 2003). There is little of the practical in Taylor's writings, just food for thought.

39. Terry Cook, "Rites of Passage: The Archivist and the Information Age," *Archivaria* 31 (Winter 1990–91): 171.

40. Tom Nesmith, ed., *Canadian Archival Studies and the Rediscovery of Provenance* (Metuchen, NJ: Society of American Archivists and Association of Canadian Archivists in association with Scarecrow Press, 1993).

41. James M. O'Toole, ed., *The Records of American Business* (Chicago: Society of American Archivists, 1997).

42. Janet Fyfe and Clifford Collier, eds., *Symposium on Archival Education : proceedings* (London [Canada]: School of Library and Information Science, University of Western Ontario, 1980); Nancy E. Peace, ed., *Archival Choices: Managing the Historical Record in an Age of Abundance* (Lexington, MA: Lexington Books, 1984); Bureau of Canadian Archivists, *Toward Descriptive Standards: Report and Recommendations of the Canadian Working Group on Archival Descriptive Standards* (Ottawa: Bureau of Canadian Archivists, December 1985).

43. Bruce W. Dearstyne, ed., "Archives and Public History: Issues, Problems and Prospects," *The Public Historian* 8 (Summer 1986); Lawrence J. McCrank, ed., *Archives and Library Administration: Divergent Traditions and Common Concerns* (New York: Haworth, 1986); and Michele Valerie Cloonan, ed., "Recent Trends in Rare Book Librarianship," *Library Trends* 36 (Summer 1987).

44. See especially Athan G. Theoharis, ed., *A Culture of Secrecy: The Government Versus the People's Right to Know* (Lawrence: University Press of Kansas, 1998); David Stricklin and Rebecca Sharpless, eds., *The Past Meets the Present: Essays on Oral History* (Lanham, Md.: University Press of Maryland, 1988); and H. G. Jones, ed., *Historical Consciousness in the Early Republic: The Origins of State Historical Societies, Museums, and Collections, 1791–1861* (Chapel Hill: North Caroliniana Society, Inc. and North Carolina Collection, 1995).

45. Barbara Craig, ed., *The Archival Imagination: Essays in Honour of Hugh Taylor* (Ottawa: Association of Canadian Archivists, 1992).

46. Examples include Sissela Bok, *Secrets: On the Ethics of Concealment and Revelation* (New York: Pantheon Books, 1982); Janna Malamud Smith, *Private Matters: In Defense of the Personal Life* (Reading, Mass.: Addison–Wesley, 1997), one of particular interest with its assessment about access to the literary archives of the author's father (Bernard Malamud); Richard E. Neustadt and Ernest R. May, *Thinking in Time: The Uses of History for Decision Makers* (New York: Free Press, 1986); David Rudenstine, *The Day the Presses Stopped: A History of the Pentagon Papers Case* (Berkeley: University of California Press, 1996); E. Wayne Carp, *Family Matters: Secrecy and Disclosure in the History of Adoption* (Cambridge: Harvard University Press, 1998); Patricia Cline Cohen, *A Calculating People: The Spread of Numeracy in Early America* (Chicago: University of Chicago Press, 1982); and Margery W. Davies, *Woman's Place Is at the Typewriter: Office Work and Office Workers 1870–1920* (Philadelphia: Temple University Press, 1982).

47. Some examples are Louis Leonard Tucker, *Clio's Consort: Jeremy Belknap and the Founding of the Massachusetts Historical Society* (Boston: Massachusetts Historical Society, 1990); Jed I. Bergman, in collaboration with William G. Bowen and Thomas I. Nygren, *Managing Change in the Nonprofit Sector: Lessons from the Evolution of Five Independent Research Libraries* (San Francisco: Jossey-Bass, 1996); and especially Kevin M. Guthrie, *The New-York Historical Society: Lessons from One Nonprofit's Long Struggle for Survival* (San Francisco: Jossey-Bass, 1996).

48. Some examples include Jack Goody, *The Logic of Writing and the Organi-*

zation of Society (Cambridge: Cambridge University Press, 1986) and *The Interface Between the Written and the Oral* (Cambridge: Cambridge University Press, 1987); Margo J. Anderson, *The American Census: A Social History* (New Haven: Yale University Press, 1988); Martha S. Feldman, *Order Without Design: Information Production and Policy Making* (Stanford: Stanford University Press, 1989); Laurel Thatcher Ulrich, *A Midwife's Tale: The Life of Martha Ballard, Based on Her Diary, 1785–1812* (New York: Vintage Books, 1990); Suzanne L. Bunkers and Cynthia A. Huff, eds., *Inscribing the Daily: Critical Essays on Women's Diaries* (Amherst: University of Massachusetts Press, 1996); Tamara Plakins Thornton, *Handwriting in America: A Cultural History* (New Haven: Yale University Press, 1996), with many interesting references to the creation of letters and the rise of autograph collecting; and David M. Henkin, *City Reading: Written Words and Public Spaces in Antebellum New York* (New York: Columbia University Press, 1998).

49. Collecting, in general, received the most critical attention, such as with Werner Muensterberger, *Collecting: An Unruly Passion; Psychological Perspectives* (Princeton: Princeton University Press, 1994).

50. Janet Malcolm, *In the Freud Archives*, originally published in 1984 was recently re-issued. See Rick Klumpenhouwer, "On the Archival Couch: Freud and the Freud Archives," *Archivaria* 21 (Winter 1985–1986): 198–203.

51. Steven Naifeh and Gregory White Smith, *The Mormon Murders: A True Story of Greed, Forgery, Deceit, and Death* (New York: New American Library, 1988); Linda Sillitoe and Allen D. Roberts, *Salamander: The Story of the Mormon Forgery Murders* (Salt Lake City: Signature Books, 1988); and Richard E. Turley, Jr., *Victims: The LDS Church and the Mark Hoffman Case* (Urbana: University of Illinois Press, 1992).

52. JoAnne Yates, *Control Through Communication: The Rise of System in American Management* (Baltimore: Johns Hopkins University Press, 1989); Donna Merwick, *Death of a Notary: Conquest and Change in Colonial New York* (New York: Cornell University Press, 1999).

53. Stanton A. Glantz, John Slade, Lisa A. Bero, Peter Hanauer, and Deborah E. Barnes, *The Cigarette Papers* (Berkeley: University of California Press, 1996); Shelley L. Davis, *Unbridled Power: Inside the Secret Culture of the IRS* (New York: HarperBusiness, 1997).

54. Examples include C. Peter Waegemann, *Handbook of Record Storage and Space Management* (Westport, Conn.: Greenwood Press, 1983); Betty R. Ricks and Kay F. Gow, *Information Resource Management* (Cincinnati: South-Western, 1984); and Ira Penn, *Records Management Handbook* (Brookfield, VT: Gower, 1989).

55. See, for example, Mark A. Greene, "The Power of Memory: The Archival Mission in the Postmodern Age," *American Archivist* 65 (Spring/Summer 2000): 42–55.

56. The first debate was started by George Bolotenko's plea for archival work being more firmly rooted in historical studies. For his initial essay and subsequent responses to commentators, see "Archivists and Historians:

Keepers of the Well," *Archivaria* 16 (Summer 1983): 5–25; "Of Ends and Means: In Defence of the Archival Ideal," *Archivaria* 18 (Summer 1984): 241–247; "Instant Professionalism: To the Shiny New Men of the Future," *Archivaria* 20 (Summer 1985): 149–157; and "Professional Convergence: New Bindings, Old Pages," *Archivaria* 27 (Winter 1988–89): 133–142. The second debate revolved about John Roberts's writings, such as his "Archival Theory: Much Ado About Shelving," *American Archivist* 50 (Winter 1987): 67–74; "Archival Theory: Myth or Banality," *American Archivist* 53 (Winter 1990): 110–120; and "Practice Makes Perfect, Theory Makes Theorists," *Archivaria* 37 (Spring 1994): 111–121. The first essay by Roberts was a response to yet another, earlier debate about theory that commenced with Frank G. Burke, "The Future Course of Archival Theory in the United States," *American Archivist* 44 (Winter 1981): 40–46.

57. Ann A. Gordon, *Using the Nation's Documentary Heritage: The Report of the Historical Documents Study* (Washington, D.C.: American Council of Learned Societies, 1992).

58. See, for example, Jacques Derrida, *Archive Fever: A Freudian Impression* (Chicago: University of Chicago Press, 1996); Donald H. Reiman, *The Study of Modern Manuscripts: Public, Confidential, and Private* (Baltimore: Johns Hopkins University Press, 1993); Barbie Zelizer, *Covering the Body: The Kennedy Assassination, the Media, and the Shaping of Collective Memory* (Chicago: University of Chicago Press, 1992); John Tagg, *The Burden of Representation: Essays on Photographies and Histories* (Minneapolis: University of Minnesota Press, 1993); Shawn Michelle Smith, *American Archives: Gender, Race, and Class in Visual Culture* (Princeton, NJ: Princeton University Press, 1999); and Roy Rosenzweig and David Thelen, *The Presence of the Past: Popular Uses of History in American Life* (New York: Columbia University Press, 1998).

59. Barbara L. Craig, "Selected Themes in the Literature on Memory and Their Pertinence to Archives," *American Archivist* 65 (Fall/Winter 2002): 279. See also Francis X. Blouin, Jr., "Archivists, Mediation, and Constructs of Social Memory," *Archival Issues* 24, no. 2 (1999): 101–112; and Brien Brothman, "The Past That Archives Keep: Memory, History, and the Preservation of Archival Records," *Archivaria* 51 (Spring 2001): 48–80.

60. One recent example might suffice to demonstrate what I mean. Gary Nash's study, *First City: Philadelphia and the Forging of Historical Memory* (Philadelphia: University of Pennsylvania Press, 2002), tells the "story of how museums, libraries, and historical societies, beginning in the late eighteenth century, became instrumental in transmitting historical memory from one generation to another by collecting, preserving, and exhibiting what they regarded as the stuff of history." While *First City* is a book all archivists should read, it is a somewhat curious scholarly achievement. Nash emphasizes the roles of these repositories in telling stories, creating meaningful myths, generating "useful" knowledge, fashioning order and unity in society, perpetuating the frauds of bogus artifacts in order to shape a particular cultural memory, and sustaining legends as a means of getting at the truths of the past. One of the most

interesting problems with Nash's approach is that although he is studying how archives and manuscripts and other repositories acquire records,
he seems to make no effort to understand the professional issues and
standards of the various disciplines involved with such work. Nash's
interest in social history leads him to be critical of organizations like the
Historical Society of Pennsylvania for ignoring such matters, and he is
right to be concerned (although for Nash this seems to be the main criteria for assessing the performance of any collecting repository, failing to
bear in mind that there are many other reasons that records are gath-
ered). Later, Nash also displays something of a lack of appreciation for
modern recordkeeping when he writes, "In an era before modern recordkeeping and before civil service, fragments of municipal records—even
tax assessors' lists and quarter-session court records—surface in the private papers of civic leaders" (quotations pp. 10, 47, 71). While this is certainly true, Nash's idea that there is a clear demarcation between modern
and more systematic recordkeeping is somewhat fallacious, especially as
municipal records programs have been very late in developing and have
achieved checkered success. One of Nash's contributions to the history
of collecting is his analysis of the kinds of artifacts ignored and his description of other collectors, providing a more balanced sense of the kind
of collecting being performed, but Nash has made no effort to examine or
understand the evolution of archival appraisal principles and approaches.
Would a historian of science ignore scientific methods or a historian of
technology gloss over technical and engineering approaches of the period in question? Historians assume they comprehend archival methodology by virtue of being historians, or, that there is no methodology worth
examining.

61.   As Wosh suggests, we have "institutional archives vs. manuscript repositories; graduate-trained archivists vs. those with post-appointment training; national organizations vs. local and regional groups; lone arrangers
vs. laborers in large bureaucratic organizations; archival theoreticians vs.
everyday practitioners." Wosh, "Turning Pro: Reflections on the Career
of J. Franklin Jameson", *Provenance* 15 (1997): 101.

62.   James M. O'Toole, "Toward a Usable Archival Past: Recent Studies in the
History of Literacy," *American Archivist* 58 (Winter 1995): 99.

63.   Tom Nesmith, "Still Fuzzy, But More Accurate: Some Thoughts on the
'Ghosts' of Archival Theory," *Archivaria* 48 (Fall 1999): 142.

64.   Joan K. Haas, Helen Willa Samuels, and Barbara Trippel Simmones, "The
MIT Appraisal Project and Its Broader Applications," *American Archivist*
49 (Summer 1986): 310–314.

65.   An examination of the publications list offered by the Association of
Records Managers and Administrators at www.arma.org provides a sense
of this.

66.   The survey results were published at http://www.arma.org/publications/
infopro/online.cfm#six and accessed April 17, 2003, the date the results
were released.

67. Maynard J. Brichford, "Seven Sinful Thoughts," *American Archivist* 43 (Winter 1980): 14.
68. See my "An Analysis of Archival Research, 1970–92, and the Role and Function of the *American Archivist*," *American Archivist* 57 (Spring 1994): 278–288 for a discussion of the various research agendas materializing in this time period.
69. Carolyn Hamilton, Verne Harris, Jane Taylor, Michele Pickover, Graeme Reid, and Razia Saleh, eds., *Refiguring the Archive* (Dordrecht: Kluwer Academic, 2002), p. 7.
70. Tom Nesmith, "Seeing Archives: Postmodernism and the Changing Intellectual Place of Archives," *American Archivist* 65 (Spring/Summer 2002): 26–27.
71. Terry Cook, "What is Past is Prologue: A History of Archival Ideas Since 1898, and the Future Paradigm Shift," *Archivaria* 43 (Spring 1997): 45.
72. Tom Nesmith, "'Professional Education in the Most Expansive Sense': What Will the Archivist Need to Know in the Twenty-First Century?" *Archivaria* 42 (Fall 1996): 91.
73. Stephen Jay Gould, *The Hedgehog, The Fox, and the Magister's Pox: Mending the Gap Between Science and the Humanities* (New York: Harmony Books, 2003), 82.
74. Gould, *The Hedgehog, The Fox, and the Magister's Pox*, 195.

10

Putting It Altogether: Case Studies of Four Institutional Records Programs

INTRODUCTION

Although the advent of the so-called Information Age has diverted the attention of many from records to a variety of other forms of information, records are still a prime source of information for any organization. The information found in organizational records is critical to the institution. Traditionally, records with archival value (those with continuing use or of historical significance to both the institutional creator and other components of society) were needed for ongoing administrative, fiscal, legal, and research values. More recently, archives and other records have been described as possessing value for purposes of accountability, evidence, and corporate memory.

While these various values can be debated, it is nonetheless true that records are produced for particular reasons by an organization at great expense and, if for no other reason, deserve to be managed as a corporate asset. It is also true that without the crucial information often found in institutional records, an organization can make poor decisions, waste time and energy in recreating information normally found in records, and operate at less than an optimal level.

Many institutions become concerned about their records and information systems when they reach critical chronological or organizational benchmarks. They then recognize their systems' historical significance; fear that their organizational memory is becoming jeopardized by growth in size, turnover of staff, or the passage of time; face growing quantities of records or the adoption of more sophisticated information systems that challenge their ways of doing things; or encounter an administrative, legal, or fiscal crisis in part attributable to problems with records and information systems.

In recent decades, an unfortunate barrier has been erected between archivists and records managers, a barrier made more troublesome by the emergence of newer fields like information resources and knowledge management. Nevertheless, organizations often come to recognize problems with their records and information systems through concerns over such issues as corporate memory and the accumulation of older records represent liabilities because of problems of access.

Institutions generally do not acknowledge the full scope and nature of their problems. A local government authority issued a call for proposals to assess its "historical resources." The call asked for a "comprehensive assessment of archival materials." The organization wanted an identification of its "historically valuable documents, photographs and artifacts," as well as an evaluation of the "strengths and weaknesses of the collection" and the "physical condition of the archives." The local government wanted a consultant's report to describe "findings of the [archives] survey" and to outline "recommendations for the ongoing storage and management" of the archives and related materials.

The scope of the report, however, had to be much broader than what was requested, since it is impossible to distinguish between the management of current records and the identification, preservation, and use of records possessing archival value. (This is well known to records professionals through the concept of the records life cycle or continuum—even if these concepts seem to do little in resolving the professional or disciplinary separation between archivists, records managers, and other information professionals). It is impossible to have an effective records management program without an archival program; it is also impossible to have a valid archival program without a connection to records management. Records management functions ensure that records with archival value are properly identified—and the identification of archival records is crucial because these records have ongoing administrative, research, and other worth to any organization. In the case of archival records, the distinction between current and non-current records is not very helpful, since archival records have a continuing value (a currency) to the creating institution.

This chapter is an assessment of advising institutions (two local governments and two religious organizations) on how to establish or to reenergize programs for administering their records, bringing together many of the issues discussed in the previous chapters in practical applications to real-life situations. In all four cases, the institutions had a limited concept of what they wanted advice about; they mostly started out with a concern for their older records, either because of a forthcoming anniversary or obvious management and storage problems best visualized through the organization's oldest records. The first part of this extended essay considers the essential matters supporting an institutional records program and a description of the needs of four different organizations in administering their records. The second part of this essay provides recommendations for improving the administration of their records, both archives and current records, with general conclusions about the parameters of institutional records programs.

THE ESSENTIAL IMPORTANCE OF RECORDS PROGRAMS

Why is an archives and records management (ARM) program needed? Since many records have continuing value to an organization, an ARM program is the best means for ensuring that such records are maintained. The typical organization needs accessibility to both current and archival records for functions like continued public relations and marketing. Most institutions, whether for-profit, not-for-profit, public, or private sector organizations, require adequate documentation of their functions and activities to ensure compliance with external regulations and understanding of internal needs.

An institutional archives program is much more than the gathering up of older and obsolete, but interesting, records. An institutional records management program is much more than shuffling obsolete paper records out the door. The potential and necessity of both kinds of programs must be understood.

Institutional archives represent the memory of an organization, at least the part that is captured through its records. (Knowledge managers have even expanded the concept of corporate memory to encompass records, people, traditions, symbols, and other institutional features.)

Records are generally deemed to have archival value because of their administrative, legal, fiscal, or research uses—or some critical combination of these uses. Records with such continuing value are generally moved to an archives because they retain some vital use to the organization. The particular manner in which that use is determined often varies with the organization and its needs. In a highly regulated organization, for example, extra care will be given to ensuring that the organization is compliant with its external regulations and legal sanctions, and many of the records maintained as part of an archives might be kept there because of such concerns. In a less regulated organization, but one with particular constituent needs or providing critical services, an archives program may be serving both as documentation of these activities and perhaps playing a symbolic role in supporting some sense of the legacy of the organization.

Understanding an institutional archives starts with understanding records, rather than comprehending historical aspects of an organization. A record is a document capturing a transaction. Each record consists of structure (a form such as a letter or memorandum), content (the literal topic, issue, event, or activity being described), and context (who or what function originated the document). Records are usually created because of a warrant, a process requiring, regulating, or encouraging the creation. Warrants range from legal requirements to professional best practices to custom and tradition. Records are managed because of these attributes. Managing them in appropriate ways enables an organization to sustain its memory, provide accountability of its activities, and to preserve significant evidence of its origins, evolution, present activities, and potential future directions. Records serve both broad cultural or symbolic roles as well as more utilitarian functions to enable the present functioning of an organization.

Records encompass both organizational records and personal papers. Understanding the nature of personal papers and organizational records includes the key to determining how to design institutional archives. Such an archives should exist not merely as a repository of interesting old documentation, but as part of a rigorous formulation to document in a thorough manner the critical or most important activities of an organization. The value of the archives—as organizational memory and as a source for documenting its history, ensuring compliance, and other aspects—stems from approaching the process of gathering archival records in a well thought-through manner.

The traditional values of a records management operation encompass at least five broad functions. Records management can help an organization achieve fiscal economy in the management of its records. Records are expensive to produce and, if not managed properly, can be far more expensive to maintain. A simple memo or letter can cost an organization many dollars to produce, but the *loss* of a crucial letter or memo can be much more expensive—in lost time tracking it down and recreating it (if it is even possible to do so), or in lost business or a lost court case.

Records management can assist an organization to achieve efficiency in its control and use of records. This encompasses both better access to existing records and helping to ensure that appropriate records are created in the first place. Organizations are literally drowning in records and information generated from records and other sources. Without efforts to strengthen control of records that must be kept or to destroy those records that don't need to be maintained as soon as possible, the effectiveness of organizations will be diminished in the modern Information Age. And, in the present Information Age, the ability of an organization to compete and to fulfill its mission depends to a large extent on its ability to manage its records and the information contained in them.

Records management can enable an institution to eliminate useless or obsolete records and discourage the creation of unnecessary records. Only a small portion of an organization's records needs to be maintained beyond ten years (or even after six or three years) after their creation. Maintenance of unnecessary records makes it difficult for an organization to use its needed records, as well as adding financial costs that could be effectively avoided.

Records management can help an organization select appropriate recordkeeping systems. In this day and age, electronic recordkeeping and other flashy information systems are available. To make the best possible selection and use of such systems, an organization must understand its records needs. Technology, without a careful assessment of its best use, is not the solution, and, indeed, it can turn out to be a problem.

Finally, records management can provide a valuable, continuing service to the organization. Employees constantly need information from their records, as well as to keep their records as "under control" as possible. Records management is the key to meeting these important needs.

An archives program also provides essential services to the organization. These services are often described by archives professionals as identifying, preserving, and making available for use records with archival (continuing) value. A better way to characterize these services is in the notion of corporate memory, evidence, and accountability already mentioned.

The most logical, visible, and crucial function of an archives is to provide a corporate memory for the institution, especially if it is undergoing personnel and other changes that occur as an organization ages. Such an organization can no longer rely on the memory of its long-term employees, but must be able to retrieve older information from its records on an as-needed basis. This also requires that the right records be identified as worth preserving by the organization.

An archives also helps an organization to be accountable to its constituency or regulatory agents. It preserves records that may be useful when the organization needs to demonstrate or defend its past actions and decisions. In order for an organization to be accountable, it must have accountable recordkeeping systems—meaning that they are responsible, implemented (used as intended by the organization), and reliable. Such concerns have become more critical in the post-Enron/Arthur Andersen age of new accountability (much of it mandated by new federal legislation).

Accountability is achieved by preserving the organization's most essential evidence, another crucial function of an institutional archives. Evidence can be defined in a variety of ways, from a purely legal definition of what is acceptable in court to information regarding a past action. In the broader sense, evidence is the result of a particular record's data, structure, and context, and it results every time an organization records a transaction. Every transaction must be captured, maintained as long as is needed, and usable whenever needed. If such transactions are not maintained carefully, what makes them valuable as records to the organization can be lost.

Archives and records management programs support a number of basic functions crucial to any organization. These programs, working together or combined (the ideal arrangement) into a single administrative unit, can support at least five necessary institutional functions.

Archives and records management programs and their staffs perform records analysis. An institutional records management program conducts systems studies, surveys records and recordkeeping systems, and schedules specific retention time periods for each series of records through appraisal.

Archives and records management identify records vital to the continuing operation of the organization. Vital records are those without which the organization cannot function or which would be difficult and expensive to recreate in case of loss. These are records that, if destroyed by some unexpected event, would significantly reduce the organization's ability to function in order to meet its mission and to serve its clients.

Archives and records management provide records retrieval and design functions. Forms management is an excellent example of this area of activity. The vast majority of records are created through the use of forms. If forms are poorly designed, they can lead to substantial problems in the maintenance of records. Forms management also provides a crucial means by which records throughout an organization can be managed through retention schedules and other similar activities.

Archives and records management provides for records security and preservation. Some records contain privacy or proprietary information, and therefore require special handling throughout their existence and special treatment when destroyed. Archival records also require special environment and handling in order to ensure their long-term preservation.

Finally, archives and records management administer programs that ensure the adequate administration of an organization's records. They develop, use, distribute, and revise as needed policies and procedures regarding the management of an organization's records. Crucial to this function is the development of a records liaison system that maintains a network of staff involved in managing an institution's records. Given the increasing decentralization of records creation and management evident in most modern organizations, this function is more than a necessary one.

What follows is the description of records problems encountered by four organizations—two government and two not-for-profit (religious) institutions—that reflects the importance of records programs. Although there are many other organizations (such as for-profit business enterprises) that could be considered, these case studies were included because they represent real-life work by the author. The kinds of records challenges described are typical of all organizations, although the scale of the problems, the nature of external rules and regulations affecting records generation and maintenance, and the motivations for resolving such problems may vary.

CASE STUDY ONE: A LOCAL GOVERNMENT AUTHORITY

Befitting a thirty-year-old organization, there is a considerable quantity of archival and other records. These range from administrative records to photographs and publicity materials. There is no question that these records are essential to the local authority's ongoing administration, and the records are generally comprehensive in scope of its responsibilities and activities. The older records are called upon for speeches, public relations and media relations, and analysis of long-term projects. The nature of the authority's function and importance in the late twentieth century development of its region also merit the maintenance and preservation of the archival records. If the local authority does not preserve and manage these records, it runs the risk of damaging its relations with portions of the public who might want access to these records for historical and other research purposes.

A major problem with the local government archives (and records in general) is how they are defined and viewed. This problem is typical of most organizations, but it must be rectified or important records with continuing value to the organization might be lost. Archives are generally viewed in the authority as the "old" records. Archives are also considered to consist of a select few record types and forms. The records stored in the vault in the finance department are what many in the local government perceive to be the archives, including board minutes, files on the acquisition of older companies and other entities to form the authority, and copies of grant and project files. While these are important records, they do not represent all of the archival records or even the most important ones. There is also a lack of knowledge about what these records represent and whether other related records exist; both problems undermine the ability of the authority to be able to effectively use its older records.

The physical condition of the records ranges from satisfactory to excellent. Given that the records are mostly less than thirty years old and that the impact of electronic recordkeeping systems has been minimal to date, the physical condition of the records is good. However, the greater problem is that intellectual control over the existing records is less than satisfactory, whether they are piled up in offices in the headquarters, stored in other facilities, or held a commercial records service. Related records are stored in more than one location, and records overlapping in function, origin, and topic are scattered throughout the local government facilities.

Both the marketing and media relations units hold very closely related records with their slides, photographs, and public relations material, and while they know of each other's holdings, the lack of descriptive information makes finding needed records and information extremely difficult. The possibility of records being removed, lost, and mishandled is also very likely in such an environment. So although the archival records are now in reasonably good condition, they could be easily lost or mistreated. The local government's corporate memory is in jeopardy.

The engineering division has made a valiant effort to administer its engineering and related drawings, and its efforts are a good sign of the kind of staff support that can be found for assisting an archives and records management program. The division has set up a storage area, where engineering drawings are stored in flat cases and arranged by original contract number. A master index of drawings has been developed, and microfilm copies of the drawings have been made and filed on aperture cards in order to provide access without wear and tear on the originals and to be able to make prints on demand. A sign-out system is in place, and it appears that there is careful follow-up on any original drawings that have not been returned in a timely manner.

Such efforts may be a rarity within the local government, and they reflect the limitations of the current approaches used to manage records. There are some records, such as old blueprints, that are extremely brittle and that are revealing signs of deterioration; these are unique originals and their loss cannot by made up in any other fashion. Yet, no steps are being taken to deal with these records, attesting either to a lack of resources available for such purposes or a lack of knowledge about how to proceed. Although there are means by which these drawings could be stored or copied, the lack of knowledge of the engineering division of records management and archival principles probably prevents such actions.

There are other problems—from poor environmental storage conditions to failures to capture important records from various contractors and vendors working with the local authority. Engineering and architectural firms using CAD software have been required to transfer CAD records to the authority upon the completion of projects, causing problems for the authority in the maintenance of its projects and revisions to the drawings. Another major problem is the impossibility of knowing the extent of the local authority's archives or being able to locate the archival records efficiently or effectively.

The purpose of an institutional archives is to do more than to provide a mechanism for saving old records. An archives program exists to preserve records crucial to maintaining an organization's corporate memory, enabling the institution to understand from where its current activities derived, as well as to find information about past activities. An institutional archives also identifies and preserves records that help an organization to be accountable to its constituencies and to protect the evidence required by regulatory and other agencies. Institutional archives seek to identify the primary functions of an organization and to ensure that records vital to understanding and documenting such functions are maintained as long as they are needed.

It is impossible to be able to tell whether the archival records adequately document the local authority's primary functions, although it is likely that not much has been destroyed due to the relative youth of the organization and the utilization of the commercial records center for off-site storage. Except for some clusters of older records found in scattered places, records with archival value have not been identified.

Significant gaps in the local authority's records will probably develop. Although the existing records retention schedule identifies some records as "permanent," it fails to provide adequately detailed descriptions of records that might possess continuing value to the organization. At the least, the schedule is not a surrogate for a comprehensive view of the local government's records universe, a purpose that such a schedule should be able to meet. There is no focus for archival records, and, as a result, there is no way to determine if adequate archival documentation exists; determining this will require some careful records surveying after identification of the essential authority functions.

An even greater problem at this point is the lack of any intellectual control over the authority's archival records. An institutional archives exists to provide needed and timely information. At the moment, there are only a few individuals who have determined the need to develop areas of expertise about older activities of the authority, and these individuals are called upon to provide information when needed or to point to where necessary records may exist. This arrangement leaves too much to chance. As the authority becomes older, a corporate memory dependent on such a process will become flawed. An archives program, staffed by a professional with adequate information about the location, nature, and content of archival records can provide a much steadier and more reliable source of information.

Problems with the authority's archives stem from the difficulties associated with the management of all the local authority records. The identification, preservation, and access of archival records requires a good records management program that can provide for the orderly transfer of archival records to an archives operation, or the development of a locator system that can lead anyone needing access to archival records to their location. Problems in records management range from issues of creation to concerns about access and use to staffing of the records management unit.

The most immediate records challenge faced by the local authority is access to records, along the same lines as the difficulties confronting staff with the archival records. If records needed are not found within a few minutes, then the prospects for locating them within a reasonable time (less than an hour) are bleak. This problem has a high visibility, with a majority of offices heavily cluttered with records. A typical office has file cabinets jammed with records, records boxes of all shapes and sizes stacked around the desks and in hallways, and loose records piled high in corners and all available space. While some of this records clutter has to do with office renovation, the majority of it appears to be a manifestation of the records not being well managed.

Some staff members complained about other staff removing records at will as they needed them and not returning them in a timely fashion or at all. While staff members make efforts to take charge of the records in their immediate custody, there is a discernible lack of authority regarding who has ultimate responsibility for records management issues. The physical condition of records indicates chaos instead of order. This is not an accidental or natural result but rather the direct outcome of the absence of records systems and administration responsibilities for these systems. It is difficult to imagine that substantial time and resources are not wasted in trying to locate records when they are needed.

The lack of control with the paper records also indicates substantial problems with creation of records and development of adequate recordkeeping systems. Although there is a forms program associated with the records management unit, most departments create their own forms as they need them, using their own computer equipment and resources. Since a high percentage of any organization's records are forms driven, this lack of control is a serious problem for an orderly records management program.

The forms management operation is completely reactive; it works on forms development or revision when a unit or division requests assistance. This type of reactive operation means that the records management unit will not have a thorough knowledge of the extent and nature of forms used by the various offices. This is a major problem given that forms management is absolutely essential to the management of records throughout the organization.

There are other similar problems. While most of the local authority is not yet automated, the absence of any systematic process for developing or selecting electronic recordkeeping and information systems does not bode well for the future. Departments are scanning documents, considering image systems, and exploring other options without necessarily understanding existing requirements for the retention of their records. As the authority becomes more automated, the potential for records problems will increase exponentially. While electronic systems can provide faster and more efficient access to records, they can also—without proper judicious selection and design—speed up the development of records problems. The issue to consider is the care with which records concerns are evaluated as new recordkeeping and other information technology is acquired. It is easy to seek solutions in the acquisition of new hardware and software; however, in reality, such solutions are not possible unless the problems that have plagued the local authority in the management of its paper-based records systems are resolved.

Records management problems at the local authority can also be seen in the inadequate use of the records liaisons (or coordinators). Records liaisons were appointed in the late 1980s when the records management program was established, but there are serious problems with how these liaisons are being used. For one, the scope of activities and responsibilities of these individuals seems focused on boxing, inventorying, and sending records, through the records manager, off to the commercial records center.

The records liaison function also seems to have several other inherent flaws. First, the records liaisons do not necessarily understand the existing records retention schedule that they use as a template for boxing the records. At times, they need to interpret the schedule fairly broadly. Second, they sometimes mix records from different records series and with different records retention schedules in order to fill a box. This is a violation of basic records management and archival principles—destroying evidence that is generated by contextual relationships and making it difficult to dispose of records in an orderly fashion. It can also cause major problems down the line when records need to be located or destroyed. If records have been removed from their context as well, this can lead to problems with their use as evidence and in their general interpretation.

Third, the records liaisons do not meet regularly to share mutual concerns or to develop solutions, and they receive no instruction or additional training in their records responsibility capacities. A few seemed to have had some meetings or received some instruction, but there is no question that it was sporadic at best. In fact, there is an even greater problem here. The records liaisons have often been assigned their responsibilities as an additional mandate with no accompanying resources or even any expectation of what it is that they were supposed to accomplish.

The problem with the records liaisons is rather surprising, given that the local authority has a reasonably good records management manual. The manual includes a good working definition of records management with all the proper components described as part of this definition. The benefits of records management are well described. Responsibilities for the division records coordinators are articulated. If there are any flaws with the manual, they are the result of being too focused on the inventory and scheduling functions and, more importantly, with a lack of educational and training opportunities to get the manual into the hands of employees so that they will understand how to use it for their benefit.

There are many other responsibilities of records management that need to be addressed in addition to administering the records schedule. It is quite possible that the manual is more reflective of wholesale borrowing of its contents than either understanding or acquiring the necessary resources to implement it in an effective manner. In other words, its content is good, but its execution has been very poor. This poor execution may have as much to do with the fact that division records liaisons are given their responsibilities as just one additional set of requirements, and the lack of an aggressive records management program provides the liaisons with the perfect opportunity to pay little attention to records concerns.

Indicative of the broad problems associated with the local authority's management of its records is its lack of information on all phases of the administration of its records. Departments purchase records supplies individually (adding to the costs of such supplies by not buying in bulk as an institution), and no one seems to maintain reliable figures on the financial aspects of the administration of records. In other words, if money is being wasted, it is even difficult to determine the extent of such waste.

There are other serious problems as well. The authority does not have a disaster plan for its records. In the event of a fire or other natural disaster occurring, or mischief by an employee or visitor, there is now no standardized procedures to direct immediate and authoritative response. Moreover, crucial records are not being systematically identified and reformatted (through some sort of imaging process) for duplication and off-site storage.

The nature of the microfilming that is being done should also cause concern for the authority, and it is again symptomatic of the larger records management problems. Microfilming is not being used to support an organization-wide vital records program, but instead is being used to produce multiple copies for access and reference. The engineering division tries to microfilm all records related to a project one year after the project is completed, primarily so that its staff can gain access to the records as quickly as possible. While this is an appropriate use, it is not the priority use.

Moreover, the authority's microfilming operations seem to be operating with only a modicum of knowledge about industry standards and best practices governing microfilm quality control. Its notion of quality control is checking processed film to be sure that what was filmed is complete and the images are clear. However, there is no readily apparent knowledge of production standards such as those supported by the American National Standards Institute (ANSI), standards absolutely fundamental to ensuring that the microfilm produced will hold up over time.

A larger problem with the authority's records management operation can be seen in the matter of how unaware staff members are of external regulations and guidelines for such functions as microfilming. Understanding ANSI standards is part of this problem. The records management unit is utilizing an outdated external manual for its microfilm operations. Their knowledge about the range of microfilming seems fairly limited, stressing the use of rotary and planetary cameras but not considering other approaches, such as computer output microfilm or other imaging systems. The local authority is rife to be taken advantage of by vendors trying to sell the latest technology applications, before it has even managed to establish its own priorities and to identify its main needs.

The local authority's records management is extremely limited in scope, far too limited to be of much use as it continues to evolve and as it adopts and adapts new forms of recordkeeping systems. The local authority is focused on the scheduling of records and off-site records storage. Both are adequate in theory, but both are of limited worth in application. The authority has confused its use of a commercial records center as being an adequate records management program; such use can only be satisfactory as part of a comprehensive records management operation.

What the authority does in records management will not expand beyond its present limited nature as long as the current staff is kept in place. The present records manager formerly was a clerk-typist. In modern organizations employing increasingly sophisticated electronic information technology and dealing with difficult legal and related records issues, an individual without relevant experience and education will not be of much use in new records management approaches and techniques. Just as serious is that the current records manager is also functioning in other administrative services.

The remaining staff includes a micrographics technician and a clerk-typist. This is an extremely poor staff complement for a unit with such important and challenging responsibilities. While the records management unit need not be a larger unit—provided that it is supported because the local authority has deemed records management to be a priority for its operations—it does require energetic, informed, and professional leadership.

The nature of the records schedule suggests many of the problems of the present authority's records management program—if it can be called a functioning program. The records retention and disposition schedule is a broad, general schedule arranged alphabetically by the title of the records series. It is a fairly standard schedule in that it provides the records series title, name of department creating or maintaining the record or official copy of the record series (although not indicated clearly), disposition information with room for additional comments, and a "remarks" column that is not used. There are two problems with this schedule, the source of its authority and the level of information provided, preventing its effective use.

The authority's records schedule was adopted from an external source. Unfortunately, there is not even good control over the records generated in the development of this records retention schedule, a sad commentary on the inadequacies of the local authority's current records management program. A records management operation should maintain files on the records of all administrative units as well as on its own policies and procedures. It is now impossible to go back to evaluate how the records schedule was developed. The schedule is used purely for opening up more space in the local authority's offices by providing the rationale for the transfer of records to the commercial records center. Authorizations to destroy records identified through the schedule seems to be the result of an uncertain process, in which a division head and records manager sign off to approve such destruction, but there is a murkiness about who else ought to review such disposition decisions.

The use of a commercial records center is a perfectly acceptable mechanism for dealing with the off-site storage of records. The commercial alternative can provide excellent storage and retrieval services along with maximum security for the records at a relatively modest cost. There are limitations, however, with what the center can provide because it cannot be a substitute for a quality internal records management program. In fact, the use of such a commercial records center without a respectable records management program can lead to the storage of records that don't need to be stored and, obviously, increased financial expenditures.

The best use of the center will continue to be for the storage of non-current records needing storage before final destruction. Even in this function, its use will only be optimal if the local authority adopts a more comprehensive and aggressive records management program. The authority needs to enlarge the scope of activities of its records management program, from just a focus on the cycling of paper records to encompass planning and implementation of all aspects of the administration of recordkeeping systems—from electronic to paper and from current to archival records.

CASE STUDY TWO: A SMALL MUNICIPAL GOVERNMENT

With little distinction made between current and non-current records, the archival and other records of this municipality are maintained in two basement rooms of the main municipal building. An interest in reformatting the records led the municipality to seek outside advice, and it became obvious that there were other concerns and issues regarding the use and maintenance of the archival records that required a broader assessment of the city's records. Reformatting, whether accomplished through traditional approaches such as microfilm or through the use of newer digital technologies, must be decided upon and utilized within the context of records management needs and current records uses. There is no reason to focus on a small portion of the city's archival records for enhanced preservation or access if no provision is being made for overall administration of the municipal records.

The municipality's original interest in reformatting is interesting and revealing. It reflects intentions to preserve older paper records showing signs of deterioration and to provide enhanced access to the records that will ease the burden on the municipal zoning officer (the official who has assumed most of the records management and archival administration responsibilities) in terms of retrieving information from the paper records stored in the basement of the municipal building. Both are worthy objectives, but there are other issues the city needs to resolve, including the fact that preservation and access can, in reality, be quite opposite in their purposes and outcomes.

Adequate care for any government or organization's records requires the existence of some basic elements. First and foremost, the government must be aware of laws regulating the records and be interested in providing acceptable maintenance of these records. This municipality seems to possess these critical elements. However, there are other elements that are essential as well, such as records management expertise, records storage, and intellectual control over the records. In these, the municipality has some serious deficiencies.

The city government relies on records and archival management advice from the state government; the state provides general guidelines for the administration of local government records and archives, mostly in the form of requirements for records retention periods, housing of archival records, and basic functions like reformatting. A local government must possess continuing expertise on records management and archival administration in order to interpret and effectively use the state government guidelines.

It was easy to determine some salient characteristics of the municipal archives. Council minutes, dating back to the 1870s, are the most regularly used of the municipal archives—by current council members governing the municipality, high school students doing local history research, and other members of the public who need access when they work with the city government. Most of the requests for these records are for the previous five to ten years. The continuing use of these records, the backbone of the history of the municipal government and the city, demonstrates the value to the government of some sort of internal archives program. The municipality has rightly identified these records as part of a permanent archives, since these records provide documentation about the critical decisions and activities of local government. Except for the earliest volumes, the council minutes are generally in good condition and can withstand careful and moderated use by researchers and municipal officials. They are also prime candidates for reformatting because they are reasonably homogenous in size and format.

There is also a moderate-sized set of local maps and architectural drawings stored in one of the main municipal building basement areas, across the hall from the other records storage area containing the city council records. There are some important records in this group. There are, for example, architectural drawings of the municipal building that are important for any work on or within the building. There are also drawings related to other important structures within the city, and, at present, it seems as if these are the only publicly accessible drawings related to these buildings.

These records need to be reformatted in order to protect their critical evidence of current value to the city. These records do not just possess archival value; some clearly have value as vital records, records critical to the functioning or reconstitution of an organization, especially in protecting the legal and financial rights of an organization and of the individuals affected by its activities. The city needs to pay particular attention to records falling within the parameters constituting vital records.

These records have been identified as being permanent, in accordance with the requisite state laws and regulations. The present condition of these drawings is poor, especially since they are stored in an area that is also the staff smoking zone. The proximity of the smoking area to the storage of fragile records is a "disaster in the making." Secondhand smoke will discolor and damage the records, and there is an enhanced opportunity for a fire (this also may be a violation of the local fire code). Some of these drawings are on paper that is fading or that is becoming brittle, and the constant rolling and unrolling of these records is rapidly weakening them.

A careful inventory and identification of the most critical of these maps and drawings will focus attention on those requiring some sort of reformatting. Reformatting requires costly preparation and filming or digitizing because of their special size, colors, fading, paper quality, and other related physical characteristics. As a result, the initial focus of reformatting should remain on the council minutes, resolutions, and ordinances.

The zoning officer, who has taken a sort of unofficial authority for the archives, has made efforts to conform to the statewide guidelines for the management of local government records. This individual has used the statewide retention and disposition schedule for local government records to identify those records with archival value. The zoning officer has maintained some additional records (that is, records *not* required by the state government as archival records), based on her sense of the interests in use of older records produced by the city.

Even with this sensitivity to the potential use of the city's records, the current approach to municipal records management is more reactive and piecemeal than planned and proactive. For example, any decision for reformatting should be made based upon the ability to utilize the reformatted records in a variety of ways that will promote good city government, better community understanding of its government and its functions, and public relations and educational activities, such as the study of local history in the local schools.

The zoning officer also has made efforts to develop usable storage conditions in the basement of the municipal building, although these storage conditions are still very inadequate for the maintenance of records with continuing value. The state government's retention schedule for municipal records provides for administrative and legal; data processing; personnel; payroll; general financial and purchasing; tax collection and assessment; police, fire, and emergency services; public health; public works and engineering; waste management and sewage disposal; planning and building; zoning code enforcement; library; parks and recreation; and municipal health department records. However, only a small span of these records is represented in the records stored in the two municipal building basement storage areas—although the backbone of the city's government history are well represented with the city council records. The municipality needs to develop a citywide records management program, enabling it to make effective use of *all* records with continuing value to the city and the community.

While there have been efforts to provide better care for the municipal archives, there are *glaring problems* with the municipality's management of these records. These problems require attention to both the reformatting of selected records *and* to other means to improve the administration of these records. The first and foremost goal is gaining some improved intellectual control over the records in the municipal building. At present, the city relies on the general schedule provided by the state archives. What the city needs to do is to develop a detailed inventory of the existing archival and other records, not just in the basement areas but throughout the municipal offices. This inventory could be used to ensure that no records are being destroyed that are valuable to the city and the community, and that the city is in conformity with the state government requirements.

An inventory needs to include such information as the records generating agency, title of a particular records series, general description of the nature of the records, the date range of the records, and the physical location of the records. Conducting an inventory of the archival records will help identify gaps in the records. The importance of having an inventory came to light during my visit, when historic ordinances and resolutions of the city council were discovered. It had been assumed that the ordinances and resolutions prior to 1948 had been destroyed in a flood. In looking through the records in one of the basement storage areas, three volumes of these ordinances and resolutions, spanning 1854 into the 1920s, were found. It is possible that a more thorough inventory process will uncover even more records and fill in other documentary gaps. This type of process should be a priority for the city.

The municipality also needs to reconsider its current records storage methods. The zoning officer's efforts to find some space are commendable. However, these spaces have serious limitations. The problem with sharing space with an employee smoking area has already been discussed. There are also other problems. In both basement areas, there are water pipes that are close to the records, making the prospects of water damage great. This is a particularly dangerous situation since water could leak and go undetected for a considerable period of time (such as over a weekend when the building is lightly staffed at best). Reformatting critical records could allow the municipal government to store its original records in a more suitable commercial records storage area that protects these records from further deterioration (primarily by restricting the use of the originals).

The current storage areas have other major problems. Many of the records are on the floor. Some of the bound volumes that should be stored flat are standing upright, placing pressure on their spines. Some records, such as the older boxes of correspondence, are still housed in the original, highly acidic boxes and folders. Standards for records storage generally include provisions for elements such as flood and water protection, adequate shelving (both in terms of materials used in their construction and design), security, pest management, mechanical and electrical equipment, fire barriers, environmental controls, and fire detection and suppression.

Guidelines from the state government provide that a municipality can seek storage of its records in another repository provided that repository meets certain standards. For the city to meet *any* of these requirements, it must give more attention to the quality of records storage, but only as part of a group of strategies intended to provide a stronger foundation for the management of the municipal records. The city can seek advice from the state in terms of legal requirements and relevant professional standards if it pursues storage in a commercial records center.

CASE STUDY THREE: A DIOCESAN ORGANIZATION

With the impending sesquicentennial of its founding, the diocese's archives and other records have taken on even more significance than usual. These records will be needed for preparing a history as well as for exhibitions about the organization's history, and for public relations and other similar activities to support the celebrations. However, it must also be noted that while such uses of archival records are important, they pale in comparison to the other kinds of values attributed to all records. Moreover, while the publication of an anniversary history can be a notable event, the strengthening of the diocese's archives and the overall management of its records can have a continuing importance to the diocese that far outweighs publications, exhibitions, and festivities marking the event.

The diocese's move to developing an electronic information network with full electronic mail capability and access to the World Wide Web represents yet another reason why the diocese needs to be very mindful about records and archives issues. While at the present the only major recordkeeping system that is electronic is the primary financial system, it is also true that electronic mail capability will enable the diocese staff to transmit digital forms of records as well as to create new record forms for transmittal via the network. This increases the need for a strong and visible records management program in the diocese to grapple with the issues of electronic records management. Currently, the archives program is geared only to working with the older paper records.

The diocese is clearly dedicated to supporting an archives program. Their primary problems have been the lack of professional staff and the lack of a comprehensive archives and records management program for the administration of all vital records—those with archival value as well as those possessing other value to the diocese.

Considering that the diocesan records have been accumulated without the benefit of a formal records management program or any kind of formal mechanism for the identification of records with archival value to the diocese, there is an impressive quantity of records. As a consequence, many records are included as part of the archives that would have been destroyed under a typical records management program (such as routine financial records like cancelled checks). A program that reactively accepts *any* records sent to it is hardly a program at all; it reflects the lack of a specific mission and an inadequate use of accepted professional standards.

There are other serious problems with the current diocese archives, although many are likely the manifestation of lack of a clear mission or use of adequate professional standards. The diocese archives does not possess policies and procedures governing its performance. While there is a notebook containing draft policies and procedures, none of them have been officially implemented. Many of them are copies from other archives programs or from the archives and records management literature. Many of them even represent outdated sources. Especially crucial is the need to develop policies that protect confidential information found in certain records and that enable diocese employees to allow access to records with any degree of confidence. Without clear guidelines, it is surprising that so few serious incidents have occurred.

Failure to use policies and procedures is as much due to the absence of a records management program as to any other factor. Records management is the set of procedures used to manage *all* records—from the point of creation to final disposition (i.e., destruction or maintenance as part of the archives). As noted earlier, the absence of a records management program considerably weakens the possibility of identifying and appropriately maintaining core archival records. Without such a program, the organization runs the risk of either maintaining records that do not need to be (adding to the already substantial financial burden of records management), or of creating an environment in which individuals make decisions regarding the records' maintenance and destruction without the proper knowledge of the legal, fiscal, administrative, and other reasons why the records should be kept or destroyed. Given the immense quantity of privacy-sensitive records in an organization like the diocese, the potential of serious problems occurring is multiplied.

The absence of the broader records management program also is a major contributor to the lack of knowledge about the records held in the current archives storage areas. Despite the existence of detailed lists of records, there are still significant weaknesses in what is known about the diocese's records. There has been no effort to consider which agencies and units of the diocese have been thoroughly documented, even though there are many records relating to the bishops' administrations, clergy, and the parishes. This also results from a lack of understanding of the basics of archival appraisal (or records management scheduling) whereby records are carefully examined for their potential continuing value to the records creators and other potential users.

At the very least, the diocese needs to have its archives unit develop an acquisition policy and records retention schedule, identify the core administrative records needing continuing maintenance, and describe which (if any) records from non-diocese agencies it would accept. A records retention schedule will enable the diocese to destroy unnecessary records, free up space, and make it easier to administer the important records with longer-term value. In this regard, it is similar to the brief record retention guide provided in the diocese's *Guidelines for Parishes* (although it needs to be more detailed and more complete than the general advice provided here). The acquisition policy for the archives will enable the diocese to determine what it wants this program to represent. The diocese should not accept non-diocese records (even if closely related to this region's Catholic community) *until* it has made substantial progress in caring for its own administrative records.

Compounding this problem of the knowledge of the diocese records is the description of the records. What passes for descriptions are box and file folder lists. While such inventories are certainly a part of archival description, information about the originators of records, reasons why records are created, activities documented by the records, and other such data must be captured. The use of basic word processing software for keyword searching of the lists is handy for retrieval purposes, but it is hardly the best means by which to retrieve records or for the valuable information found in these records to be available to the diocese or outside researchers.

In examining these partial inventories (partial in the sense that they only represent a part of an archival finding aid), it is obvious that there are other problems stemming from the lack of a thorough knowledge of archival science or recordkeeping systems. There seems to be, for example, a mixing of records by both originating office and some sort of crude library subject classification scheme. In one instance, a dissertation is grouped with certain records because the subject relates to the records held by the archives. In another instance, all photographs are held in one record group because they are photographs, when in fact they should be administered with the records generated by the creating office. This present arrangement reflects the lack of application of one of the most basic of all archival principles—provenance.

The greater problem is that many records are probably of extremely limited or no value, including checkbook stubs, paid invoices, and bank statements. These kinds of records are generally not kept because the represented fiscal activities are captured in other core financial records. A thorough reappraisal of many of the records currently included in the archives is needed.

The physical storage of records is another serious problem confounding the development of a viable archives and records management program for the diocese. Here there are layers of problems. First, and most obvious, there is not enough space for the storage of the records or the acceptance of additional records. In fact, it appears that records—except the smallest quantities—are not being accepted into the existing archives. The space constraints create other problems. There is, for example, woefully inadequate space for staff and volunteers to work on the records.

This influences the second problem—the issue of security for the records. While the various rooms where the records are stored are kept locked when no staff is working there, it is virtually impossible to provide any reasonable security in the rooms where the archives are now stored. A staff person must move from room to room, and there is no direct line of sight over the spaces where the records are stored. Researchers, whether employees of the diocese or outsiders, are required to work in cramped quarters among the archival records, violating long-held security standards for such programs.

The third problem concerns the preservation of the records themselves. It is obvious that there is no control over humidity, temperature, or dust and dirt in the spaces the records now occupy. Some of the problems are even more egregious. In one records storage area, there were open water pipes, one of the standard hazards when records are stored in building basements. Even the use of acid-free records boxes is compromised when many of the records are still stored in their original, highly acidic folders.

Since the current archivist maintained an elaborate record of research and reference requests, it appears that the archives are a vastly underutilized source. At present, the records are primarily used by genealogists. There is little information about administrative use, although requests could be more systematically evaluated in order to determine a more precise view about current, recent, and past use. While there is an interest in utilizing the archives for the upcoming celebrations for the sesquicentennial, an archives and records management program could suggest many other ongoing uses of archival and all records. Moreover, if the diocese commits to working out policies for access and the like, it could then market the records for potential research by historians and other scholars. This could have some benefits for the diocese, benefits both for positive public relations and for what the diocese could learn from historians, sociologists, anthropologists, and others who use the records.

While these types of problems are serious, and certainly must be resolved if the diocese is to develop effective mechanisms for managing its records, there are positive features with what exists. The most positive is that the diocese administration is interested in learning how to improve the overall administration of its records. Beyond that, some of the crude efforts to manage its archives have been steps taken in the right direction. Most of the records held by the archives are in reasonably good condition, and the container lists will help considerably in developing better descriptions and better control allowing for appropriate access to the records. The current archivist is already providing some basic advice to diocese agencies about how to transfer records into the archives, using the right type of boxes and making container lists, a process that has contributed to a heightened consciousness in the diocese about records. With such actions, and the impending sesquicentennial of the diocese's founding, there is a momentum that can be used to make significant strides in improving the diocese's management of records, especially those with archival value.

CASE STUDY FOUR: A RELIGIOUS ORDER

The records challenges faced by this religious order are very similar to those encountered by the diocese, although the order is just beginning to come to grips with instituting a records program. One different challenge is in evaluating the publications held in the archives, since the accumulation of such materials seems to have developed as a kind of temporary or surrogate institutional archives. Although there is a rich array of published material, it is not clear whether it represents a comprehensive set of the order's publications or publications about the order. One of the problems is that much of the present archives holdings consist of publications—yearbooks, newsletters, special programs, and anniversary histories.

While such materials should be included, they should not be considered to be the most critical or dominant part of the holdings of an archives. These publications will, however, help the order with activities critical to reestablishing a modern archives operation. They will be useful for providing historical material for determining other records to be acquired, in building vital reference works needed in the order, and in providing information about the order to individuals outside who need historical data.

Work with the publications can proceed in a straightforward manner. A careful inventory must be made of the publications, along with an analysis of what should be included in a comprehensive set of the order's publications. When the order gets to the stage of preparing an appraisal or collections development policy, it will need to determine not just that it will house a complete set of the order's official publications (which it should) but whether it will also include publications about the order to serve as a reference collection. The close proximity of the library in the college affiliated with the order suggests that a partnership with the library could be developed, in which the library builds a comprehensive collection of publications about the order and the archives collects a comprehensive set of publications officially released by the order.

Another challenge concerns the present photographic collections in the archives. These holdings, coming from both personal and organization sources, may be the richest aspect of the present archival holdings. They appear to document well the many activities of the order, and they represent a rich set of resources for exhibitions, publications, and Web sites. However, these documents represent an extremely complex and labor-intensive set of responsibilities. Many of the photographs need to be identified. Many are in scrapbooks with highly acidic backings, and they need to be disassembled and stored in archival storage folders and boxes. Many of the photographs have come from private gifts, but lack any documentation about their origins. And, of course, the photographs need to be described so that they can be more accessible for research and reference purposes.

The archives program needs a modern accessioning system. In order to tackle the challenges presented by the photographic holdings, the order needs to approach them in clearly demarcated stages so as to not overwhelm the redevelopment of a full-fledged archives program. The order's new archivist should first do collection-level descriptions of each set of photographs, indicating the general nature of the subjects and their origins. As part of the general description, the archivist should indicate the range of problems represented by each collection—especially how much needs to be done to identify subjects and the degree of conservation needed. The archivist should then create priorities as to which collections will be worked on—indicating those that could be worked on by volunteers—and which should be sent to a conservation facility for additional treatment. As a means of assigning priorities, the archivist could also use the potential of certain of the photographic collections for exhibitions and related activities.

When evaluating the photographic collections, the archivist should consider the breadth of their coverage and sources to determine what gaps exist in documenting the order's history. This is especially important, given that the accumulation of materials now constituting the archives has not occurred in a planned or systematic fashion. The following major questions need to be addressed:

- Are there other important photographic and visual sources concerning the order which are not included in the archives?
- Are these other photographic materials the result of administrative units of the order or part of personal collections?
- What are the principal gaps in the visual coverage of the order's history?

The results of such an analysis can add to the development of an appraisal or collections development policy, and help guide the order in acquiring other photographs or visual sources critical to providing a history of the order.

Another challenge derives from the lack of recognizable official records of the order. While the archives are presently filled with valuable and interesting materials, there seem to be few official records of the order, such as records of the governing council. This problem generates from three sources: the origins of the archives, the lack of an official position of archivist, and the lack of development of a comprehensive records management program that encompasses all of the records of the order.

The origins of the archives dates from the work of a cleric who, as an avocation, began collecting documents, statistics, ephemera, publications, and other materials related to the history of the order in the 1930s and continued into the 1980s, and the transferal of these and other sources to the order's college library. His work is evident in two ways. First, there are the bound volumes of "source books" containing original documents and other such sources and "date books" with chronically arranged statistics and facts relating to the order. Both sets of volumes will be of immense value to the renewed and continuing work on the archives. Second, the materials in the present archives reflect the cleric's acquisition efforts, whereby he seemed to sweep up anything related to the order's history. While this has certainly saved documents and other materials that might have otherwise been lost, his acquisitions now require a careful re-appraisal to determine what should remain in the order's archives.

The origins of the order's archives are typical with those of other religious institutions and groups, and even non-religious bodies. As long as the organization is willing to admit the weaknesses of what was done in this formative period and to take steps to correct the problems, the work of such pioneers can take on its true importance. His efforts undoubtedly saved much that would have been lost without his work, but his efforts did not constitute a comprehensive archives program. Therefore, in addition to the reappraisal of what he collected, the order needs to microfilm the bound volumes as a record of the formation of the archival holdings. After this, the order can consider splitting apart the "source books" and placing these materials with other related documents and materials.

The order might also consider transcribing the "date books" in order to create a more useful reference work, one that can be updated and corrected as new work on the history of the order is completed. Microfilming the bound volumes should be done early in the reorganization of the archives, since they are showing signs of deterioration, both from the nature of the materials the cleric used in assembling the volumes and from their repeated use. Transcription of the date books is an activity that should occur much later, perhaps using volunteer labor.

The examination of these four organizations suggests some standard ARM problems, ranging from the lack of qualified staff to precise articulations of the real scope of challenges in administering institutional records.

LESSONS LEARNED FROM LOOKING AT THE REAL WORLD

It is never too late, no matter what the challenges or issues, for an institution to rectify problems with the administration of records and information systems. Examining real-life situations suggests the kinds of practical solutions to records and information management problems that every organization must implement—solutions suggesting basic principles guiding archives and records management operations.

For example, every records management and archives program must be related to the mission of the organization, in order to be successful. Records are a by-product of the activities carried out by an institution striving to meet its mission, as well as crucial references for aiding an organization to understand and to strive for its mission. A local government authority possesses a mandate to provide "safe and efficient" services ensuring a "better quality of life" in its geographic region. Such a mission requires a good archives and records management program and effective information systems. Safety, efficiency, and fiscal responsibility cannot be met if there is inadequate documentation regarding the organization's functions. Records management and archives programs provide an organization with corporate memory, accountability, and evidence—all essential for meeting the type of mission it has set for itself.

WHAT EVERY ORGANIZATION NEEDS

Even as modern organizations dramatically shift their recordkeeping systems to electronic-based approaches, records management and archives will continue to provide important services to an institution. As such a shift occurs, it is crucial that records management and archives be in place to ensure that recordkeeping not become so decentralized and unregulated as to create a chaotic environment for the maintenance and use of an institution's important records. The assistance archives and records management provides for the emerging modern institution includes the following:

- recognition of records as a distinctive business asset;
- connection of records to organizational goals and objectives;
- control of records in an increasingly complex work environment;
- design of good recordkeeping systems so that they can assist an organization to capitalize on its knowledge and to be in a constant learning situation;
- an increase in responsibility of individual records creators for the records; and
- a shift from an abiding concern with technology to a concern for the record and its importance to the organization.

Most of all, any organization must understand that records are extremely valuable. Records possess value if they affect corporate decisions. Records have value because they cost money to create and maintain. Records have value if, for whatever reason, they need to be kept for lengthy periods of time. Records provide critical information for the institution's operation and self-understanding.

In order for records, including those with archival value, to remain valuable to an organization, an organization must take certain steps, including the following:

- hire a professional archivist and records manager;

- place the archivist and records manager in the administrative circumstance with the most direct access across the organization;
- establish a records management program in which all requests for computer equipment and software must be evaluated by the records manager to determine that technological solutions are compatible with the regulatory and other records management issues;
- ensure that the records manager develop guidelines addressing records management and archival needs that can be used for developing or evaluating all contracts between the organization and other parties;
- create an advisory board for the archives and records management program;
- develop a system for regular training of records liaisons and staff about basic records management issues and practices;
- create and maintain a current records retention and disposition schedule;
- evaluate outsourcing the storage of non-current records in a commercial records center;
- consider establishing an internal archives program or outsourcing the archival records to an established archival repository;
- acquire an automated system for the management of records;
- develop a suitable budget for hiring consultants for other records management and archives work as needed and provide resources for continuing education;
- develop a long-range plan for the revitalization of the institution's records management program.

All of the preceding chapters in this book have been intended to assist organizations to achieve such objectives.

WHAT THE VARIOUS ORGANIZATIONS NEED TO DO

Organization One: The Local Government Authority. Why is an archives and records management program needed? There are at least three major reasons. First, since many records have continuing value to the organization, an archives is the best means for ensuring that such records are maintained. Second, the nature of the authority requires continued public relations and marketing, and archival records are essential to such functions. Third, the wide diversity of projects requires that an archival program be established to ensure adequate documentation of the authority's most important projects.

The present records management program is located in the administrative services division. Although this is not an inappropriate administrative location, it is difficult to assess this arrangement because the records management program was dormant for a period, and it has been restricted to maintenance of a records disposition schedule, removal of non-current records from offices, storage in a commercial records center, and destruction of obsolete records. This is an extremely curtailed vision for records management, because the absence of an archival program suggests an incomplete vision of the life cycle of records.

The administrative services division—which includes other responsibilities such as clerical support, office automation, and telecommunications—could be an excellent administrative location for the revitalized records management and archives unit. These other functions are all closely related to archives and records management functions, although the key is still organization-wide support via policy and directives.

There is a very decentralized view of records management throughout the local authority. Each division appears to have resorted to its own resources to do the best it can to manage its records. Although some have done better than others, none have done as well as they could or should have. There is inconsistent knowledge about the general records disposition schedule. Even those divisions that know about it generally do not understand why the retention schedule has developed in the fashion it has. There is also inconsistent knowledge about the external regulations that might affect authority records—and such guidelines must be known in order for it to be a compliant organization. The main records concern of many employees appears to be restricted to the removal of obsolete paper records or the reformatting of paper records to reduce storage space needs, provide security, or have multiple-reference copies.

Generally, an organization like this local authority has several major options. The first option is to not do anything about its records. The authority is clearly not interested in this option because it has already secured the services of a consultant. If the authority were to take no additional action to reinvent its records management program or to establish an archives program, then the condition of its records and the availability of its archival records would deteriorate at a much quicker rate. Reaching its thirty-year mark, the local authority is at a critical juncture in the administration of its records, especially those that have archival value. Records will only continue to grow in volume—and as the volume increases, there will be a decreasing chance to gain efficient control over them. The local authority will also continue moving toward the use of electronic information and recordkeeping technology. If it moves in this direction without satisfactory control over its current records, there would be a greater possibility for chaos, loss of valuable evidence and information, and the chance for legal, fiscal, and other administrative problems.

A second option for an organization like the local authority is to enter into an agreement with an existing archival repository to serve as its official archives—although this option does not solve any of the problems involving the administration of its current records. This option should also not be considered for several important reasons. To be successful, the authority would have to possess a good records management program. Records to be transferred to the archival repository would have to be regularly evaluated and transported, a process that can only work smoothly if there is a records management program in place, with sufficient resources and authority. Any second party serving as the repository would doubtless require some substantial resources for staff support and housing of the archival records in appropriate storage facilities and supplies. At best, the local authority should re-evaluate the possibility of such an arrangement within a year or two of hiring the new records manager and archivist, based on a thorough internal evaluation of its archives and current records needs.

The third, and most viable, option is for the local authority to hire a professional archivist and records manager to head a revitalized records program. Such a revitalized archives and records management program should be responsible for a much wider array of functions. It should:

- prepare records appraisal and maintenance of records retention and disposition schedules;
- work with advisory committee to ensure state-of-the-art records management program;
- develop and support policies to ensure preservation of the authority's archival records;
- develop and use standards and procedures for records management, including advice on electronic recordkeeping and information systems and records storage equipment;
- maintain best practices related to specific types of recordkeeping;
- work with commercial records center to ensure its proper and most efficient use;
- serve as clearinghouse of information for all records-related issues, such as imaging systems;
- act as lead on the development and maintenance of disaster-preparedness plan and vital records program; and
- educate and train all local authority employees, especially records liaisons, in basic records management and archives issues and activities.

The crucial action to be taken by the local authority is the hiring of an archivist and records manager. Without an internal, knowledgeable professional, it will be impossible to improve the records management program or to establish an archives operation.

For an archives and records management program to be successful, it must be located in a division with responsibilities that cut across all administrative units. The local authority must delegate authority to the archivist and records manager so that other administrative units comply with rules and regulations regarding the administration, maintenance, and use of records.

It is especially important for the records manager to work closely with the information systems and management staff in the development and acquisition of new electronic recordkeeping systems. There is no possibility for resolving the local authority's records management concerns if these two units are not carefully coordinated. A records management program must be established in which all requests for computer equipment and software are evaluated by the records manager to determine that technological solutions are compatible with regulatory and other records management issues. In establishing this relationship or process, care must be taken so as to not to make the records manager an obstacle to the authority's efficiency in making records and information management decisions. The archivist and records manager must have the ability to learn about records-related purchases, since such purchases are often the best and most timely indicators of records needs.

The records manager must also have the responsibility for reviewing all contracts and requests for proposals to ensure that archives and records management issues are fully addressed. Such contracts and bids need to reflect external records management regulatory requirements as well as provide the type and form of records that the local authority deems necessary to have for its archives or for temporary governance of a project or ongoing function. The records manager should develop guidelines addressing records management and archival needs that can be used for developing or evaluating all contracts between the authority and other parties. This kind of policy development will be a priority activity for the archivist and records manager. Other types of policies to be created range from micrographics specifications to access and privacy guidelines. First in this type of work should be a thorough evaluation of current records management policies and procedures.

One way of developing wider local authority knowledge of the records management program is to establish a visible oversight body. In some institutions, advisory boards are created primarily in order to approve records retention schedules and disposition of records. A typical arrangement is for a representative of the administration, auditor or other fiscal officer, legal counselor, and historian or archivist (often an external member) to advise on the identification of archival records. In this case, an advisory board should be established to provide a greater range and variety of advice. Such a board could be used in order to establish records policies and procedures, review training and other educational materials for advising division records liaisons and other training venues, analyze records needs, and recommend new directions in recordkeeping systems. The advisory board, most importantly, should be composed of sufficiently important local authority officials who can lend the records management and archives program the support it requires and deserves.

The local authority needs a small records management unit with a network of division records liaisons. The records liaisons should be given management responsibilities beyond inventorying of records and the enforcement of the disposition schedule. This will only work, however, if the local authority establishes and supports a system whereby the records liaisons are given these responsibilities but with release time to attend to them in addition to their normal duties. The records liaisons must also be trained to discern and troubleshoot records management needs and problems. This means that the new archivist and records manager should probably have monthly meetings devoted to two hour to half-day training sessions and bi-weekly meetings to discuss records needs and issues. The records manager might also wish to develop a newsletter for communication and a small professional library that can be used by the records liaisons.

At present, the records and disposition schedule is the main tool to be used by the records management program. The schedule should be carefully evaluated to determine whether the recordkeeping systems still exist, the descriptions are adequate, and, especially, whether they have changed in any substantial manner (such as becoming automated). The new records manager should make an effort to locate the older files of information compiled when the original schedule was assembled. At the least, the schedule should be revised to include more specific information, including a description of the recordkeeping system, external regulations, and explicit statements about any records of archival value.

The local authority needs to reevaluate its use of the commercial records center. Such use can only be at an optimum level if there is a thorough, professional records management program in place. An evaluation of the nature of the records currently stored there should be conducted in order to ensure that only scheduled records are there and that records are regularly destroyed rather than stored beyond their required retention periods. The local authority also needs to make sure that divisions are sending records to the center—that is, that records of various series and retention periods are not being mixed together in the same boxes—and to determine how the divisions and their units are using the center's services after the records are stored there. For example, if divisions are consulting certain records on a daily basis it may be an indication that the records should not be stored off-site. The local authority's priority should be to ascertain how the commercial records center can fit into its records management and archives program, not the other way around.

The commercial records center should not be used to house the archives. The local authority should gather additional data about its archives as it evaluates the current records retention and disposition schedule. With this new information, it can identify the possibility of creating a facility for storing its records on one of its properties. This will be difficult, since the archives need to be maintained where the records are used most (possibly at the local authority headquarters). Although there are other options for entering into an agreement to house the archives at a local archives repository, it is advisable that the local authority first establish its own records management and archives program and determine its needs and priorities before beginning such discussions. It may be possible to acquire resources for renovating a joint facility for both current records and archives storage.

As the local authority moves to reevaluate its records retention and disposition schedule, it should carefully consider the prospects of automating the schedule. Although this topic has already been discussed, it is extremely premature given the other issues concerning the local authority's archives and records management program. The acquisition of software should occur as part of the normal development of the records operations. Such software will certainly assist the authority records management program to provide life-cycle tracking of all records and to maintain location information about recordkeeping systems and archival records. However, it is premature to consider the use of such software given the current nature of automation at the local authority. Software purchasing should occur at the appropriate time and not drive the program before it is ready to cope with such concerns.

Organization Two: The Small Municipal Government. Here, we must start with more basic concerns. The city needs to understand that digitization is more an access approach than preservation approach (although there is continuing debate about the role of digital preservation). Digitization will only aid the preservation of older archival records by lessening the use of the original documents. By adopting a holistic view towards the management of its records, the city can place actions like digitization or other reformatting into a larger context that will enable it to make better and more cost-effective decisions regarding any actions concerning its records.

The city should set aside some modest funding for sending its designated records manager to records management continuing education workshops and institutes. While the ideal solution for the municipality would be to hire a professional records manager and archivist, the small size of the government and the lack of availability of financial resources work against this as a viable recommendation. The city could improve its records management immensely by clearly designating an individual with official responsibilities for records management and then supporting that individual in obtaining appropriate training as it becomes available. There are opportunities for continuing education offered through the state government, regional archives, and records management professional associations, and workshops offered by such national professional associations as the Society of American Archivists and the Association of Records Managers and Administrators.

The city should focus on both the council minutes and ordinances and resolutions for strategic management and reformatting. These records provide the most long-term and comprehensive portrait of the history and work of the city government, as well as function as an invaluable resource for local history and other community-based research. Most other records will be referenced in these two series of records. At some point, such focus does, however, require a more in-depth indexing of the records for personal and corporate names and subjects; the large number of personal, place, and organizational names, as well as other topics on each page, necessitates more than two or three index terms per page—provided as a baseline service by the digitization vendor contacted by the city.

The designated records manager needs to work both with other city agencies and the necessary state agencies to identify which engineering and architectural drawings and maps may possess vital value to the ongoing work of the city government. There are two benefits to focusing on the city's vital records. First, it may help to identify which drawings and maps should be digitized or microfilmed for ease of reference and preservation. Second, by consulting with other city officials about vital records, the city government staff will gain a heightened awareness of the importance of the better management of records in general.

The city should compile an inventory of *all* records in all city agencies and then compare this inventory for (1) utilization of the state archives records schedule for local governments and (2) instituting records management approaches to all records. Conducting this inventory can also facilitate an understanding of proper records management within the municipal government. The inventory can also ensure the government that all records with continuing value can be identified and administered in appropriate ways. Current gaps in the most important records—such as council minutes and ordinances and resolutions—might be filled in by the discovery of misfiled and misplaced records. The inventory will also help the city support other uses, such as research by local history students.

The city needs to improve the storage of its original archival records either by improving the current basement areas or by storing the records (after reformatting) in some other facility. The city must find some space for its records, storage that is away from staff smoking areas, water and steam pipes, and that has adequate shelving and security. There is no means by which the city can find environmentally stable conditions within the main municipal building, so that archival (acid-free) storage materials should be sparingly applied. The city might opt to find commercial records storage within the region for select of its records after they have been reformatted.

Organization Three: The Diocese. The diocese needs to obtain professional archives and records management expertise. There are current professional practices that ought to be used in the diocese's activities that are not being carried out due to the lack of professional expertise. The diocese needs to hire an experienced archivist and records manager who can reorient the current program or expand the range of activities currently supported. Without a resident professional archivist and records manager, the diocese will not be able to change or improve its current work with its records. The professional can perform a detailed evaluation of the current archives operation by reexamining the current holdings and general practices against records held in other locations or still maintained by offices. This person should be responsible for advising on the establishment of a more comprehensive archives and records management program, as well as charting its implementation.

The diocese must expand its current archives program to become one that includes responsibility for all records. In one sense, this is a rather philosophical recommendation. Yet, it is also extremely practical because (1) *all* records are corporate assets requiring management, (2) a comprehensive records management program is the *only* effective means by which matters such as privacy and security can be guaranteed, and (3) records with archival value can *only* be definitely identified and secured if the universe of records created and maintained by the diocese is consistently considered. Having such a records management program will bring other advantages to the diocese: cost savings, better negotiating with vendors who provide information technology and software solutions to records administration, and better planning for reaping the fullest benefits from the important information provided by records.

The diocese must establish a records advisory committee with responsibility for the overall administration of its records, advising the chancellor about the actions needed as well as authorizing the development of records retention schedules and appraisal decisions. For records to be properly managed, any institution must ensure that legal, fiscal and auditing, administrative, and research or historical factors are constantly considered, both in designing new recordkeeping systems and in evaluating the products of these systems through critical points in their life cycle. An advisory committee, meeting quarterly, could develop general policies and procedures, as well as evaluate and approve records retention schedules allowing for the disposition of certain records. Furthermore, the diocese can use this advisory committee to have at least one individual from outside the diocese—a historian or researcher knowledgeable about the diocese and Catholic history in the region, or an archivist or records manager knowledgeable about archival and records management principles and procedures—involved in tracking the reestablishment of the diocese's records program.

Better modernized storage areas for the diocese's archives must be secured. Although the storage spaces in the basement of the main diocese building are far from adequate, there are actions that might be taken to rectify some of the problems. After clearing as many of the non-archival records from these areas as possible, the diocese should consider removing the false walls, rerouting water and other related utility lines away from the storage areas, and adding moveable shelving to provide a higher volume, more secure, storage area. An environmental systems expert could also be hired as a consultant to determine what might be done to the existing storage areas to provide stable temperature and humidity controls. However, the diocese should be prepared to hear that these rooms are not viable for reengineering to produce the needed environments, and that it might have to look elsewhere for adequate storage.

Even taking such actions will not resolve the diocese's needs for additional storage space for its archives and other records. The space in the basement of the main building is severely limited, and the diocese will need to consider off-site commercial records center storage for the maintenance of its inactive, but not archival, records. The diocese might consider other properties it already owns for the expansion of the archives. If the diocese has any plans to build a new facility or to renovate an existing structure, the archives and records management program should be given more and better space. A professional archivist and records manager would be responsible for all these activities as part of his or her normal duties.

While better space for records should be the first priority, the diocese must also take into consideration the needs of its researchers and staff. At present, researchers work in cramped, inadequate spaces among the records; this creates security problems as well as a public relations nightmare. Staff has no place to work with the records holdings. If the diocese recruits a good archivist and records manager, better working quarters will need to be found, preferably not in the basement. Better lighted, more spacious, and more attractive space for offices and research rooms should be located somewhere in the main building, ideally on the first floor and accessible to the elevators for the delivery of records.

The diocese needs to reappraise its current archival holdings, including a thorough evaluation of the extent of records documentation held or not held by the archives. In the past fifteen to twenty years, archival appraisal has taken on more sophisticated approaches, with new articulations of values and approaches such as the archival documentation strategy and macro-appraisal. When the archivist and records manager is hired, one of his or her first priorities should be to evaluate the current holdings, weed out and destroy inactive and non-archival records, determine the nature of records still held in offices, and develop new strategies for the full documentation of the diocese. This is invaluable both for cleaning up existing spaces and for supporting the production of a good finding aid to the diocese archives.

An inventory of all archival records should be completed and published as one of the products of the sesquicentennial celebrations. Establishing a strong archives and records management program should be the first priority of the diocese and a high-level objective for the diocese's celebration of its sesquicentennial. Another objective is the publication of a basic guide to its archival records. If an archivist and records manager is hired early enough, a guide could be published by the time of the anniversary celebrations. The publication of such a guide ought to be as valuable to the diocese as the publication of an official history; in fact, the two could be useful companion volumes.

The diocese needs to move cautiously in developing an exhibit area or museum function as part of its archives program. Because of the impending anniversary, there is some sentiment about having an exhibition space attached to the diocese's archives or even to see a museum developed. However, the diocese should be careful because such activities can be both notoriously expensive, and they consume considerable time and other resources. One professional staff person supporting the archives and records management program cannot administer *both* an archives and museum program. Having a small exhibition space associated with archives and records management is certainly a manageable function, but it needs to be seen as supporting the broader mission of the diocese's records operation and not the other way around. At present, the real problem is that the chancery building is not suitable as an exhibition area, and placing it in another structure (such as the rectory across the street) would stretch a program with a very small staff.

The diocese needs to establish partnerships with other cultural and historical organizations in the region. Having partnerships will enable the diocese's archives to do a number of additional activities, such as working with a historical manuscripts repository to acquire the archival records of non-diocese organizations with importance to the documentation of Catholic history in the region. Another fruitful partnership would be between the diocese and local universities, especially those with a graduate archives education program, for the purpose of supporting fieldwork opportunities for archives and records management students. Such partnerships should develop normally out of the work of the newly hired archivist and records manager.

An adequate budget needs to be provided for the continuing support of the archives and records management, including a revolving fund for records-related fees. A salary and fringe benefits package for a professional archivist and records manager obviously needs to be provided. In addition, funds are needed to include purchasing a computer with appropriate software, archival supplies, and related office support materials. Funds allocated for travel to related diocesan records programs, conferences, workshops, and other educational venues are very important. Providing such funds will be crucial both for keeping the professional archivist current with new approaches and techniques, as well as be an inducement for recruiting for the most qualified archivist and records manager.

The diocese must *first* create an archivist and records manager position, develop a suitable job description, and advertise and recruit for this position as soon as possible. This person's first year responsibilities should include developing a long-range plan for the development of the archives and records management program, reevaluating and redesigning the physical storage space for the archives, and developing a full set of policies and procedures to manage the diocese's records and archives.

The archivist and records manager should then begin the process of reappraising existing records and developing an acquisition policy. He or she should immediately develop a full set of policies and procedures for the management of records, allowing for the disposal of useless records and better assessment of current records needs. The new archivist and records manager cannot be expected to resolve all of the problems and concerns during the first year, but at the least he or she should be able to recommend a more realistic and more professional mission, clean up existing storage areas, establish and start work with a records advisory committee, and draft a working long-range plan for the continued development of the diocese's archives and records management program.

Organization Four: The Religious Order. A standardized records management program needs to be put in place for all of the order's administrative records, so that records of archival value can be routinely and regularly moved to the archives at appropriate times. The present archives holdings tend to be an accumulation of valuable (but not necessarily the most valuable or complete) sets of records for the order. Part of this is due to serendipitous collecting, and part stems from the lack of any standardized records management program with records retention schedules and approved policies and procedures. Such a records management program would cover all administrative records, starting with a complete inventory of all such records and the development of a retention schedule indicating the nature of the records, how long they should be maintained, and the reasons they should be managed.

The records management program should pay careful attention to the criteria that must be applied to the records of organizations and programs affiliated with or administered by the order that have been closed, an issue the order is aware of as it considers the range of records concerns. In addition to a retention schedule covering its administrative records, the order also needs to develop schedules, policies, and procedures ensuring that records of affiliated institutions also are well maintained. The order needs to decide when or if certain records with archival value will be sent to the main order's archives or maintained on site because of continuing value at their point of creation. In developing such schedules and policies, the order will reduce the risk of losing valuable records when an affiliated program or organization is closed or undergoes substantial changes.

A key to the success of a records management program, one encompassing a full range of archival functions, is creating an advisory group for the program and investing the professional hired to carry out the program with authority to make decisions about the administration of the order's records. Generally, such an advisory group includes the

- chief administrative officer (or his representative)
- fiscal officer
- legal consul
- a person well versed in the history of the organization.

One of the keys to the advisory group's success (and ultimately the archives program) is that it meshes well with the organization's culture and provides the archivist the latitude for administering the archives and records management program.

The main functions of this advisory group are to advise on and approve policies and procedures concerning the management of records and their access and use—especially records retention schedules dictating which records are sent to the archival repository and what are ultimately destroyed. A good practice is to have this advisory group meet quarterly to consider such matters as the

- progress of the records management program;
- performance of the records professional;
- needs for additional policies and procedures or revision of existing ones;
- new issues or concerns regarding the management of the order's records;
- other matters that emerge with the establishment and evolution of the records program.

Another key to establishing an efficient and effective archives and records management program is in creating and filling the position of archivist. A records professional, someone with substantial graduate training in the administration of archives and current records, is necessary to provide guidance to the records operations and to serve as a resource for advice to the order in all aspects of records creation. Without a professional working within the order, the management of records is subject to inconsistent practices and to the use of non-standardized approaches to managing both archival documents and current records. A records administrator needs to have expertise about the nature of records systems, the organizational and other mandates for the creation of records, and the present and continuously changing nature of archival and records management standards. A professional archivist and records manager position is also needed for building a working staff, applying consistent practices from college work-study students, volunteers, and paid support staff.

The responsibilities of the archivist would be varied. He or she would work with the records advisory group to develop and implement archives and records management policies, carry out appraisal of the order's records, prepare descriptions of the records, and perform or supervise reference to the records. The archivist would also be responsible for creating and maintaining a Web site about the order's archival program (assuming the order wants to publicize it). The archivist also would be responsible for developing and running workshops and other training programs for individuals within the order who may have responsibilities affecting the creation, maintenance, and use of the order's records. Workshops would be necessary and helpful as various archives and records management policies are developed. Finally, the archivist would be a source of advice about archival and records management issues within the order, requiring him or her to maintain professional contacts, stay current with the professional literature and standards, and attend professional conferences and workshops.

The order has a number of options in staffing an archives and records management program. It can create a professional position, write a description, and advertise nationally. The advantage of doing this is the ability to bring someone in quickly who possesses both the necessary expertise and the relevant professional experience. The disadvantage is hiring someone who does not possess adequate knowledge about the order itself. While the priority ought to be on hiring someone with sufficient records knowledge and experience, the order's interests in creating a exhibition program as well as in using the archives as a substantial component for preserving its corporate memory suggests the need for hiring someone from within the order or someone who already knows about the order.

Another challenge is defining the scope of the order's archives program. At present, the materials in the archives presents mostly non-administrative records and personal items related to the history of the order. In reestablishing the archives program, care must be given in defining its mission. The program should focus on the order itself, stressing both administrative records and papers related to individual brothers and related programs and activities of the order. Consideration should be given to other institutions related to the order, especially its institutions of higher education. Historically, colleges and universities have developed and maintained their own institutional archives, and these two schools should be encouraged to do likewise in a manner that is cooperative with the work on the archives of the friary.

The question is, just what role should the order's archives play in nurturing these other academic archives? Many options present themselves, but the archivist hired to take responsibility for the main order's archives should develop guidelines for the related university records programs. Those schools (and any others) should be encouraged to hire their own professional archivists or, if they already have archivists, to work in a cooperative fashion—to ensure that the order is fully documented and that none of the programs assumes overlapping or unnecessary work.

Formulating a mission statement should be the preeminent focus in the early stages of establishing an archives program. The mission statement should indicate that an archives program is intended to serve several major purposes, including

- providing a corporate memory for the order;
- providing accountability for the organization in its daily responsibilities; and
- ensuring that key records providing continuing value to the organization are identified, preserved, and made available for use.

The mission statement will need to address the potential uses of the archival records, especially when and if individuals from outside the order will have access to them. The mission statement, with the addition of a policy governing access, should address both legitimate confidentiality issues and needs to enable use of certain records supporting good public relations. Certainly, personnel records will need to be ensured confidentiality, but the order will want to enable others to use certain records for historical and genealogical purposes. Given the order's strong connection to its region, there will be legitimate requests for access to some of the records by those interested in local history. Through the employment of a professional archivist and the work of an advisory committee, reasonable access requests should be honored without there being any possibility of breaching confidentiality.

At present, the existing archives only serves the occasional genealogical request or administrative inquiry about some dimension of the order's history. Developing a more comprehensive records program will enable the order's records to play a more important and appropriate role in the ongoing work the order.

Another challenge is dealing with the increasing use of electronic information technology to generate and store records. It is obvious, with computers present everywhere, that the order is using such technologies to create records. The use of e-mail, for example, can generate large amounts of correspondence and other records, some of which needs to be captured for archival purposes. Another example is the responsibility for maintaining the order's Web site, making sure that substantial changes are documented so that nothing of historical value is lost. Once a records program is established and a professional archivist is hired, attention should be given to the impact of the information technologies on the order's records. Then, appropriate policies and procedures need to be put into place.

The management of electronic records is a hotly contested topic within the archives and records management disciplines, with many different perspectives being presented and a variety of solutions, from technical to procedural, being proposed. By establishing an official archives and securing a professional to administer the program, the order creates the best opportunity for engaging such issues generated by new technologies.

At this point in its history and in the status of its present archives, the order need not feel it has a crisis caused by technological issues. Rather, the order needs to approach electronic records management and related issues by establishing an organization-wide records program, one that enables matters like electronic mail or the creation and maintenance of financial files in electronic form to be seen as part of an overall effort to administer its records. The archivist will have to address electronic records as he or she surveys and schedules records for their maintenance.

The reliance on electronic systems, which is probably restrained and limited in an organization the size of the order, can be evaluated after a records program is established and other needs addressed. If the archivist discovers a records system that is electronic and in danger of being lost, perhaps because of a change in a software product or vendor's contract, then it will need to be dealt with as quickly as possible. Otherwise, priority should be given to other more pressing matters, such as the establishment of an organization-wide records program and securing appropriate space for storing valuable records and other materials.

Another challenge is identifying records supporting legal and fiscal requirements that the order has to meet. In most organizations, the vast majority of records are created due to some external warrant. The warrant can generate from legal, fiscal, or best practices requirements. A records management program, including an archives, is the best means by which to guarantee that the external requirements are well known and met. A records professional, by virtue of his or her education and experience, becomes an expert in knowing what requirements, both internal and external, lead to the creation of records and governs why and how they should be maintained. The evidence derived from an organization's records plays a critical role not just in building and sustaining a corporate memory, but in enabling individuals within the organization to work in accountable ways.

Why and how a particular organization has to be accountable varies from organization to organization, as each fits into larger institutional structures or provides different services with different requirements. A pharmaceutical company functions in a much more regulated industry because of its important role in the health care industry, but all organizations have some external requirements affecting their work. The order's records professional would become an authority in such regulatory and other issues affecting the organization's records.

An advisory committee representing fiscal, legal, administrative, and historical perspectives is also necessary so that the order is ensured that its records can assist it in meeting external and other regulations—from governmental to business guidelines. Some records will have archival value and be maintained in the order's archives in any event, but other records with short-term value will still need to be managed in a systematic fashion. In addition to an archives facility, the order might want to store records of temporary value (needing to be kept less than ten years) in a commercial, off-site records center. Such decisions will arise as a full-fledged records management program is put into place.

Another challenge lies in creating excellent space for the storage and use of the order's archival records. The main requirements for such storage space are that it provides

- stable environmental conditions (temperature and humidity);
- dust and pollutant-free conditions;
- fire-resistant conditions;
- protection from rodent and insect infestations; and
- security from theft and loss of archival records.

In addition, the space should include comfortable conditions for staff working with the records, as well as good reference room facilities for individuals conducting research in the archives. Both areas should be well lighted and wired for computer use and reading.

Given the nature of the order's present archives, it is doubtful that immense spaces are necessary. In the present archives storage area, there appears to be approximately one thousand linear feet of materials; these represent largely unappraised materials, some duplicated materials, and materials that will not necessarily remain in the archives. Based on discussions, the archives storage area should accommodate about three thousand linear feet of materials. Given the potential for using movable shelving, the overall space requirements are not substantial. More problematic is developing storage space that is close by both staff work areas and public reference areas. The idea of using some of this space for exhibitions adds another challenge to developing the archives facility. Given the quality of the renovations of the older structures, the old garage and adjacent work buildings could be renovated to accommodate archival storage along with work, reference, and exhibition areas. The idea of a combined exhibition area and archives brings together nicely the memory function of the archives program.

The best archival storage space should be reserved for the archival records. An allusion was already made to the possibility of using commercial records storage facilities for non-archival records that are no longer actively used but still need to be stored for a limited time before they are destroyed. Commercial records centers provide low-cost storage for inactive organizational records, charging annual fees for each cubic foot of records stored and additional charges for retrieval of records and their ultimate storage.

Once a records management program is established with comprehensive records retention schedules, the order might consider storing inactive records of no archival value in such a facility. This will enable the archival storage space to be used more effectively. Commercial records storage firms also provide security for confidential records as well. If the accumulation of such inactive records is small (less than fifty cubic feet), then the order might consider storage on site as part of the archives facility.

In designing the archival facility and the exhibition space, priorities must be determined carefully. It would be easy for the exhibition area to overwhelm the archival records program. Since archival records are essential for the order's corporate memory, the exhibition area will be an excellent means by which to display both some of the most important documents as well as interesting and significant artifacts related to the order's history.

The rich photographic documentation already in the existing archives will be useful for exhibitions, and good exhibitions (especially those that can be reproduced in some fashion on the order's Web site) will also help to attract donations of additional valuable archival documentation. However, the order will need to determine, in a careful manner, whether the archivist's main responsibility will be to direct the development of an archives and records management program or support changing exhibitions and related public programs. Small, changing exhibitions about the order's history certainly can be within the scope of the archivist's responsibilities, but if the order wishes to develop a more comprehensive exhibition about its evolution it will need to consider additional staffing.

If priority is given to developing the archives and records management program, the museum function will need to take a second-level priority. The identification of good materials for exhibitions will require that the archivist become familiar with the order's records and be able to select those that will best reflect the order's history and support the display of related artifacts.

Comments have already been made about making sure the archives program is administratively situated so that it reports directly to the chief administrator of the order. Many of the reasons for this can be ascertained from the roles and functions already described. Most critical, however, is the fact that the archivist will have responsibilities across the order since every unit creates records that need to be managed and sometimes archived. The archivist will need the authority to work with everyone, and the people in the order will need to know about the records program and understand that it is a sanctioned activity.

None of this suggests that an archivist is an absolute free agent in dealing with records. The advisory committee described earlier will help set the policies and procedures by which the archivist's responsibilities and duties are defined. Decisions concerning matters of confidentiality and other sensitive issues will require special safeguards both to protect the order and the archivist. And, of course, the archivist will be obliged to work within accepted professional standards and practices. Even with these limitations, however, the archivist needs to know that he or she has the endorsement and support necessary for work to be done in a satisfactory and timely matter.

The key to having a successful archives and records management program is hiring a professional archivist or arranging to have someone educated in the field to assume the duties of an archivist. However, the scope of the program to be created by the order will determine whether other individuals are necessary to support its development.

Equipment needs have already been partially described. There are a number of such needs that the order will have to consider, including:

- *Computers.* The archives will need a top-of-the-line personal computer with high-speed modem, large memory and RAM, scanner, laser quality printer, and professional suite of software. Whoever is hired as an archivist should be allowed to research and assess the specific needs and make the decision about the computer to be purchased. The order should also consider purchasing a laptop for the archivist so that he or she can work with records and other materials off-site. The order might also consider acquiring a computer for use in the reference room by researchers, especially as it prepares and makes available finding aids on the Web.
- *Shelving.* The archives area should be shelved over with movable shelving to accommodate something in the range of three thousand linear feet of materials. There should also be some shelving (perhaps for several hundred linear feet) placed in the archivist's office for professional literature and in the reference room (also several hundred linear feet) for archival finding aids and other basic reference works on the order.
- *Furniture.* The reference room should have two to four large library tables and chairs that could accommodate up to eight researchers in a comfortable fashion. The archivist's office should have at least one large work table for working with archival records. There should also be a separate processing room with chairs and at least several large tables for work by students and volunteers on the archival records.
- *Microfilm Reader.* If the order envisions having some of its records microfilmed (especially those that are fragile), there should be one microfilm reader-printer available in the reference room. Since this is certainly not an immediate need, the archivist should be allowed to investigate the specific type of reader-printer when the time is appropriate for its purchase.

- *Archival Storage Supplies.* Once the archives facility is ready with shelving, a large quantity of archival storage boxes and folders should be acquired. All materials should be placed in appropriate sized boxes. The particular array of box and folder sizes can be determined by the archivist after a more accurate inventory of the records is made.

Many of the activities and functions described could be worked on cooperatively. Below is a brief enumeration of the kinds of cooperative activities that can be considered as the archives program is established and develops.

- Work-study students with neighboring colleges and universities to provide archival training and experience;
- Consortium of archives and special collections departments in colleges to work together on documenting the order's history in America;
- Commercial records center use for storing inactive, non-archival records;
- Joint hiring with the nearby college for archivist position to work on both the order's archives and the archives of the college; and
- Workshops on archives and records management topics co-sponsored by the order's archives and other nearby archives programs or through other of the order's colleges and universities.

Obviously, once the order has hired an archivist, it should encourage him or her to take every opportunity to seek cooperative ventures benefiting the development of the order's archives.

THE ESSENTIAL CHARACTERISTICS OF RECORDS PROGRAMS

For an institutional archives to be successful, it must possess some particular attributes and play certain important roles. These include the establishment of an organization-wide records management program; the hiring of a professional archivist; the vesting of an archives program with administrative authority; the availability of a suitable archives facility; the preparation of a manual of policies and procedures for archives and records management; the creation of a Web site for publicizing the records program; and the securing of sufficient funds to support the ongoing functions of a records program. Each of these attributes and activities is described in more detail below.

Organization-wide Records Management Program. For an institutional archives to identify the most important records possessing continuing value, it must be part of or connected to a records management program. Although records management programs focus on the administration of active records (those still being used at the point of creation), they also enable organizations to carry out a variety of other important activities, such as to:

- develop a full picture of their records and needs for their management;
- ensure that legal, fiscal, and administrative uses of the records are being accounted for;
- identify records with archival value through the process of assigning time lengths for the maintenance of all records (records schedules);
- advise on procedures for managing records in all offices; and
- keep all organizational staff aware of legal, fiscal, or other changes that might affect the nature of records and recordkeeping systems.

For a variety of historical and other reasons, there are separate professional associations for archivists and records managers, but the increasing use of new electronic information technologies have blurred some of the distinctions made between their work.

Professional Archivist and Records Managers. An institutional archivist must have the services of an individual educated about archival and records management work and the nature of records and recordkeeping systems. This individual oversees all aspects of the archives program, including

- appraising (identifying records with archival value);
- arranging and describing archival records;
- handling reference requests;
- making decisions about additional preservation needs of the records; and
- promoting the purpose and services of the archives.

In the case of an institutional archives, the archivist will have responsibility for both records management policies and procedures as well as for seeking manuscripts and other materials related to the organization from outside sources. The archivist also will need to serve as a clearinghouse of information about records matters for the organization, requiring him or her to

- attend professional conferences;
- stay current with professional literature and standards; and
- develop networks so that other experts may be consulted regarding the organization's records (e.g., utilizing a conservator for the repair of certain archival records beyond the normal cleaning and storage).

Archivists usually enter the profession with a graduate degree in history or library and information science with an emphasis on archival studies.

Administrative Authority. The success of the archives program is dependent on the archivist's having sufficient authority within the organization. The archivist should not have to negotiate every aspect of work on archival or records issues; it should be well known within the organization that the archivist is vested with authority to make decisions about all aspects of records management. Such authority usually requires two components. First, the archivist should have as direct tie to the chief administrative officer as possible. This means different things in different organizations, but the crucial concept here is that the archivist be able to seek advice and make decisions about records matters quickly and easily. Second, there should be an advisory group overseeing the work of the archives and the archivist. Again, while this may vary from organization to organization, such a group is usually comprised of individuals who can deal with the administrative, legal, fiscal, and research aspects of archives. Some organizations will have one or more experts from outside serving in the group, and the nature of these experts may vary as well. This advisory group obviously advises the archivist and usually has the authority to set records policy with the archivist's assistance.

Archives Facility. Every institutional archives program must have an adequate archival facility. Such a facility enables the storage of archival records and provides space for researchers and the archival staff. Storage space must allow for the maintenance of records in an area that has stable temperature and humidity controls; is free from dust, pollutants, insect, and vermin; and has an adequate security and fire-suppression system. Public research and staff work areas should be well lighted and wired for computer and other equipment.

The archives facility should also be accessible to people in the organization and the public; it should be near the primary working areas of the organization and encompass adequate parking. There also needs to be handicapped accessibility. The facility should be easy to find and well designated by signage.

Most institutional records programs have contracts with commercial records centers for the storage of inactive records that will be destroyed at some point without coming into the archives. Commercial records centers can save money and free up valuable storage and office space for the use of more important records and other functions. However, commercial records centers are only a viable option if the organization has a records management program with well-developed records retention schedules.

Policies and Procedures Handbook. All institutional archives programs produce policies and procedures handbooks that cover all aspects of archival and records management work. They generally include policies and procedures directed to individuals working within the organization, researchers who come to use archival materials, and volunteers and other staff who may work within the archives. Besides providing an opportunity for an institutional archives program to bring together existing professional standards, such policies and procedures handbooks cover the following:

- records retention schedules;
- procedures for transfer of records to the archives;
- access policies;
- guidelines for arrangement and description practices;
- researchers rules and forms;
- disaster-preparedness plan in case of emergency; and
- appraisal criteria and collection development policy.

The nature of such handbooks will change as an institutional archives program is established and matures. Most programs, working with their advisory group, will identify and add new policies as circumstances warrant them.

Web Site. With the advent of the World Wide Web, most archival programs have set up Web sites in order to reach a wider segment of the public and to make their services and holdings more accessible. These sites usually include the following information:

- location;
- hours of operation;
- mission;
- nature of archival holdings;
- special events;
- telephone; and
- e-mail.

Some archives have made full-texts (digital reproductions) of certain important records available on the Web. Others have created educational packets for use in grade, middle, and high school history and other classes. Some programs have created virtual exhibitions (sometimes based on real exhibitions held at their institutions) based on or highlighting their archival materials. Not all institutional archives put up publicly accessible Web sites, especially if their records are generally reserved for internal use only. Whether an institution develops such a Web site for its archives depends on the scope of its operation and the definition of its constituents.

Sufficient Budget. The size of the budget for an institutional archives always will depend on the scale of the archival program. At the least, there needs to be

- a full-time professional;
- some support staff (at least a part-time secretary);
- a personal computer (with printer and scanner);
- funding for professional conferences and professional publications; and
- a discretionary budget for the purchase of software and other equipment as needed.

CONCLUSION

I can imagine two criticisms that can be made of this chapter (and perhaps of the entire book), one concerning matters of technological issues and the other the seeming emphasis on archival records.

First, some will read this and be critical about its lack of discussion of solution options—such as the acquisition and implementation of records and information management software or a broader reliance on commercial records centers and assistance provided by these services. Both are important considerations and valuable options for gaining improved administration over an institution's records. However, organizations—including both their administrators and their staffs—must first develop some basic understanding of the nature and importance of essential records issues. Without such understanding, decisions to adopt software or engage the services of commercial records centers may only compound the records and information problems of the organizations. Indeed, some of the new areas, with all their flashy attributes, such as knowledge management or e-commerce or e-government (or any word where "e" has been prefixed), won't work well unless those mundane traditional records are well managed.

Second, some may be annoyed at the emphasis on archives, preferring more focus on information or, at least, current records. As I have suggested above, it is counter-productive and artificial to divide archives from current records from information and knowledge management functions. A current record can be not only an archival record, but may also be critical in an organization's corporate memory and its hard-acquired knowledge. Such matters seem more obvious in the embattled trenches of organizational offices where staff seek to accomplish their tasks, meet their mandates, and administer the records and information critical to being successful.

Index

About the Author

Richard J. Cox is Professor in Library and Information Science at the University of Pittsburgh, School of Information Sciences where he is responsible for the archives concentration in both the master's and doctoral programs. He has been a member of the Society of American Archivists Council from 1986 through 1989. Dr. Cox also served as Editor of the *American Archivist* from 1991 through 1995, and he is presently Editor of the *Records and Information Management Report* as well as serving as the Society of American Archivists Publications Editor. He has written extensively on archival and records management topics and has published eleven books in this area: *American Archival Analysis: The Recent Development of the Archival Profession in the United Sates* (1990)—winner of the Waldo Gifford Leland Award given by the Society of American Archivists; *Managing Institutional Archives: Foundational Principles and Practices* (1992); *The First Generation of Electronic Records Archivists in the United States: A Study in Professionalization* (1994); *Documenting Localities* (1996); *Closing an Era: Historical Perspectives on Modern Archives and Records Management* (2000); *Managing Records as Evidence and Information* (2001), also winner of the Waldo Gifford Leland Award (2002); co-editor, *Archives and the Public Good: Accountability and Records in Modern Society*; *Vandals in the Stacks? A Response to Nicholson Bakers' Assault on Libraries* (2002); *Flowers After the Funeral: Reflections on the Post 9/11 Digital Age* (2003); *No Innocent Deposits: Forming Archives by Rethinking Appraisal* (2004); and *Lester J. Cappon and Historical Scholarship in the Golden Age of Archival Theory* (2004).